The New Nonsense

The End
of the Rational Consensus

CHARLES FAIR

SIMON AND SCHUSTER

NEW YORK

Designed by Edith Fowler
Manufactured in the United States of America
1   2   3   4   5   6   7   8   9   10
Library of Congress Cataloging in Publication Data

Fair, Charles M.
    The new nonsense.

    Bibliography: p.
    1. Civilization, Modern—1950–   2. Human behavior.   I. Title.
    CB428.F34   901.94   74-8028
    ISBN 0-671-21822-0

*To my father, who
would have liked it*

Contents

Introduction

This is, as its title says, a book about nonsense—in particular the kinds which most appeal to us today. Parts One and Three are about nonsense as a way of life, as therapy, and as a mother of institutions.

Part Two considers three items of the New Nonsense in detail: UFOs; ESP or psi phenomena generally; and the perennially popular ideas of Dr. Velikovsky. Do UFOs exist? Are the Russians about to revolutionize modern warfare with their psi machines? Can we project our thoughts along a fifth dimension and foresee the market crash coming next week? Was there really an explosion of psychic energy in a nearby bookcase one day when Drs. Freud and Jung were having a heated discussion? Is it safe to assume, with Velikovsky, that a good deal of our petroleum fell down recently from the sky?

Some of these ideas have established quite a following—and there is always the possibility, of course, that not all of them are rubbish. Our government seems to be discreetly funding research in ESP on the chance that it may have some military potential. The sightings of UFOs go on and on. And now a few scientists are beginning to have second thoughts about Velikovsky. So I felt I should try to show why these items of the New Nonsense may actually be that.

In fact, if some of what I have called nonsense proves not to be, neither my main argument nor the attitude of the believing public will be much affected. It is important to know why we should doubt Dr. Velikovsky's ideas, but more important to understand why millions of supposedly educated people have not done so.

The real question is what the resurgence of nonsense in our era means. What connection, if any, does it have with the revolutionary spirit of the age? And what, therefore, may it prophesy?

PART ONE

i

Nonsense and Revolution

Although nonsense is sometimes revolutionary and revolution invariably generates its own, we do not see them as having any special connection—if only because revolutions are sporadic and nonsense perennial. Men rise up against the state for good reason; they believe in nonsense just because.

By nonsense we usually mean the absurd ideas entertained by others—either simple mistakes, such as the belief that toads cause warts, or matters of fervent conviction, such as that all Reds, Jews, Trotskyites, or advocates of the fluoridation of water are public enemies and should be executed. A certain amount of claptrap seems almost necessary to our mental health, and so flourishes even in ages in which it shouldn't.

Revolutions, on the other hand, are supposedly practical and work on a threshold principle. Abused beyond a certain point, people will rise up; short of it, they will not.

Neither of these ideas, I believe, is correct. Though in a sense endemic, nonsense also waxes and wanes. It was waning toward the end of our own Middle Ages, and suffered severe setbacks during the seventeenth and eighteenth centuries when science began and the persecution of witches was finally given up. Ignoring the current view,* one would have to say that such progress as we have made toward more just government and a more humane social order has chiefly occurred in more modern times. Some ages, in short, have made a little more sense than others—nor was the result, as we tend to think, just better technology.

* That we have made no progress at all.

On the commonsense theory, revolutions never occur spontaneously but always from some combination of weakness and provocation. One way or another, it is entrenched privilege, acting through its natural instrument, bad government, that brings down the house. The nonsense-proneness of the public is not a factor in the situation except insofar as the ruling class can take advantage of it to postpone the inevitable.

This theory fails to account for two important facts. One is that a people can become revolutionary (as we did, for instance, in the 1960s) under conditions not nearly as bad as those they put up with only a few decades earlier. The other is that conditions are *always* bad, so the question becomes not why revolutions occur but why they don't occur far more often.

One can hardly think of a time when men have not had reason to distrust or actively dislike their social superiors. The instinct for survival guarantees that most of us are violently competitive, even with our friends, and master rationalizers when it comes to justifying any outrage we or our tribe may have committed in our own interest. It is part of our biological heritage that aristocrat and commoner alike should lay down their lives for the collective good; but the same instinctive tic, acting in behalf of the individual, his class, or his next of kin, causes these same citizens, in times of peace, to struggle without cease or mercy to get the upper hand of one another. Societies are thus almost by definition unfair, the wonder being that anything resembling justice or mercy has come to exist in any of them.

While the everyday view sees men as nonsense-prone by nature, it also assumes a direct relation between ignorance and superstition. Those who know least tend to be the most suggestible. Conversely, when fear of the unknown is reduced by general education, suggestibility also diminishes and epidemics of nonsense become next to impossible. But if that is really the case, astrology should not be making a comeback today; there should be no revival of satanism, witchcraft, or Oriental religions; no scientology; possibly no psychoanalysis.

In fact, as I will try to show, there may be more of a connection between nonsense and revolution than we realize, nor is it a directly causal one. Men do not become revolutionary because inflamed by nonsense, or nonsense-prone because caught up in revolution. Both states of mind have a common origin and tend to appear together.

For more than a hundred years, but most rapidly in the last few decades, faith among us has been declining. Some of the results of that change are clear enough; others, less so. In giving up the consolations of our traditional religion, we have exposed ourselves to an ever-increasing pressure from what Freud called the Id—the subrational instinctive self. In particular we have inflamed the instinct of self-preservation, since as conscientious agnostics we can no longer placate it by assurances of life beyond the grave. One curious feature of that situation—the one we least understand, and which I will try to explain later—is that we have failed really to adapt to it.

Whereas some men seem able to live comfortably with the idea of their own mortality, the majority of us evidently find it quite difficult. For one thing, agnosticism involves not just the problem of death, but that of day-to-day meaninglessness; it lays upon us the burden of self-creation, and the signs are that we may be cracking under it. Among other things, it has profoundly affected the way we bring up our children. It has also brought into being a new species of extremist. And today we are beginning to see its ultimate product, the Perfect Amorph, the man open to, or capable of, anything.

What characterizes this century, even more than technics, is its unsettled emotional climate. For fifty years we have seen the temper of everything change—superficially, because of new ways of doing things; essentially, perhaps, because of a slow-gathering mass of fear. The technology that has brought us physical comfort and power we now hold responsible for our *Angst* as well. For whatever reasons, the feeling is there, manifesting itself in some as "floating anxiety," in others as alienation, anomie, Sartrean

15

nausea, depression,* or what, in schizophrenics, is called a "defect of pleasure."

No doubt many of our psychiatric difficulties are due to the pace of change or at least aggravated by it. But the fact is that basic anxiety seems often to be independent of our personal circumstances, thriving in rich and poor alike† and in the sheltered as well as the exposed. It is simply the legacy of the death of God. And in proportion as we suffer from it, we incline to other sorts of emotional excess. It is not exactly that we are victimized by our feelings. We cultivate certain of them half-deliberately in order to rid ourselves of the main one.

For normally, of course, emotions are fluid states which easily convert themselves into their "opposites"—fear into rage, grief into desire or hilarity, hopelessness into last-minute hope. Indeed, when they cease to do so (as in melancholia or some anxiety neuroses) we regard them as pathological. Much of the extravagant, driven behavior of men today is an attempt to escape the same sort of emotional fixity. Our basic aim is to avoid being engulfed by our fears, since fear is, of all emotions, the most unpleasant and the most crippling. Our basic dilemma is that, as skeptics, we cannot avoid stirring it up in the first place. Because we tell it, the Id knows, and knowing, will never let us alone.

From that point on, the problem becomes not how to achieve happiness but how to blunt our anxiety or transform it into feelings we find more bearable. Depending upon our temperament, almost anything may do; and in that light, a great many very different ways of life begin to look like the same sort of expedient. The executive who works a sixteen-hour day, knowing his next coronary is just around the corner, and his hippie-dissident son or promiscuous, much-divorced daughter have more in common than they imagine, as do the twenty-year-old junkie from the ghetto and

* It is reported in the medical literature that since about 1910, melancholia has been on the increase and "hysteria" declining in the Western world. Hysteria, long regarded as a last manifestation of Victorian repression, may actually have been the first manifestation of modernity.
† This was shown literally to be the case, in a sociological study done in New York City some years ago.[1]

the middle-aged middle-class drunk. The street people or habitués of swinging-singles bars have their own concept of Nirvana, but is it so different really from that of the dropouts who take up Yoga and organic gardening? The object in all cases is to break the grip of fear—to put the relentlessly renewed energies of our survival instinct to some use or, failing that, to waste and dissipate them (and ourselves, if need be), in the process.

It was appropriate that the Nazis called their system "dynamism." The age as a whole is dynamic. And with us the Rage to Live also becomes a Rage to Believe. Hence we incline in two directions at once: toward strange supernaturalist ideas which revive our hopes of life everlasting, and toward an increasingly brutal success ethic* or, in the extreme, to violence outright. Along with news about wholesale theft in high places, we learned in 1973 that rape, murder, and aggravated assault were up in this country.† It is almost as though one were following the rising emotional pressure of the times on a set of steam gauges.

Exactly the same sort of pressure, for instance, that has produced our recent increase in political assassinations; in purely inspirational killings (à la Charles Whitman, or Manson, or the heroes of Truman Capote's *In Cold Blood*); or in such teen-age "fun" activities as vandalism, sniping, and arson is also responsible, I believe, for the so-called Sexual Revolution. From the crude eroticism of our books and movies and the incessant, increasingly gross way we pursue pleasures of the flesh in real life, one would think an epidemic of lust was sweeping the world—but is it, really?

---

* Competitive success being one of the principal ways we appease our survival instinct here and now. Obviously to be smarter, richer, and higher in the pecking order than one's fellows improves one's chances of outliving them, as well as filling life in the meantime with pleasant distractions, among them a sense of one's own superiority.

The value we set, in this country, on being a "good competitor," and the violent energy we put into outdoing one another—in sports, in business, in intellectual matters, even in cocktail-party conversation—is part of the same pattern. What we like to regard as vitality may in fact represent a continual overdraft on our energies of a kind which our children are already refusing to make.

† Because crimes against property—rational crimes—were down in the same period, the Nixon Administration, which published these statistics, considered them "encouraging."

*new
sexuality*

Have men and women suddenly become all that much sexier? Or is the Pill, as some say, chiefly responsible? There is no clear evidence that we *are* sexier; indeed, from the reports of Masters and Johnson and other clinicians, it would appear that our urge to libertinism often far outruns our performance. And the Pill cannot be a major incitement, since the Sexual Revolution and the boom in divorce began decades before it was available. In reality, our "swingerism" may be a matter of borrowed ardor, deriving a good part of its energy not from our overdeveloped gonads but from our undercontrolled fears.*

Those whose temperamental bent is toward the conversion of fear into rationalized hatred become activists of various kinds. The plight of women in a male-dominated world has never been good. Indeed, in this country only eighty years ago it was much worse than it is now. Yet American women, who today enjoy more freedom and more rights than their sisters almost anywhere else, are among the most belligerent on these very points. I do *not* mean they have nothing to complain about. I mean they are complaining for reasons they themselves only half understand—and would as soon leave that way. The surpluses of anxiety they suffer along with the rest of us have driven some of them to become militants; and it is neither here nor there that the situation they are protesting against—lower pay scales for women, job discrimination, sexual exploitation, household slavery, etc.—is far less grievous than it used to be. The main thing is that they have found a "defense" that works.†

The same applies to student revolutionaries who denounce the American corporate establishment as a heartless imperialist monster. The sort of imperialism the New Left is talking about is

---

* Since fear or anxiety is a natural antagonist of Eros, particularly in the male, it follows that the conversion of fear into amorousness is a chancy business. Having seen the would-be lover through the preliminary stages of conquest, it may then betray him in bed—as happens, apparently, only too often.

Hence our vast literature of sexual self-help, dealing with impotence, clitoral anesthesia, and similar obstacles to romance.

† Anxiety is, of course, an emotion one must chiefly suffer oneself. Rage is an emotion more likely to transfer one's sufferings to others. Hence withdrawal is a very poor solution to the problem of *Angst*, whereas systematically indulged hatred is a very good one.

already all but dead.* Conversely, when it was in full vigor, very few denounced it. And while the domestic practices of big business are frequently deplorable, the fact remains that the working-man today has more recourses and gets more consideration than he did even as recently as 1930. In short, we became revolutionary not during the 1930s but in the relatively prosperous '60s—the era of Medicare, unemployment insurance, Social Security, and the Fair Employment Practices Act. The reason may simply be that we had become psychologically ready in the meantime. Revolutions, I believe, have a timetable and an inner momentum of their own, only tangentially related to the more or less chronic evils which it is their declared purpose to do away with.

History on the whole supports the conclusion that revolutions seldom realize their supposed aims. Not until eighty years after the French Revolution did anything resembling democracy come to France; and of all major Western governments founded upon the principle of representation, the French has remained the least secure. In Britain, in Scandinavia, in the United States, the course of political change has been far less violent, and the resulting systems have been far more stable. In ancient Rome, in Nazi Germany, and in modern Russia, revolution led to more systematic oppression, not unaccompanied by signs of mass insanity. Again, I do not mean to say that revolutions never accomplish anything or have no rational justification to begin with. Any society that truly understood itself—which is to say, the nature of its leadership and the actual purpose of much law and custom—would be revolutionary most of the time.

But the fact is most societies are not, even with exceptionally good reasons for being so. The French had as much cause to revolt during the last years of the reign of Louis XIV† as they did in

---

* In fact the post–War II world has shown that the most prosperous nations are not those with colonial dependencies and large arms budgets, but those (like West Germany and Japan) which have negligible arms budgets and do most of their overseas business not with colonial countries but with high-technology nations like themselves.
† Whose death in 1715 was celebrated, I have read, with bonfires and rejoicing.

1789; like the American public of 1930, they were just not, in other ways, ready. They had not built up the required head of steam; practical incentives alone were not enough. Besides an awareness of injustice and governmental mismanagement, they needed to be deprived of a most fundamental metaphysical security, for only in that way would a general decontrolling of the Id occur and an over-powering pressure of bad feelings build up, at last enabling a handful of gifted fanatics to dynamite the state. Professional revolutionaries, like the causes of revolution, are always to hand; whole peoples ripe for revolution are another matter, the problem being what ripens them.

We pretend that it is because the notion of a divine Providence gives purpose to our existence that we find religion such a comfort; but that can hardly be so, since the most religious of men have never been able to state what that purpose is. It is a "mystery," and what sort of consolation is that? No, the real consolation is not purpose but the promised continuity of our own existence after death, *in perpetuo*. For in that idea man has a club with which to batter down the Id. He may fear death on occasion when specifically threatened with it, but death in the abstract, in the shape of a nagging day-to-day awareness of his own mortality, ceases to trouble him. Once destroy that security and (as Lenin, and Dostoevski before him, well understood) you will have on your hands a restless, unstable, potentially revolutionary populace, whatever the conditions it happens to live under—though the worse those are, of course, the better.

What we managed to show in the 1960s was that a country could become revolutionary even when conditions, although not good, were hardly worse than usual, and in some ways better.* Perhaps if President Johnson had succeeded in bringing on a major crash, that, combined with the war in Vietnam, the unbalanced

* It could be argued that the aims of the Vietnam war were no more questionable than those of the Korean war, which elicited almost no protest at all. And Army studies made during World War II showed that the majority of our draftees did not understand that conflict, many thinking it unnecessary or a "phony." Yet there were no riots; they went. The new age had simply not matured.

budget, the dollar crisis overseas, race riots, and the renewed inflation, might have done it; we'd have had something like a complete social collapse. Conditions, in short, do help. One of the final precipitating causes of the French Revolution was a poor harvest and steeply rising bread prices. (See Chapter IV.) But in eighteenth-century France, as in twentieth-century America, the essential factor seems to have been a properly receptive state of mind. Until men were seized with an anxious embittered skepticism and made sufficiently volatile and prone to violence, the sheer energy needed for rebellion was lacking, nor could conditions of themselves stir it up. Conversely, once the *philosophes* of both eras had convinced us of the death of God, once a mechanistic view of existence had established itself in different ways in the several classes, the energy for rebellion did gradually become available.

And as that occurred, there was in both societies a remarkable outbreak of nonsense. Even the *kinds* of nonsense are quite similar. Mesmerism, which swept Paris in the 1780s, has much in common with Freudian hypnotherapy and Janov's scream cures. The mystical elements that crept into mesmerism as the Revolution approached closely resemble the hocus-pocus which Dianetics added in becoming scientology, a development of the 1960s. (Dianetics was a crude derivative of psychoanalysis.) And Mesmer's notion that "animal magnetism" depended upon a universal fluid or erotic *Äther* anticipated Wilhelm Reich's orgone. (See Chapter IV.)

The basic difference between France then and America now is that atheism (as distinct from anticlericalism) is perhaps more general among us. Old faiths die hard and hold out longest among the poor and ill-educated. In *Battle for the Mind* Dr. William Sargant suggested that it may have been Wesleyanism that prevented the equivalent of the French Revolution from occurring in England during the 1840s, when the condition of the industrial workingman was probably at its worst and when revolutions on the Continent did occur. In France, just before 1789, it seems to have been chiefly the city folk and the educated who ceased to go to church. The lower orders, although disenchanted with the clergy, as with their secular overlords, were not quite ready to go it without God Himself—this also being true of the Russian peasantry of 1917. In both cases the revolutionary leadership backed off from an extreme atheistic position—Robespierre pausing in the midst of the Terror to celebrate a day in honor of the Almighty, and the Soviets wisely deciding not to try to wipe out the Russian Orthodox Church but simply to propagandize the rising generations away from it.

In Western Europe and America, the history of the last two centuries has essentially been that of the spread of skepticism and its consequences. If it is true that societies become revolutionary not merely because of an accumulation of evils but also as a result of a rising wave of anxiety and related bad feelings set in motion by the collapse of faith, then the French Revolution was clearly premature. It lacked the necessary popular base. Except for the Jacobins and the Parisian rabble, Frenchmen were perhaps insufficiently convinced of the pointlessness of existence or the improbability of God and an afterlife to plunge themselves into the sort of nihilism which Hitler and his party were said to have created in Germany or which is in fact becoming prevalent in modern America.

From about 1750, as skepticism became general in the educated classes, there sprang up among them a sort of second religion which reached its apogee with nineteenth-century liberalism. The essence of it was that man could live without God—must prepare himself to do so, since the sciences were making atheism inescapable. Henceforth the survival and progress of society must depend upon a rational consensus whose function would be not merely to order the material world but to conserve the decencies of traditional Christianity as well.

To Ortega y Gasset the liberal position appeared "acrobatic"; to Matthew Arnold it was a dream. It assumed that man was capable of a purely reasoned unselfishness; that he needed no promises of eternal bliss or threats of eternal damnation to keep his always turbulent Id under control. It took no account of the fact that when those threats and promises were removed, society might become so disturbed that it would in time resort to a kind of violent self-simplification (as Germany did) or (like modern America) go mildly insane. The men of J. S. Mill's time did not foresee the Age of Anxiety;* nor did they understand, any better than we do, what such an age portends, because they and we misread, as if deliberately, the basic principles of human nature involved.

How else can one explain the perennial popularity of Rousseau's absurd notion that man is born good and ruined by society[2]—i.e., other men? That we are endowed with undeniably strong instincts, many of them blindly selfish and destructive; that they have an immense power to warp our thinking, causing us to rationalize as just and noble actions that are obviously nothing of the kind—that the instincts, in short, are an inborn source of violence, chicanery, and self-justifying rubbish—are facts we know from daily experience. But if we are to believe in a rational consensus, we cannot face them. Some new theory of human nature is required. In its latter-day form it is called environmentalism, and some believers of this school go so far as to say man *has* no instincts. The common thread in Rousseau and his doctrinal descendants is that conditions make the man—a good system a good man, a bad system a bad one. Crime is not a matter of personal responsibility but a product of poverty or "broken homes." The private struggle, each with himself, with the animal inside him, has been given up. That, after all, was the old Puritan approach. Today the solution to what we trivially call "personality problems" is external: a "shrink," a change in conditions, better group affiliations—something outside of ourselves which we can use, as good Skinnerians, to give ourselves "positive reinforcement." If we can find "socially acceptable goals" then we will be motivated (by reinforcement) to do more along the same lines. In effect this amounts to using our environment as a way of holding ourselves together—realizing ourselves (as Dewey put it) through our "relations"; becoming a kind of human putty.†

---

* Dostoevski, however, did, and many of its consequences. And in such Victorians as Walter Bagehot, who in his *Physics and Politics* tried to fathom "the secret of progression," one detects the beginning of some uneasiness about the future.

† Or "other-directeds," as David Riesman called us in the 1950s.

Marx (who largely begged the question of human nature) would have considered the Puritanic notion of struggle with self part of the propaganda of the Church, intended to turn our eyes from injustices we suffer here and now and rivet them upon essentially imaginary questions relating to the health of the soul. For liberals à la Mill, the admission that the instincts do, to some degree, constitute innate evil and a threat to man's sanity was possibly too close to what they regarded as the superstition of Original Sin. Worse, it was an admission that cast serious doubt on the powers of reason itself.

For if man's hold over his given adaptive nature was so shaky, if the Id, over and over again, could drive him into the grossest nonsense and self-deception, as well as into the grossest inhumanity toward his fellows, what chance was there that the reign of reason would ever come? So to make its arrival seem more likely, the powers of reason had to be exaggerated and those of instinct played down.

Hence Rousseau, the most irrational of philosophers, became to democracy what Hegel was to Marx. And to the extent to which he himself managed to "let it all hang out," Rousseau was prophetic of the twentieth-century communards and New Left types described, for instance, in Elia Katz's Armed Love.

A more recent line of thought, developed in different ways by Freud, by Carnap and Wittgenstein, by B. F. Skinner and the early behaviorists, even by the mathematician Kurt Gödel, casts doubt not only on the ultimate powers of reason but (if we conceive the essential self to be rational) upon the existence of the self itself. Conscious autonomous decision-making I, we are told, is a fiction. The question here is whether we are talking about a "law" of human nature or about the psychologically crippled state into which men today happen to be falling.

It is important, in this connection, to make a clear separation between matters of logic or physics and those which actually have something to tell us about our psychic makeup. Immense amounts of nonsense have been written about the philosophic implications of Werner Heisenberg's Principle of Indeterminacy. Epistemology

24

—the problem of what we can or cannot know of the world out-side ourselves—is not to be confused with the problem of our freedom to investigate these questions, or to control our own behavior. Quite typically, however, we do confuse them. Freud's notion of the feeble Ego, trapped between Superego and Id, is taken as a corollary of Gödel's demonstration that no mathematical system, working solely from its own postulates, can prove its own tenability; or of Heisenberg's, that the exact position and velocity of an electron cannot be known simultaneously. All these are taken as corollaries of the theorem supposedly proved by logical positiv-ism—namely, that no moral system can be shown to be objectively preferable to any other. If ultimate uncertainty and the inherent weakness of reason can be shown from so many directions, on what ground is reason left to stand?

The last bit of it appears to be cut away by Skinnerian behav-iorism which tells us that our actions are in no understandable sense willed but simply the resultants of our conditioning and our present circumstances.* So reason has no real freedom, and even if it had—if it were the instrument of Free Will—its powers to penetrate the world of phenomena are almost too feeble to bother about (in which case, the successes of science become something of a puzzle).

The impression one gets is that in this century we have been using the whole highly developed apparatus of thought, bequeathed us by the last, to explain away powers of mind and imagination, not to say of character and moral choice, which we are ceasing to cultivate and therefore ceasing to have. As the principle of indi-vidual responsibility or of individuality itself becomes more and

---

* As readers of Skinner's *Beyond Freedom and Dignity* already know, all be-havior, human as well as animal, reduces to what he calls "contingencies of re-inforcement." If I do something society approves of, I will be "positively rein-forced" and accordingly do more of it. (Money makes the mare go.) If society does not approve, it will "negatively reinforce" me. People who persist in doing "negatively reinforced" things are criminals or lunatics. Skinner favors a world of "automatic goodness" in which, presumably, rewards for the good (socially acceptable) are maximized, and criminals and lunatics are put on special rein-forcement schedules to get them back on the right track. Should those meas-ures fail there seems no reason, under Skinner's view, not to kill them. Except for its laboratory language, it is hard to see what in his system is new.

more problematical, we are forced, if only to save face, into devising theories which demonstrate that really those human attributes never existed.

But then, if we are not to believe in essential evil, we are driven to the Rousseauesque notion that man's instincts are basically good. If we haven't the power to make ourselves virtuous, the only sensible course is to assume virtue is innate. And really to give up the old struggle *is* a relief. The life of continual inner hardship which the Puritans regarded as inescapable if man was ever to attain grace has few attractions for us.

The spiritual disciplines of today, including such things as Mind Control, are all aimed at *releasing* powers, tapping subliminal forces which are the Real You. (See Chapters II and III.) Unloose the Primal Scream, roil up the oceanic depths, set aside the ordinary supernatant self with LSD or mescaline or by means of alpha control or Transcendental Meditation, and amazing revelations will follow; new powers; greater health—automatically. Has that not been the wisdom of the East for centuries? (And with what result? one might ask—although the question is now considered Philistine. Salvation is not always visible in the form of things like justice or capability—sometimes not even in the art or philosophy or character of those who have achieved it.)

By the same reasoning, intellect proper is not to be trusted; not even—given its poor powers—deserving of much respect. The great advantage of anti-intellectualism, especially when combined with a permissive attitude toward the more basal self or Id, is that it permits us to hold any hodgepodge of opinions we like. Since the Id is a wellspring of primitive wishes, including those automatic dramas we call fantasies,* we need never be at a loss for colorful contradictory ideas, in particular those which justify whatever, at the moment, we most want to think or do.

---

* In contrast to imagination, which takes effort—is something we *do*—fantasy is something the Id does to us. In contrast to those we imagine, the dramas of fantasy are apt to be crude, their characters dimly outlined, their action summary and violent. Movies like *A Clockwork Orange* are fantasies; and it is significant that in ordinary speech we usually fail to make a clear distinction between fantasy and imagination—having, perhaps, in our inner lives no experience on which to base it.

Hypocrisy, contrary to the popular view, is not disappearing among us. It is just becoming much easier, and assuming forms such as "sincerity" which one can't quarrel with because they have almost no content. With the passing of our traditional morality, we find we can dispense with the virtuosity once needed to put a good face on our actions. We have no trouble convincing ourselves that drugs or promiscuity may be curative—almost forms of self-discipline. After centuries of a reluctant Christianity we are entering an era of willful personal belief, and in the short run at least, that is simplifying everything. Not only do we feel free to live according to any set of values we choose;* there is no need for them to make any ultimate sense. The important thing is for us to *like* them, for them to give us good "vibes." Obviously this is a considerable departure from the world of Mill and nineteenth-century liberalism, and one Mill or Walter Bagehot or even such determined skeptics as Henry T. Buckle would scarcely have welcomed.

A hundred years ago, most educated people, and many of the semi- or uneducated as well, seemed to agree on certain fundamental propositions. The Victorians considered that much of what they believed could be explained, and those who disagreed had the task of demonstrating, by logic and evidence, *why* they disagreed. This way of doing things was thought a great advance; indeed, it was the essence of the idea of Progress, if by the latter one meant something besides inventions and manufactures. The Victorian rational ideal gave man a special place in animal creation; leaving aside the supernaturalist assumptions of Christianity, it supposed him to be a creature with unique powers of self-management. Nor were these given, merely. They needed to be developed (hence the Victorian emphasis on Character and Enlightenment); but once they had been, they would presumably enable him to resist whatever unseemly behavior or idiotic imaginings his more primitive nature might try to force upon him. He was, in short, perfectible, and not in useful skills alone.

Because of his survival instinct, did he yearn to live forever? Of

* For statistical evidence of this pluralism of beliefs, see Chapter V.

course; but if there was nothing really to suggest he might, he was prepared to see his wish to do so as a superstition. Was the personal God of our ancestors after all a dream? If the facts seemed to say so then, like Matthew Arnold, he would bow to rational necessity. To have progressed or become civilized meant that at last men might be able to face the truth of things, however unattractive, without losing their poise or humanity, and without perjuring their reason. It was a difficult ideal, but for a time there were signs that it just might be taking hold.

The Victorian Age was paradoxical in that, in the midst of a brutal industrialism, it produced many liberals and reformers who, although believers no longer, were more Christian in their acts than their Christian ancestors had ever been. And notwithstanding a renascence of the irrational in art (Poe; Rimbaud; Wagner) and an outbreak of sinister tastelessness and political dogmatism (Marx; Burne-Jones; jigsaw Gothic), the age also produced men of the greatest intellect and sensibility, not to mention a working class apparently far more susceptible to cultural uplift than our own.*

Since that time, a trend in the opposite direction has set in. One can date it from World War I and the Roaring '20s. In retrospect, the war appears to have been an explosion not merely of Teutonic ambition but of the whole Western psyche. In *The Strange Death of Liberal England*, George Dangerfield describes the "fever" of strikes and violent Fem Lib demonstrations that broke out in Britain in the years just preceding 1914. It is surprising to recall that in a country seemingly as tranquil and secure as England then was, suffragettes set off a bomb under the Coronation Chair in Westminster Abbey, mutilated Sargent's portrait of Henry James, burned churches and hospitals, and staged hunger strikes so prolonged that they had to be force-fed rectally. One of the more militant—red-haired, green-eyed Emily Davison—flung herself under the hoofs of the King's horse at Epsom and was killed.

In 1913 there was a rash of what we would call UFO sightings in the skies over Britain. Some of the reports read exactly like those

* See below, page 136.

which appear today in publications such as *Argosy* or the NICAP bulletins. (See Chapter VII.) These queer apparitions were not, however, thought to be visitors from Out There; they were German spy craft or, in Dangerfield's phrase, "mythical dirigibles."

From these and similar events, one gets the impression that men and women had tired of the brief reign of reason and in their various ways, half-unconsciously, were setting out to get rid of it. As Dangerfield put it: "For nearly a century men had discovered in the cautious phrase, in the respectable gesture, in the considered display of reasonable emotions, a haven against those irrational storms which threatened to sweep through them. And gradually the haven lost its charms . . . Men with a defiance they could not hope to understand began to put forth upon little excursions into the vast, the dark, the driven seas beyond."

In effect, the Victorian rational consensus—short-lived, restricted in its membership, and imperfect in all its works as it had been— was over. The era when each would lapse back into himself, reconciled to those very instincts against which the Church had perennially warned him—victimized, almost with his own consent, by the "irrational storms" within—was soon to be upon us. It began with the horrible fantasy-acted-out of the war itself—a masterpiece of gruesome mismanagement costing millions of lives, billions in money, and an incalculable sum in damage to the spirit. As I remarked in an earlier book,* it cut the taproot of idealism, and much that we have seen since has simply been the withering of the tree.

Among the more fortunate, the feeling right after the war was one of lightness, almost light-headedness. A weight of unnecessary striving, of age-old intimations of Higher Purpose, had suddenly been lifted, and in their new emptiness men felt free to think and do as they pleased. The result was a brief golden age of juvenility.† I can still recall bits of it from my own childhood: the parties and drinking and glamour; the talk of "affairs" and the Millennium; the sound of the saxophones Scott Fitzgerald wrote about; the boyishly pretty, desperately sophisticated girls; Helen Morgan on her

* *From the Jaws of Victory*, Simon and Schuster, 1971.
† Perhaps at that not so brief, since in other forms it seems to be continuing.

piano, dying of booze, as my father and so many of his friends were doing—as Evelyn Waugh in London and Fitzgerald on the Continent and innumerable *bons vivants* everywhere were trying to do.

The so-called moral revolution of the 1920s was essentially an exercise in willful personal belief, and in its way no happier or more genuinely free than the drug culture and commune life of forty-odd years later were to be. Our chief wish was to indulge ourselves, and then as now, we easily persuaded ourselves that it was safe and sensible to do so. Society would not suffer, nor would our children. We would, in fact, be healthier for not being as "repressed" as the Victorians. Besides the good example we set our offspring by our sexual license and generally relaxed manners, the little dears might actually profit from growing up in "broken homes."* Parental authority would not weigh as heavily upon them; they would be even less "repressed" than we (as has certainly proved true).

These developments followed naturally from the fact that there had ceased to be any central code which men felt bound to honor. For a time, the specialized codes of science appeared to be an exception, but even they are in question now, as is Father Freud, physician to the New Sick. One result of the lapse into willful personal belief was that respect became increasingly difficult to take advantage of because increasingly nobody had any, for anything. The worker, once gulled into seeing his employer as a true superior, now began to see him with the unclouded eye of instinct. Respect for social betters was nonsense; the thing to do was organize and do battle with them for a bigger slice of the take.

In effect—and to the substantial benefit of the working class, at least in the democracies—each man was beginning to view the world in the light of what he most feared and most wanted, all questions of principle aside. But the eye of instinct is blind to many details of character and motivation; it is apt to overlook fine distinctions and concentrate upon the immediately useful or gratifying. It is concerned not with persons but with results. So class

* My own parents had this notion.

hatreds, like racism* and the reaction to it, allow for no exceptions; and in a class war, no matter how many concessions the dominant may make to the dominated, neither side really relents; peace never comes.†

In other words, the same inner changes that made the fortunate, in the 1920s, into fake revolutionaries‡ made the less fortunate into real ones—the lower middle class into potential or actual fascists; the workingmen into militant unionists, members of the *Front Populaire*, anarchosyndicalists, the doomed left of Spain and Germany. Something like this had been in the making since 1848, but the fake revolutionaries—the libertines of circa 1925— permitted themselves only a hint of awareness of that fact in their fanatic dread of Communism. They could not see the connection between their own liberated behavior and that of the native lower classes. If the latter were becoming restive, the trouble had to be foreign influence—Bolshevik agitators, the example of the Soviet Terror. It was almost the first piece of nonsense I learned at my mother's knee: that the only thing wrong with this otherwise perfect Republic was the Communists—domestic or not, it really didn't matter; their mere existence anywhere hung over us all like a curse.

In America this notion was to become the basis of an unending propaganda campaign, an instrument of rascals, and the unchallengeable premise of a foreign policy that was to last, with a few enforced zigzags, for over fifty years, embroiling us finally in the most disastrous and embarrassing of all our wars, in defense of "democracy" in South Vietnam. It also bred its counternonsense— the view among children of the Great Depression that Communism was not the Devil after all but the key to decency and social progress. It didn't count that Joe Steel killed millions of his own citizens, wiped out the best of his generals in the Purge Trials of

---

* It is interesting that anti-Semitism began its recrudescence in Germany with the Lasker inquiry of 1873. Note that the Germans had then just won a war —the Franco-Prussian—so that the usual explanation for Nazi anti-Semitism does not apply here. There was no Versailles Treaty or inflation to blame.
† Hence the worker reluctance that is contributing to our inflation today. See Chapter V below.
‡ A moral revolution without morals is a fake.

31

'37, supported tendentious science in the person of Lysenko, and rushed to sign the Berlin–Moscow pact with the Nazis in 1939.

One could likewise overlook the outcome of the various Five-Year Plans, the cumbersome confusion of collectivized agriculture, the intrusion of politics into literally everything. It did not even matter that in Spain, while the fight against Franco and his German-Italian allies was under way, the suicidal persecution of splinter parties or individual deviants continued among the Loyalists with strong Soviet encouragement. The suggestion of disingenuousness, not to say of gross stupidity, in all this carried no great weight with the young American intellectuals and their working-class friends who wanted to believe that *some* social system somewhere worked better than our own. The fact that to most of them their adopted Mother Country, Russia, was no more than a rumor supported by faked statistics was a distinct advantage, as it would be to champions of Mao and Ho and Ché thirty years later.

It is clear from this distance that the Victorian rational consensus never really took in the first place. It seems to have been more a hope than a *fait accompli* shared and believed in by millions and so likely to endure. In its heyday, the reaction against it had already begun. Art and the masses were never quite convinced that reason, rather than instinct and emotion, was their true friend. From World War I on, that lack of conviction spread to almost everyone. We were ready for the New Nonsense.

ii

On Being a Believer

By the New Nonsense I mean that body of contemporary ideas which, although widely discussed and taken by many with the utmost seriousness, either lack support from existing evidence or are clearly contradicted by it. What is novel about the majority of these ideas is the sudden revival of interest in them—the resurgence of nonsense itself. Astrology, for example, has been somewhat modernized, but there is nothing new about it in principle. What makes it part of the New Nonsense is its tremendous vogue. Neither Norman Vincent Peale nor Billy Graham is a New Nonsense figure;* the Jesus Freaks are. Freud does not belong to the movement, but a number of his ideas and his plagiarists do.

The notion of extrasensory perception, like that of the soul or detachable astral self, probably comes down to us from Neolithic times. By 1900, interest both in psychic phenomena and in astrology appeared to be dying, and the reign of reason seemed as secure as perhaps it ever has. Who would have predicted that within sixty or seventy years the public, ignorant and educated alike, would be drifting back into a muddled supernaturalism; that universities would be establishing chairs in parapsychology; that scientific papers and best sellers would be written about clairvoyance, psychokinesis, teleportation, and "psitrons," or sinister machines for concentrating and broadcasting "brain waves," and that gov-

---

* Some will feel that Billy Graham should be included. I disagree on the ground that he represents not a new vogue but possibly the last of a very old one.

ernment and private funding would be available for this sort of research? (See Chapter VI.)

The element common to all departments of the New Nonsense
is simply an inclination to willful personal belief so strong that it
amounts to a compulsion. Ordinarily what arouses our interest in
some fact or idea is the threat or promise we sense it holds for us;
in rare cases we may be drawn to it out of pure curiosity. Interest
is thus chiefly a matter of direct practical concern. Our instincts
for survival, procreation, or self-advancement prompt it; and if the
promptings are sufficiently relentless, we give in, the result being
either nonsensical behavior (i.e., actions too primitive or superstitious to rate as adaptive) or else intellectual nonsense—some form
of willful personal belief that tells the believer's Id what it demands to hear. Such beliefs fall roughly into two classes: those
which can be acted on, after a fashion, and those which can't.

Provided he lives in a permissive society, the man who solves his
anxiety-cum-identity problems through sex can be a "swinger" to
the limit of his God-given abilities, and it may be years before the
difficulties inherent in that solution catch up with him. The believer in Mind Control or scientology, on the other hand, knows
from the outset that certain forms of "reality testing" are not for
him. In scientology, for instance, the subject or patient being "au-
dited" is encouraged to go back in time not merely to his own
childhood but to previous incarnations. But if, in fact, we can recall who we were in former lives, we should be able to give details
(as Bridey Murphy did), and through some of these, our recollections could be checked:* i.e., scientology has the means to show
that some of its claims are sound—but no one seems to use them.
It is simply an item of faith among scientologists that we *do* re-

---

* As was done in Bridey's case with quite conclusive results. I know a man in
Boston, a Mind Control graduate as it happens, who remembers that he was
a German burgher in one of the Hanseatic towns. I suggested that, if he
couldn't go there, he might write a letter to the keeper of the town's archives
to see if by any chance his former name, birth and death dates, date of marriage, etc., were on record. He said this project sounded "very interesting" but
did nothing about it. When I last talked to him, he told me he had been
telepathically exploring the Sargasso Sea and had found a submerged temple
there.

member our other lives, as well as everything that has happened to us in this one, and any factual inquiry into either of these propositions is considered unnecessary.

The same I found to be true of Silva Mind Control. Basically, the Silva method teaches people to regulate their own EEGs, or "brain waves"—a skill that Yogis apparently developed centuries ago. (In fact, a scientific paper about it, published by Anand in 1961, appears to have started the vogue for biofeedback or alpha control or, lately, Transcendental Meditation.) It is quite likely that this skill has many of the good physiological effects claimed for it: lowering blood pressure and stress-hormone levels, easing anxiety, and in many cases dramatically relieving such seemingly psychogenic disorders as trigeminal neuralgia (*tic douloureux*). What brings the customers in, however, is not benefits such as these but metaphysical returns to which the physical are incidental. Only discover the soul's powers and those of the body will improve automatically. Like the scientologists, Silva's people put much emphasis on reincarnation, ESP, and related matters. Alpha control, it turns out, is essentially a technique for the rediscovery and freeing up of the spirit. The novitiate is told that he can learn to "project" his thoughts to almost anywhere, particularly if he has some benign purpose in doing so. He can, for example, "see" the body of a distant invalid not previously known to him, diagnose its trouble, and send it telepathic help. If it is to the benefit of humanity,* he can also project himself to other planets, to other solar systems in our galaxy, or even to other galaxies. In Mind Control sessions, he is repeatedly assured that these are powers he himself can develop, and that in only four days of intensive training at a total cost (in 1972) of $150. (Advanced courses are also available.)

Once into Silva training myself, I became particularly fascinated by the possibilities for space exploration that it opened up. Having a scientific background, I was, however, disturbed by what seemed to me certain technical difficulties. A graduate of the course, a young electrical engineer, attended one of our sessions to demonstrate a surefire mnemonic technique that is one of Silva's side of-

* A phrase often used in the Mind Control litany.

ferings. During our lunch break, I asked him why it was that ESP seemed to work at any range. Why could one "project" one's thoughts to Hong Kong or Betelgeuse and get back as clear and prompt a return as from, say, Metuchen, New Jersey? Just as in radio transmission, wasn't the speed of light a limiting factor over astronomical distances, and the signal-to-noise ratio a problem even over some distances here on earth?

In ESP, he told me, there *is* no noise, so messages can come in clearly from any distance.* And whatever radiation is involved goes faster than the speed of light; therefore it is possible to travel astrally to remote galaxies and back within quite small intervals of time. Could he tell me how small? How fast did ESP "radiations" go? He replied that he didn't think the question ought to be put that way. We might be dealing with another dimension altogether, a set of invisible shortcuts by which the astral self could get from anywhere to anywhere else in microseconds or less. In "projecting" our thoughts, we simply bypassed ordinary space.

These views were similar to others I had read about, for instance in Arthur Koestler's *Roots of Coincidence.* (See Chapter VI.) True, many in the field concede that ESP is capricious, but, as Mr. Koestler says, that may be because it is "governed by unconscious processes which are not under voluntary control." The noise, in other words, is not on the airwaves but in the sender's or receiver's head. Mind Control seems to work on the assumption that much of that noise is what we naively call thinking—the conscious mental effort associated with "fast" beta waves in the EEG. The Silva method teaches us to minimize those; so for the initiate, ESP or thought projection should be as static-free as FM and thousands or millions of times more powerful.

If *that* was so, I could only conclude that a revolution was at hand—one which would obviate much of the hardware now used for travel and communication. Instead of spending billions of dollars to send rocket-propelled craft lumbering off into space, we

---

* Nor is there, as with light, any spherical dispersion, apparently, because the intensity of the messages does not fall off as a function of distance. Hence the receiver has no threshold problems either; no message is too faint to get through.

might now visit the same places in a fraction of the time and at practically no cost at all. The crucial first step was a controlled experiment which would demonstrate to conventional scientists and the world at large that thought projection actually works.

While I was taking the Mind Control course, an exploration of Mars by means of unmanned spacecraft was under way, and plans for further explorations had been announced. Here, then, was a perfect opportunity. As I saw it, a group of Silva graduates could get together, project their thoughts to that planet, examine it, and compile a report describing in detail what they had seen there. Copies of the report could be filed with NASA, the Library of Congress, *The New York Times*, etc. If those data matched the findings made on subsequent conventional spaceflights, ESP would have proved itself and the whole universe would in effect have been opened up for study—not by NASA-operated instrument packages, but by teams of scientifically trained swamis, each putting himself into his alpha or theta state and sending his thoughts wherever he had decided it might be most rewarding for them to go. And José Silva, of course, would go down in history as a figure overtopping Isaac Newton.

It seemed to me that these were tremendously exciting ideas. If thought projection has the powers claimed for it, and if, as I'm assuming, it is to the benefit of humanity to learn more about Mars,* then this sort of data gathering should certainly be possible. To my amazement, however, none of those taking the Silva course seemed to share my enthusiasm for this project. They weren't interested in space in the least; they appeared to be mainly interested in what Mind Control could do for their insomnia, or their sex lives, or in aiding them to "program" their children, while asleep, by ESP (an application of the method I found rather creepy).

For a while after graduation from the course, some went on with their medical "readings," getting together regularly in what they

* I put in this qualifier because it is part of Silva doctrine. Evidently there is some cosmic law which forbids the nonbeneficial use of psychic powers. This belief, however, is confined to Silva and his group. Another school sees enormous potential for evil in ESP and urges we develop psi weapons with all speed (Chapter VI).

called cottage groups to send telepathic help to friends or relatives of the various members. But a year later, that was dying down, and there were signs that the subjective benefits of alpha control were not what they had been, either. One woman, who six months before had been able to use it instead of the usual shot of Novocain when she went to have her teeth fixed, and who maintained that she had been relieved of a nearly lifelong depression, has since had a serious relapse. Her anxiety and depression are back, and the dentist again has to give her Novocain, but she insists she got *something* out of the course. Like the Yogis, she finds alpha control a help, but one has to keep at it. It's like doing push-ups.

At the time I was beginning to see the scientific implications of Mind Control, I wrote to Mr. Silva himself, proposing the Mars experiment just described. In a letter dated September 14, 1972, he said his organization was "willing to go into a project if NASA co-operates with information; if not, no sense spending time and money if our findings cannot be verified. It seems that we first need to verify objectively, subjectively found information. . . . I think that the project would be a lot easier if we knew what we were looking for. Better still, if our survival was threatened and information was needed for survival, and if such information was out there somewhere in the universe, these are the conditions that are ideal for success with mental projection. If you still feel we can accomplish something, let me know how you want to participate in this project. . . ."

It seems that during the Grissom-Young space shot in the 1960s, Silva sensitives had done some ESP tracking of the vehicle and its occupants and submitted the results to NASA, which had not replied. (Silva's letter to me included copies of some correspondence on this matter.) I thereupon wrote to a friend of mine at NASA to see if better relations could be established. In his answer, my friend said: "NASA has been exposed to much of this stuff. There is now some *sub rosa* work that is officially denied but is tolerated. The Mars caper may be too sci-fi-ish and *visible* for NASA to get involved with"—and there the whole matter rested.

Two points about it particularly struck me. One was Silva's

statement that if our survival was threatened, and pertinent information "was out there somewhere in the universe," then the conditions for exploring space by thought projection were "ideal." Why should that be? Were we here confusing our motive for developing ESP powers with a law limiting the powers themselves? It is quite likely that one of our strongest motives for believing in ESP is, in a primitive way, religious. Thought projection equals soul travel. To be capable of it means to have a soul—a self possibly immune to the laws governing the body, and so capable of living indefinitely. Besides placating our instinct for survival in this way, ESP evidently serves the same purpose more directly. From a strictly scientific standpoint, there is no *a priori* reason why, if we can "project" our thoughts at all, we can't send them just anywhere. What Mr. Silva seems to be saying is that we don't *want* to send them just anywhere; there has to be something in it for us, "information needed for survival," or we're not interested.

In short, the teachings of Mind Control appeal not to the disinterested curiosity or imagination of the faithful, but to their fantasy—essentially to a kind of valetudinarian selfishness. To heal others by thought projection is a demonstration of the mind's more-than-earthly powers and a prelude to healing oneself. ESP will work if it meets the requirements of instinct—if relief from pain, enhancement of basic pleasures, or mitigation of our fear of death is the object. Once we become convinced that it will work to these ends, the question of whether it works at all is taken as settled. No further test, such as the Mars experiment, is needed; on the contrary, the believer has everything to lose and nothing to gain by it. Suppose the experiment should fail? Suppose, on closer examination, it turned out that ESP is simply a phenomenon like static electricity, obviating any need to reinvent the incorporeal immortal self? No Mind Control graduate in his senses would welcome that result, which is no doubt why so few seem interested in pushing verification of the method any further than is absolutely necessary. The majority are not just incurious but anticurious. This, I suspect, is the law Mr. Silva is really talking about: ESP works when it must—when we have an overpowering need for it to do so—but not, like gravitation, when no one is looking.

The second point that struck me was NASA's extreme reluctance to become involved in the same sort of "reality testing." One obvious reason is that the scientists at NASA haven't time for such nonsense—but the experiment I proposed would take very little. One of them might send a two-page letter to Silva telling him what sorts of thing the next Mars shots would be on the lookout for. Several years later, when the shots had been made and the data were in, a couple of experts could spend a day or two comparing Silva's findings with NASA's. A summary showing the hits or misses made by ESP could then be released to Silva's people and the press, and that would be that.

Perhaps the feeling at NASA is that to give even this much *Lebensraum* to a topic such as thought projection might be dangerous to its "image" as a hard-science agency.* People out front might begin to think NASA itself was harboring a few cranks. Anyone who has watched them in action knows that scientists are exceedingly touchy on all questions relating to their own intellectual respectability—a phenomenon interesting in itself. Why should men supposedly in possession of methods and ideas of such power, and reputed, moreover, for their hardheadedness and extreme independence, be so nervous about the good opinion of their peers, let alone about the misconceptions which the general public might form of them? Have they too become a bit shaky in their ultimate beliefs, retreating (as men of declining faith often do) into an aggressive orthodoxy? Is that why, like the laity but for opposite reasons, they have no wish to put ESP to the test? It is conceivable.

A few scientists have apparently done a complete turnabout on such questions as psi phenomena or the catastrophe theories of Dr. Velikovsky. (See Chapters VI and VIII.) And particularly in Palo Alto and other West Coast centers of learning, the testing of psychics who can allegedly cause small objects to move merely by willing it, or who can "project" their thoughts so as to perturb elaborately shielded magnetometers, seems to have become a thriving scientific sideline. The research community remains sharply

---

* Hence, of course, to its future funding.

divided as to the respectability, or even the sanity, of some of these inquiries, but the fact remains that they are being made.

The climate of any era is notoriously hard to resist. Given the climate of ours, it is natural that nonsense should try for a double appeal, offering the most ancient of consolations but in "scientific" form. Conversely, doctrinaire materialism, the once united front of the learned, is showing cracks here and there. If thanks to the philosophers and the *Zeitgeist*, and despite its own successes, science is beginning to have doubts, one can certainly sympathize.

iii

Touch Hate Feel Etc.

The Mind Control classes I attended consisted of some two dozen people, including a sniffish young housewife, a writer for *The Boston Globe*, a hippie contingent (who dropped out after the first day), a massive fiftyish divorcée with dyed red hair, a professor whose hobby was parapsychology, a homosexual and his boy companion (a refulgent acne case), a young woman in skintight leather clothes who ran a dance studio, and a retired manufacturer who dabbled in witchcraft and was said to have started an orgy club. During our get-acquainted session, everybody told what he was there for. A recently widowed lady said she hoped to get over her insomnia. The woman who ran the dance studio wanted to learn how to manage her teen-age pupils better. The manufacturer wanted something new to occupy him.

But behind all these stated purposes one felt there was another. We were looking for contact—with others; with a Higher Purpose. We wanted to go to church again, to throw our troubles on the Lord, and the Silva course perfectly anticipated these leanings. The young man addressing us looked like a preacher. He stood in a sort of pulpit; he roused us to a brotherly warmth for one another; and when the heavy work of training began, he read us the words of the master from a huge loose-leafed tome set before him on a lectern. The effect was quite marvelous. We immediately found ourselves caught up in a revivalist enthusiasm, talking together during coffee or lunch breaks as though we had known each other for years. It seemed remarkable that such empathy could develop so quickly among total strangers—the pity being that it should last only for those few days, which of course no one believed at the time: we were friends forever.

Though a number of us had mild to acute personality tics, none, I think, was really a clinical case. Quite a few, however, described themselves as having lately passed through a crisis of utter loneliness or alienation. It struck me, as I listened to them, that that kind of loneliness, which a generation or more of writers have been telling us is our national disease, is something we bring on ourselves, by mutual agreement. It's not that we're so bent upon privacy; far from it. The compact I'm speaking of is the one that says we will each go it alone, without God, with a minimum of ideals or illusions and a maximum of attention to the needs and fears and desires of Number One. This is radical egoism, a minimal philosophic position and in the end a minimally civilized one, reducing all relationships to arrangements of convenience—all friendship to mere acquaintance,* all love to sexual or familial use, all activity to profitable activity (even if the profit be sexual or psychological rather than monetary).

Many of the people taking the Mind Control course were, I think, casualties of this way of life. For years, without knowing why exactly, they had suffered from a certain crushing of the spontaneous in themselves; had drifted into an unbearable, almost animal, isolation which neither community work nor socializing nor adventures in sex nor business success nor motherhood nor anything else seemed to alleviate. And when the crisis came, they found they had no one really to tell about it—no one who would be more than they had always been to others: a casual presence, a sounding board. Essential pragmatism had caught up with them. They had become *unable to communicate*.

If one can believe all one reads and hears, this is *the* problem of our time, although on the surface it would hardly seem so. In the

---

* Based often on simple proximity; hence the friends-on-the-job who change with the job.

past it must have been worse. Throughout most of history, communication has chiefly been one-way—from the top of the social or familial order down—the only reply sought* usually being some form of acquiescence. With the democratization of everything, family life included, in this century, all that should have changed; and if sheer talkativeness is any index, it has.

A visitor from some other age or country might conclude that we had become one of the most promiscuously confiding peoples on earth. In planes or buses or bars, at meetings or cocktail parties, it is difficult not to run into some slight acquaintance or total stranger who will tell you his life's story, often in the most embarrassing detail. Why do we do this? Not because others listen, but precisely because they don't. Damning or humiliating as our revelations may be, we know that nothing is apt to come of them because our vis-à-vis gives them no real importance. They are about us, not him; if he absorbs what we are saying at all, he will have forgotten most of it ten minutes later.

As a result of this strange "block," this deafness to one another's most vital news, we have been obliged to create a new profession, or rather to modernize and vastly expand an old one—that of the listener-helper. In Protestant America,† that was all the foothold psychoanalysis needed—psychoanalysis and, of course, heaven knows how many other therapeutic systems based on similar principles, from psychodrama and Buchmanism to Encounter and Scream.

If I seem to be ridiculing these developments, it is not because I am callous to the sufferings which are their reason for being, but because, bedeviled as we are, we seem to prefer some bizarre simplification to the plain truth. As agnostics we want all the goodies that a materialistic existence can provide. At the same time, we cannot see‡ where the materialistic view of ourselves is leading— where it has already led. If they happen to be contrary to our will-

---

* Or even permitted.
† Protestant and Jewish, since neither religion includes the confessional.
‡ As in the slang phrase "I can't see that," meaning that I dislike something to the point of making it literally invisible.

ful personal beliefs, the most obvious conclusions escape us. It seldom occurs to us to connect Dostoevski's theorem—that if God
doesn't exist, anything is permitted—with the continuing per capita increase in crimes of gratuitous violence. Crime, of course, does
not disappear in religious societies; we are disappointed to find,
however, that in the more lenient atmosphere of our present Welfare State, crime, often of a quite senseless kind, is flourishing.[3]
Why should it not? In a world effectively without principles, a
Skinnerian moral vacuum in which one of the going ideals is to
"let it all hang out," it follows that some of the things hanging out
are going to be pretty ugly.

To admit that, however, would be to question the life of instinct
as a whole, including some of the presumably more harmless pleasures which, as law-abiding skeptics, we permit ourselves. One could
argue, for instance, that "swingerism," carried to its logical extreme, becomes as brutal in its way as the indulgence of pure
aggression (to which it is physiologically not unrelated*). But this
would be to reintroduce a kind of moral unease that would ruin
the healthy normality we feel is just within our grasp.

One way around this difficulty is to revive Rousseau's fantasy of
Original Innocence, which of course makes the present boom in
violence and the "rip-off" unnecessarily hard to account for. Like
other fantasies, however, this one is meant not to explain anything
but to make us feel better. The fact we perhaps least want to face
is the one long asserted by our religion: namely, that man is *not*
born good, and that what we call wholeness or "integration" is not
really a goal but a battle—at best a balancing act, a perpetually
unstable reconciliation of forces which, unreconciled, simply tear
us to pieces, sometimes not just individually but en bloc, whole
societies at a time.† We tend to see inner conflict as a clinical disorder, when in fact it is almost a first law of human psychic life,

* As also shows up in our slang ("screw" for swindle, etc.) and in the institution of rape. The close relation between sexuality and ferocity is suggested by
various kinds of evidence. Rage and desire have similar physiological signs; the
cries of lovemaking are like those of fighting, etc.
† As the modern Germans have reason to know, and we in America are just
finding out.

given that we have "drives" or instincts which are frequently at odds with each other, and the faculty of reason or impersonal awareness which is frequently at odds with all of them.

Whatever names we give to the various components of our nature, this would seem to be the conclusion forced upon us by our daily experience. But if we accept it, how is happiness in any ordinary, straightforward sense possible? This is the difficulty; for happiness *must* be possible. It is the dream and last recourse of Man in "materialistic" ages: to achieve what was once called grace or blessedness, not merely through things but just by *being himself*— simple old Adam who, it goes without saying, enjoys his possessions and status, and grabs what he can of both. The idea that once he gets them he may still be unhappy is totally unacceptable because it leaves us with nothing—no God, no life to come, and no guaranteed prospects, even in this one; no hope of surcease in any form. So some variant of Rousseau's myth is absolutely required—an ideal of uncomplicated normality which we insist *is* achievable, although almost no one comes close.* By the same reasoning, any unfavorable turn that our daily battle with ourselves takes is "abnormal"; he who continually loses and makes strategic retreats is a "neurotic"; the decisively defeated are insane (extreme cranks, psychotics, etc.). Having assumed there is a "normal" condition in which man, simply by being true to his given nature, becomes happy and good, we are forced to see 90 percent of human behavior as in some degree abnormal and society as a sort of vast outpatient clinic—a *Weltanschauung* that psychiatrists have, not unexpectedly, done much to encourage.†

Another, rather paradoxical consequence of this view of our-

---

* We are so clever at imitating one another, though, that our sameness in mannerisms and even in ways of thinking makes "normality" appear a more realizable condition than it is. Actually, it is by our knack or tic of imitation that we hide the deviant in ourselves from public view, only to have it burst embarrassingly out of hiding in such occurrences as the Watergate affair or a sudden attack of exhibitionism.

† Indeed, psychohistory, as it is all too appropriately called, is rather a vogue just now. The genre appears to have started with Freud's *Civilization and Its Discontents*, and in the hands of such practitioners as Norman O. Brown, it extends the sickroom atmosphere of our age backward to envelop much of history.

selves has been to trivialize our concept of sickness: i.e., everybody is a little sick (deviant) but, except for the usual hopeless few, nobody is *very* sick. Our signs—anxiety, depression, various psychogenic sexual disorders—may be quite severe, but normality, we feel, is never far away. So while our "clinical picture" might appear to classify us as raging misfits, amazingly enough four days of alpha-control training may snap us right out of it. As a matter of fact, even a kind of massage may do it—the kind invented by Ada Rolf and known as Rolfing.

The idea underlying Rolfing derives, apparently, from the psychiatrist Wilhelm Reich's notion of "character armor." We wear our inner strains in our facial and skeletal muscles, so a trained eye can read the man in his posture and the way he moves. Reich appears to have regarded "character armor" as a symptom which would clear up when other, more fundamental problems were solved. The key, in his system, was better orgasms, and the key to those the orgone box (also called an accumulator). The box sopped up a cosmic sex principle (orgone) the way an antenna sops up electromagnetic waves, and the patient inside the box was thereby infused with new sexual élan. As his orgasms improved, his tensions let up and his "character armor" melted away, leaving him supple and unrepressed and erotically in top shape: in a word, normal.

In Rolfing, if I understand it, one does not attack the armor via the character but vice versa. By skillfully kneading various muscles, the Rolfer breaks up the patient's outer tensions and so his inner ones. What could be simpler than that? Scream therapy, developed by Dr. Arthur Janov, and Encounter, as practiced at Esalen and elsewhere, are nearly as direct. In Scream,* the patient purges himself of early, crippling traumata by yelling; in Encounter, by all sorts of means—including, it is said, sexual intercourse with the teacher, if that seems appropriate (which I gather it often does).

Encounter is thus of particular interest since it incorporates

---

* See, for instance, Janov's book *The Primal Scream*, itself a fine example of the uninhibited shit-fuck style of self-expression which is supposedly one of the benefits of Scream.

many of the methods that Scream and Rolfing use to demolish "character armor"; and its concept of communication is about as close to nature as one can get without running seriously afoul of the law or ending up (as at least one graduate has) dead. In 1970, a course given at the Esalen Institute in Big Sur, or by Daniel M. Casriel, M.D., in New York, cost the client about $35 for the initial consultation and $15 to $20 for each succeeding group session. According to an article by Bruce Maliver, a psychoanalyst, in the Sunday *New York Times Magazine*, "Casriel's mimeographed information handout says it takes about 100 to 150 group meetings and 3 to 4 marathons [30-hour sessions at $100 per shot] during the course of a year to solidify new healthy feelings." The same report estimates Casriel's weekly enrollment at about 800 patients. (These figures mean that a patient taking the standard course lays out between $1,835 and $3,435, while Casriel's organization, at an estimated $20 per head, is grossing $16,000 a week or $800,000 over a fifty-week year.) The declared aim of the therapy is to break down inhibitory barriers between us, making us capable once more of emotional "involvement." It sets up primitive relationships intended to make The Other real to us in a way in which he or she seldom is in ordinary conversation, or sometimes even in bed. Lovemaking, in our alienated state, may simply not do the trick.

Here, roughly, is how Encounter works. Numbers of the afflicted gather together under the care of a "group leader." Maliver describes the experiences of a girl he calls Julia: " 'Let's get out some of that anger,' said her group leader. . . . 'I'm angry,' Julia answered in a mild querulous voice. . . . 'I don't believe you're angry,' the leader replied. 'Make me believe it.' Goaded by her group and leader Julia expressed her 'I'm angry' in a louder and louder voice. The group shouted, 'More, more, you're not angry enough!' Julia continued . . . until she was shrieking at the top of her lungs, 'I'M ANGRY, I'M ANGRY, I'M ANGRY,' and was finally reduced to . . . exhaustion . . . After a number of such sessions, Julia found that her long-standing depression had actually lifted and she told a friend, 'I'm happier than I've ever been.' The sessions were unlike anything she had ever experienced. 'I'm learning how to say what's on my mind and to shout out my feelings and be angry' she told a girl friend. . . . Three months after she began her group encounter experiences, Julia killed herself by swallowing several dozen sleeping pills."

Maliver reports a session which he attended as a paid-up participant: "First came a technique for releasing tension in which each person stood and screamed as loudly . . . as he could. 'Now wave your arms,' Schutz [the group leader] yelled above the din, 'and jump up and down in your places.' In between the . . . screaming and jumping were several periods of silence and contemplation." At the end of one tranquil interlude, the participants were told to introduce themselves to each other without words, simply by the expressions in their eyes. "Next a period of touching, shaking hands, placing a hand to a face, or one cheek to another, or hugging or grasping each other's shoulders."

After these preliminaries, things got more energetic again: "Schutz stationed 10 people a few feet apart along the walls and asked the rest of us to form lines in front of each one. The instructions were to ask yourself how dominant or submissive you felt and . . . to place yourself in your line with the most dominant person at the front. 'Of course someone else may not agree with you, and if he's in your spot get him out of there,' Schutz urged.

"The ten fights that followed were amazing not only for their . . . violence but because in many cases women fought like tigers for . . . 'dominant' spots."

More of the same developed later: "As the day-long micro-lab progressed, several very serious fights were triggered by such 'games' as breaking-in-breaking-out [of groups] and 'High Noon.' We were told not to stop them, incidentally: Schutz's rationale is that minor physical injuries are psychologically worth it, and later acknowledged that there is a weekly crop of broken bones and lost teeth at Esalen. We also took an extended 'body trip,' all 200 of us lying on the floor, imagining that we were entering our bodies and exploring them"—possibly to discover a few sore spots or loosened teeth.

"Probably the high point of the day . . . came when almost all of the group followed the suggestion that they undress down to underwear and explore each other's bodies for signs of tension and for 'neurotic muscle' areas . . . This particular exercise caused considerable amazement among the hotel staff, who were peeking through the door." (The session was held in the Jack Tar Hotel in San Francisco and at $25 a head stood to gross about $5,000.)

A more advanced form of the method Maliver describes as "Crotch Eyeballing: Special technique in nude marathons. The entire group surrounds each person in turn and closely examines his or her genitals. Supposedly this exercise reduces the shame connected with having one's privates looked at, or doing the looking." A *still* more advanced method is "Group Grope: Group gets acquainted by feeling each other. Sometimes can turn into an attack on genital privacy" (although it is hard to see how, by this time, privacy in any form could still be an issue).

The girl Julia, who killed herself, "had begun to have an affair with one of her several leaders . . . Her disappointment came when she found out that he was having sex with several other girls he'd met in the same way. . . . Apparently Julia's leader took very seriously the encounter culture principle of 'acting out' feelings"—as did Julia.

The Casriel technique is quite similar to that of the Esalen group. "Members are taught to grab hold of a feeling—whether pain, pleasure, love or anger—and to express it in a series of yells, screams and moans which increase in volume to almost unbearable intensity. . . . Doctor Casriel has a considerable staff, including a $40,000-a-year senior group leader, an ex-patient whom he describes as a 'formerly psychotic lawyer.'" It is natural that a field with such powerful attractions should become highly competitive, and by 1970 it was doing so. A man who had been ejected from Casriel's sessions as a gate-crasher subsequently set up as an encounterman himself, but seems to have found the business too heady, since he ended up being carted away to Bellevue.

Other entries in the field include such evocatively named institutions as The Center for the Whole Person (Philadelphia, Penn-

sylvania), the Explorations Institute (Berkeley, California), and
the Athena Center for Creative Living ("with intimacy labs in
Mexico and Aliquippa, Pa."). "Over 100 such growth centers,"
Maliver reports, "have sprung up across the nation in the last year
or two, all offering . . . promises of warmth, human contact, personal growth and, often, a touch of mysticism." One is reminded
of the sadomasochistic rites of later Roman times described by
Mommsen—"the wild worship of . . . Bellona to whom the
priests in their festal processions shed their own blood as a sacrifice"—with the difference that today bloodshed seems to be confined to the laity, whose sacrifice also includes a considerable out-
lay of cash. (It is probable that the Mystery Cults too levied what
they could from the membership, but as the latter was largely pro-
letarian and the Roman gross national product relatively small and
narrowly distributed, the returns from that form of Whole Person
Therapy must, by modern standards, have been chicken feed.)

The variations on the foregoing approach to salvation are of
course innumerable, the whole movement having begun roughly at
the turn of the century, with the psychoanalytic method for obtaining "a return of the repressed." Ever since Freud's ideas started
to become generally known, the notion of cure-through-purgation,
of "letting it all hang out," getting rid of one's "character armor,"
"telling it like it is," "being sincere," never "holding back," etc.,
has gained ground until today it seems to be an article of faith
with millions. The question is, does it work? Is it really based on
sound psychological principles? Has psychoanalysis, itself, worked?
In *The Crisis of Psychoanalysis*, Erich Fromm says: "The analyst
offered a substitute for religion, politics and philosophy. Freud has
allegedly discovered all the secrets of life . . . One was a member
of a somewhat esoteric sect, with the analyst as its priest, and one
felt less puzzled as well as less lonely by marking time on the
couch." He goes on to say that notwithstanding various abuses
and misunderstandings, the method *did* work. ". . . Analysts . . .
have observed a considerable number of people relieved of troubles
they complained about. Many patients have experienced a new
sense of vitality and capacity for joy, *and no other method than*

*psychoanalysis could have produced these changes."** (Italics added.) *How many* patients? one might ask.

The profession has been loath to publish statistics, and the few follow-up studies that I have seen strongly suggest that the rate of demonstrable improvement achieved in psychoanalysis does not differ significantly from the rate of spontaneous remission that has been reported for various untreated psychiatric disorders. (Note too that it was not psychoanalysis but a drug, chlorpromazine, which finally began emptying the back wards of our mental hospitals. For the psychotic, who needed it most, psychoanalysis never worked at all.) Like addiction to "hard" drugs, which is said to die out in many after the age of forty, our troubles do simply tend to pass with time unless they drive us over the edge first; and if we imagine we *made* them pass by weekly or daily confessionals, so much the better. The doctor has our money, but we have our high morale and feeling of accomplishment.

As nonsense goes, all this is fairly innocent. The theoretical foundations for it are something else again, and the transformations to which Freud's basic ideas have since been subjected are in some cases quite startling. In the same period in which psychoanalysis has been declining in popular favor, "disciplines" such as Reich's orgone therapy or L. Ron Hubbard's Dianetics (now reborn as scientology), not to mention Yoga, and Yang and Yin dietetics, have begun replacing it.

A common thread in these developments is that they add a mystical dimension lacking in Freud. Their central assumption seems to be that deep inside me is the Real Me, locked away by the repressive forces of society, and by those superficial processes we refer to as thinking. Society *teaches* us to think—mostly in wrong, irrelevant ways; and with its help we also develop this fearful Superego, this "character armor" which shuts us off from everyone, including ourselves. Stop thinking and start feeling and things will begin to come right. The quality of our orgasms—regarded by many as the acid test—will begin to improve. We will "relate"

* Encounter Group people, scientologists, Transcendental Meditators and graduates of Silva Mind Control would certainly dispute this claim.

more to everything, living or dead. In the extreme, the doors of perception may open so wide that we experience the "oceanic sense" and go to the roots of being, and know God.

In scientology, the basic therapeutic method is called "auditing," which is somewhat like Freudian analysis except that the patient's remembering appears to be more directed by the "auditor" than it used to be by the analyst. Evidently transmigration of souls is an important part of scientological doctrine, and "recovery of the repressed" can now span eons instead of the few decades of a man's present life. How are therapists going to handle such masses of data, even with the help of computers? How is the brain able to store them—in particular since scientology also postulates that we recall everything* that happened to us in this life: a fact we are normally not aware of, because 99 percent of this memory material tends to be repressed. According to one scientologist I know, there may admittedly not be enough neurons in the brain to accomplish that amount of remembering. Storage of "engrams" must, therefore, he thinks, involve some as yet unknown form of potential energy, which exists as a field or aura just outside of our heads. He assures me he can sense the quality of these auras in people—can almost see them.† My friend, incidentally, insists that he does not take drugs—in fact, he and his colleagues disapprove of them. Scientology does not believe in tampering with the senses.

For instance, I'm sure most scientologists would dismiss the kinds of therapy practiced at Esalen or by the staff of the Athena Center for Creative Living as mere quackery and sensationalism. They would be the first to admit that screaming, fighting, palpating strangers' faces, trading insults, or having mass sex is in the longer run not apt to result in much. Like the old-fashioned orgy, it may produce a temporary euphoria, derived from new feelings of freedom and personal zip, but it does not really address the problem. Neither did Dianetics, which came close to dying in the

---

* A rigorous test of this supposition would be very time-consuming. It might well take a day of "auditing" for a subject to recall everything that had happened to him in the last week. If he were 30 years (1,560 weeks) old, it would take him over four years of continuous auditing to complete the record.
† I have since met several people who do see auras.

early 1950s and is now thriving again, thanks to the religiocosmic elements it has added in becoming scientology.

Except for a few who have used astrology as a diagnostic tool (see pages 213–15 below), psychiatrists have mostly stayed away from the supernatural—a policy that may yet cost them their clientele. The aim of psychotherapy seemed simply to be to bring the patient to a state of naturalness; by resolving his inner conflicts, he became "realistic." It was taken for granted that en route he might divorce his wife, junk other old habits or associations, and become generally more forward about doing whatever the hell suited him —changes which showed that he had rid himself of the scruples, or "immature attitudes," that had so hampered him in the days of his illness.*

What the more positive or distinctively moral objectives of psychotherapy were was never made clear. Analysts such as Heinz Hartmann (in *Psychoanalysis and Moral Values*) took a sternly objective line: ". . . Psychoanalysis cannot be expected to provide us with ultimate moral aims . . . This is not to say we cannot make any statements on such aims . . . We can form a scientific opinion on what strivings they will or will not gratify . . ." —which suggests a rather utilitarian view of goodness, forbearance, and the like. In more popular works such as Karen Horney's, one read vague promises that the patient who had "worked through" his difficulties (say in two to four quite expensive years) would then be free to give or accept affection. Nor would he, in theory, be compelled to repress his aggressions as before, or refrain from doing much of anything that his new realism told him he might get away with. In short, he would have become normal. Instead of exploiting others unconsciously, as part of his neurotic "defenses," he could now exploit them quite consciously (unless you assume his native decency might prevent that).

It was perhaps only a question of time before these liberating

---

* Stated another way, one aim of psychoanalysis was to relieve residual Christians of their residual Christianity. The excuse was that residual Christians were often dreadful exploiters of one another—a situation that has not greatly changed since.

attitudes leaked over into the practice of psychiatry itself, resulting in some novel revisions in the Hippocratic code. Dr. Phyllis Chesler, a professor of psychology, recently published an article in *New York* magazine about the current vogue, "especially in New York but to a certain extent in California," for sexual intercourse on the analytic couch.

". . . William Masters and Virginia Johnson talked to many women who said that they had had sexual contact with their psychotherapists, and concluded, 'If only twenty-five percent of these specific reports are correct, there is still an overwhelming issue confronting professionals in this field.' "

Dr. Chesler quotes one Greenwich Village psychologist to the effect that doctors should sleep with their patients but only " 'very rarely. If they do they should send them to another doctor. You lose your objectivity. I know I do.' " In fact, psychiatrists themselves have been seeking psychiatric help on this question. The Greenwich Village man just quoted "says that he often treats other psychotherapists who sleep with their patients and who come to him for help in resolving the 'guilt' and 'conflict' precipitated by these relationships."

The details of some of the latter are depressing in the extreme. Dr. Chesler interviewed eleven women—nine New Yorkers and two Californians. "Seven of the women did not experience orgasm the first time; four women never did throughout the treatment. . . . Four of the therapists had difficulty in maintaining an erection." One woman said: " 'It took ten minutes. He jumped up, washed in the bathroom and was back at his typewriter. I thought . . . if anyone should know what he's doing a therapist should. If I don't have an orgasm here, then it's really my fault.' " Another said: " '. . . It was a very strange thing, there was almost no tenderness or prelove play. . . . Then all of a sudden he said, "Excuse me, I have to make a train," because his wife was sitting out in the Bronx with his kid. . . . It was probably the coldest affair I've had in my life.' " This patient clearly needed more analysis; she was not yet "realistic" enough. Neither was the one whose doctor-lover took ten minutes: " 'I finally asked him if he would marry me, and he just laughed and said no, he was more interested in my typing for him.' "

According to Dr. Chesler, two New York psychiatrists were creating what she calls "a primal patriarchal family empire," each one's consisting of a sizable harem of woman patients who not only serviced the doctor but cleaned up around the place, conformed to his eccentric schedules, and permitted their lives to be run by him in various other ways.

The question is whether many of these innovations weren't implicit in Freud from the beginning.* Freud, after all, was a pioneer—a Victorian who helped to end the age he grew up in—whereas his professional heirs are part of the result. In sleeping with their patients, they are simply approaching that unclouded realism which for decades has been the goal of the analysand. The remaining question raised by Chesler's article is how far in advance of his patients it is actually therapeutic for the doctor to be. If more and better orgasms are, as Reich and others maintain, the key to psychic well-being, it is clear that some of the patients Chesler described deserve to get their money back.

My object, again, is not to ridicule psychiatry, still less to make light of the sufferings it professes to alleviate—usually by more conservative methods than those just described. The issue is not the ethics of psychiatry as such but the future of the modern world, given that rock-bottom realism is now pretty much everyone's position. How far should realism be permitted to go; or rather (since law and the police can do only so much), how far can it be prevented from going? What is to keep us from lapsing either into an anarchic animalism or into some politically organized form of it, in which the police do finally control everything?

If the dream of educated Victorians had become a reality, this problem would never have arisen. Skinner's "automatic goodness" would work not for the reasons he supposes but because a majority of men would have developed reasoned convictions sufficiently

---

* Dr. Chesler quotes him as saying that if one kisses one's patient, there is apt to be a "lively scene"—as it turns out, a less lively one, often, than the patient had expected.

strong to enable them to act as Kant suggested.* That is, they would obey reasonable rules and restrain their natural urge to prey upon one another, not simply from fear of reprisals but from a clear awareness that by this sacrifice of immediate primal pleasures the lives of all would be made immeasurably less lonely, less embattled, less bitterly selfish and utilitarian than they now are. This, basically, is the Social Contract; but with a few possible exceptions, it has never come into existence.

The echo of the hope that it might survives among us in the shape of certain liberal institutions. The Western world did, at some cost to itself, abolish slavery, and particularly in the democracies of this century, has done much to alleviate the *de facto* slavery of the poor, including those impoverished by a combination of illness and old age.† But even as these improvements were still being made, a psychological drift in the opposite direction appears to have set in. One might date it from the First World War, after which men suddenly began to think and behave differently, as though they had decided to dispense with a whole body of notions which before 1914 most people had taken, or pretended to take, quite seriously.

The men of the Jazz Age took heart from what they thought science told them about themselves and the nature of existence, and so set about becoming radical egoists. In effect, Skinner's world of "automatic goodness" began right then; for to the extent to which morals came to be generally regarded as mere conventions or useful rules for others to observe, it was no longer men's moral convictions but simply their fear of the law or personal revenge which kept them from doing whatever they felt like.

The paradox is that this seemingly rational change in outlook immediately began to have irrational consequences. Even before Hitler and the Great Depression, the euphoria of the so-called Jazz Age had started to pass, and the Age of Anxiety set in. Amer-

* In the familiar maxim that we should behave in such a way that any of our actions could be the basis of a moral law.
† Under Skinner's view, it is hard to see how these things came about. Where was the "positive reinforcement" for anyone in freeing slaves—even, in many cases, for the slaves?

ica began to assume that world leadership which it now holds in quack medicine and various sorts of lunatic sectarianism. To judge from the number of psychoanalysts who migrated here at the time, we were also far ahead in the per capita production of well-to-do neurotics.

After we had won the Second World War and entered an era of unprecedented prosperity, our behavior became even more peculiar. First as juvenile delinquents and Beats, then as hippies, our children turned "mutinous";* some withdrawing into a passive, inarticulate, flamboyantly grubby world of their own; others taking up gang-fighting, "biking," bombing, or miscellaneous forms of vandalism. The Organization Men of the 1950s and the swingers of the '60s seemed, if anything, more jangled and disenchanted than their predecessors of the '20s had been. The age of drugs began—tranquilizers for the "straights," a whole pharmacopoeia of uppers, downers, and psychedelics for the far-out. Seers such as Wilhelm Reich and Immanuel Velikovsky turned into folk heroes. And by the end of the 1960s, Eastern religions, astrology, tarot cards, brown rice, ESP, Yoga, and witchcraft had become the rage with young people. A student taught in school about gravitation, stars, planets, etc., found no difficulty in supposing that these distant lumps of matter somehow influenced him and foretold his future.

In the same period, the boom in psychotherapy took an oddly primitive turn. Apparently not feeling up to the intricacies (let alone the expense) of old-fashioned analysis, people started trying more nitty-gritty approaches. The underlying object was to find not merely some shortcut out of our vacuous unhappiness, but one that required the least possible thought. Whether because it really wouldn't work or because (as I suspect) we were simply becoming incapable of it, sustained, conscious mental effort as a way of understanding and managing ourselves was out. We wanted to rid ourselves of unhappiness or "alienation" without disturbing the vacuity that was more than half of its cause. And inevitably, this new market for mindless cures of the mental created its own en-

* To use Robert Lindner's word.

trepreneurs—men of "charisma" who played back to the public its own prejudices, rephrased to sound like fundamental laws of human nature.*

So Encounter explicitly discourages "intellectualizing." In Mind Control, the "brain wave" frequencies one is specifically taught to minimize are the fast so-called beta rhythms normally associated with active thought. Thinking is bad—associated with stress and anxiety, hypertension, coronary disease, "alienation," etc. In Rolfing, it is not involved at all; you merely allow your "character armor" to be massaged off, and with it your psychic troubles. It's almost like removing warts. Alternatively, you can scream your disorders away in just a few sessions with Dr. Janov; or unload them on your fellow combatants in a free-for-all at Esalen. Or as a latter-day Reichian you can sit in your orgone "accumulator" and absorb cosmic sex radiations which will improve your orgasms; and as these approach perfection so, of course, will your mental health.

In short, the radical egoism of the '20s has begun turning into something like radical subjectivity a half century later. What looked like a move toward ever-greater realism was actually the reverse. Whereas writers such as Lewis Mumford and Charles Reich still see us as crushed under the dispiriting certainties of science, the last generation which was so—which had been "brain-washed" into thinking science the hope of mankind and a model of intellectual excellence—is already dead or in its dotage.

As Alvin Toffler tells us, we live in an age of increasing pluralism —in tastes, in beliefs, in standards of morals and of credibility. Far from thinking too much, the evidence is that we are thinking less and less—that our whole search is for ways to make ourselves sane and happy at the smallest possible cost in effort or responsibility. For really to think *is* to be responsible, whereas nonsense is indulgence of the more blind elements in the self. Because these generate wishes beyond fulfillment (to possess all women, exert all power, live for all time), fantasy or nonsense is their natural medium, and reason their natural enemy. But why is reason, at what

* To an extent, this description may even fit Freud, especially in his later days.

should have been its apogee, suddenly giving up the struggle? What are the consequences for our society likely to be?

We can see what the consequences were for other societies in the past. Possibly the best example is eighteenth-century France, in which one can trace quite clearly the progress from faith to agnosticism; from concern with the humanities to concern with science; and thence to concern with fake science and nonsense generally, in the decade just preceding the Revolution. The next chapter is about these developments, and about Mesmer, who was to his day what Dr. Janov promises to be to ours—a prophet who may not fully have understood his mission but did well enough from it for as long as it lasted.

iv

A Model Social Collapse

An early practitioner of the New Nonsense—if not in a sense its inventor—was Franz Anton Mesmer, an Austrian who had studied medicine in Vienna. He was also keenly interested in astrology, which he tried to put on a scientific footing by supposing the influence of the heavenly bodies to be due to electricity or magnetism. His first book, *De planetarum influxu,* appeared in 1766, and in his first experimental work with humans he is said to have used magnets.

Ten years later he evidently stumbled upon the principle of hypnotic suggestion. Instead of dropping the notion of magnetism, however, he transmuted it into "animal magnetism," a universal essence which bathed all living things. This essence was the "mesmeric fluid," or eighteenth-century orgone. Then as now, some people were orgone-rich, some not; those who were could use their own surpluses to revitalize the less well endowed. Mesmer, it turned out, was one of the fortunate few with fluid to spare.

He was in advance of his time too in proposing that many ills are psychosomatic. Consequently, anyone with plenty of animal magnetism and the clinical know-how needed to get it into others could heal their physical ailments by restoring their psyches. In the clinic which he opened in Paris in 1773 and operated with spectacular success until the outbreak of the Revolution, eleven years later, Mesmer seems to have combined his new notions of hypnotherapy with his earlier ones involving magnets. His attack on disease was thus double-barreled; besides injecting the vital

61

force into patients from his own person, he used a variety of accumulators which mechanically accomplished the same thing.

The essential apparatus, according to Robert Darnton,* consisted of "his famous tubs. These were usually filled with iron filings and mesmerized water contained in bottles arranged like the spokes of a wheel. They stored the fluid and transmitted it through movable iron rods, which the patients applied to their sick areas. Sitting around the tubs in circles, the patients communicated the fluid to one another by means of a rope looped about them all, and by linking thumbs and index fingers in order to form a 'mesmeric chain,' something like an electric circuit."

Mesmer also anticipated Reich's orgone boxes with his "portable tubs for patients who wanted to take mesmeric 'baths' in the privacy of their own homes." However, Darnton tells us, "he generally recommended communal treatments, where each individual reinforced the fluid and sent it coursing with extraordinary power through entire clinics. In his outdoor treatments, Mesmer usually mesmerized trees and then attached groups of patients to them in daisy-chain fashion."

The object of these multiple infusions appears to have been not merely sedative but purgative. Mesmer wanted (as we would say) to obtain a "return to the repressed," and evidently often did so. Darnton's account continues: "Everything in Mesmer's indoor clinic was designed to produce a crisis in the patient. Heavy carpets, weird astrological wall-decorations, and drawn curtains shut him off from the outside world and muffled the occasional words, screams, and bursts of hysterical laughter that broke the habitual heavy silence . . . Every so often fellow patients collapsed writhing on the floor, and were carried by Antoine, the mesmerist-valet, into the [mattress-lined] crisis-room; and if his spine still failed to tingle . . . Mesmer himself would approach, dressed in a lilac taffeta robe, and drill fluid into the patient from his hands, his imperial eye and his mesmerized wand. Not all crises took violent form. Some developed into deep sleeps, *and some sleeps provided communication with dead or distant spirits* by way of the fluid

* *Mesmerism.*

directly to the somnambulist's sixth sense . . . Many hundreds of Frenchmen experienced such marvels . . ." (Italics added.)

Mesmerism appears to have attracted patients and practitioners from all classes. According to a contemporary account, cited by Darnton: "There is a tub for the poor every other day, in the antechamber. . . . Arriving at the home of this famous doctor one sees a crowd of men and women of every age and state; the *cordon bleu*, the artisan, the doctor, the surgeon. It is a spectacle worthy of sensitive souls to see men distinguished by their birth and position in society mesmerize with gentle solicitude children, old people and especially the indigent."

A year after opening his clinic in Paris, Mesmer was under attack by the medical profession, which, quite naturally, begrudged him his success. A pamphlet war set in, Mesmer's opponents denouncing and ridiculing him and the mesmerists giving as good as they got. As certain medical men of our own day (notably Dr. Andrew Ivy, the champion of Krebiozen) have done, a Dr. Charles Deslon got himself caught in the middle. Feeling that Mesmer might have made a genuine medical discovery, Deslon presented him at a dinner party to twelve doctors of the faculty of the University of Paris. The presentation failed, and after a lengthy controversy in which thirty young doctors took his part, Deslon himself was expelled from the faculty in 1784—an event which, according to Darnton, "provided the mesmerists with a martyr whose effectiveness was spoiled only by his concurrent quarrels with Mesmer and ultimately by his death, while being mesmerized, in August 1786."

The Deslon affair and the pamphlet war effectively decided Mesmer's own fortunes. Sensing that the crisis called for firm yet delicate action, he let it be known that he was going to take the waters at Spa and might never come back to France at all. In some alarm, by Darnton's account, Marie Antoinette sent "Maurepas and other government officials to negotiate with Mesmer in March and April 1781." They offered him "a life pension of 20,000 livres and another 10,000 a year to set up a clinic, if he would but accept the surveillance of three government 'pupils.' "

After some dickering, Mesmer made his reply in the form of an open letter to the Queen. "He refused to be judged by his pupils; the offer smacked of bribery, and yet it was not generous enough— he now demanded a country estate . . ."

Like the schismatics in Freud's circle, Deslon soon broke with the master and set up his own clinic. He was thereupon expelled from the movement and never again enjoyed the full confidence of Mesmer himself. It was a lawyer, Nicolas Bergasse, who organized Mesmer's operations, essentially on the franchise principle. Having completed his training as a therapist, the would-be branch-office man paid a substantial fee, for which he received an "exclusive" to a particular territory. By 1785 Mesmer was living in some splendor in the Hôtel de Coligny in Paris, and according to the treasurer of the Society of Universal Harmony (as the mother organization was called) had amassed a fortune of nearly 350,000 livres. By 1789 the Paris branch alone had 430 members, and there were thriving subsidiaries in over two dozen French towns, including major ones such as Strasbourg, Lyon, Bordeaux and Marseille.*

While resembling the Freudian circle in its theocratic structure and Mind Control in its fried-chicken-chain style of organization, mesmerism was far closer to scientology in certain points of doctrine, in particular this one—that it did not exclude the possibility of a spirit world and life eternal. According to *Life* magazine, some psychoanalysts in New York during the 1960s had begun to have their patients' horoscopes cast (see page 213), but the move came years too late and for the times was already too conservative. Mesmerism, being grounded in supernaturalist ideas to begin with, more easily accommodated itself to its market. Darnton reports:

"As the Revolution approached, mesmerists tended increasingly to neglect the sick in order to decipher hieroglyphics, manipulate magic numbers, [and] communicate with spirits. . . . By 1786 even the Parisian Society had fallen under the control of spiritualists. . . ."

* Mesmer clearly got a better shake than one of his modern equivalents, L. Ron Hubbard, who currently conducts his operations from a yacht (for jurisdictional reasons, it is said) and whose people in this country practice their art in some danger of prosecution as quacks.

In this same epoch, two significant changes were taking place in the intellectual interests of Frenchmen generally. One was that public enthusiasm for science, once genuine enough, was turning sensationalist. The other was that a kind of crank Second Establishment began growing up in science and medicine. The movement started as a loose coalition of outsiders dedicated to the overthrow of learned élites and ended as one dedicated to the overthrow of the state—this apparently on the principle that if you hate one institution venomously enough you will soon hate them all.

There is contemporary evidence to suggest that a generation before the Revolution, the public did take a serious interest in science.* Thirty years later, however, Science for the Amateur had developed a distinctly "carny" atmosphere. Darnton tells us: "Scientist-magicians like Joseph Pinetti toured the country performing 'amusing physics' and various entertaining experiments. . . . The 'têtes parlantes' of the Abbé Mical elicited a serious investigation by the Academy of Sciences and a rapturous letter in the *Mercure* by Mallet du Pan about . . . the 'thousand marvels' of science in general and Parisians' general frenzy about experiments regarded as supernatural."

Besides scientific showmen, another type became prevalent: the embattled crank. Believing that they had been denied a fair hearing, men of this sort came to form a political wing of quack science. In 1785, mesmerism itself split along similar lines, Bergasse breaking with the master and setting up what amounted to a radical-revolutionary branch, with headquarters of its own. In becoming spiritualistic at one extreme and political at the other, mesmerism thus represented all the major inclinations of the age—one being a growing impatience with things of the mind.

In the last years of the monarchy, there seems to have been a sudden decline of interest in the classics.† This phenomenon is usually attributed to a general shift in interest from the humani-

* For instance, in a letter written from Paris in 1755, Oliver Goldsmith remarked, "I have seen as bright a circle of beauty at the chemical lectures of Rouelle as gracing the court of Versailles."
† In 1785, Thomas Jefferson said (writing to Madison from Paris), "Greek and Roman authors are dearer here than, I believe, anywhere in the world: nobody reads them, wherefore they are not reprinted."

ties to science; but the fact is that by then the French public was becoming chiefly occupied with fake science.

In the interim, the agnosticism that had started with Voltaire had evidently begun to affect church attendance, and even led to a most startling change in the relations between Church and state. Thanks to the infiltration of the government by Jansenists, the Jesuits fell into disfavor, to such a degree that in 1761–62 their whole educational system was dismantled and the Order itself expelled from the country. According to Buckle, "a number of their most celebrated works were publicly burned by the common hangman"—an absolutely remarkable proceeding when one considers that for generations the Jesuits had been "the spiritual leaders of France, the educators of her youth and the confessors of her kings." The charge on which they were condemned was a grotesque one, apparently involving an unpaid bill.*

The importance of this event is what it tells us about the state of mind of the country at the time: i.e., it is unlikely that any government could so summarily have rid itself of a traditional institution of the faith unless it sensed a permissive indifference in many ranks of society and an active sympathy in some. (The same may apply to the recent ban on prayers in American public schools; it was a concession made by the Protestant majority not because it was liberal but because it was no longer Protestant.)

Churchgoing, at least in the larger towns, seems to have been falling off in the same period. Many of the more distinguished men of intellect—among them Condorcet, Diderot, Helvétius and Laplace—were admitted unbelievers. As Episcopalianism and Unitarianism were one day to become in America, French deism of the time appears to have been a sort of shadow religion, supported by those not quite ready to give up hope of another life and anxious, in any event, to maintain appearances in this one.

---

* Especially in revolutionary eras, the charges on which a society gets rid of people or institutions it no longer wants are apt to be absurd. When Robespierre was condemned under the summary proceedings he himself had instituted, his *décret d'exécution* accused him of wanting to "put on the throne the son of Louis Capet and in that way betray the mother country," as though that were a far greater crime than any he had actually committed.

It is natural that the French Revolution should   the
characteristics of the decade just preceding it—the chief of these
being an absence of real intellectual content and an overwhelming
excess of primal emotion, most particularly fear. For in revolutionary eras, I believe, it is the climactic decontrolling of that emotion
which, by the mechanism of conversion described earlier, unlooses
all the rest, exploding into the vindictiveness and sheer wanton
fury that are the means to power of men such as Mirabeau and
Danton, and not infrequently their undoing as well.

Once started, a revolution is quite apt to have this blind character because it arises in a people already half-blinded by their
feelings. The need to *do* something has grown on everyone to the
point of seeming a kind of fate. The general attitude is "Let it
come down"; and when it does, the result is essentially a free-for-
all, a doctrineless scramble for power and revenge in which the
behavior of millions may become as primitive or automatized by
the Id as it is during a street fight. Given some critical sign of
weakness on the part of the regime, some culminating threat or
outrage, the whole of society simply blows up, every faction falling
upon its enemies or competitors until the weakest are eliminated
and some group capable of consolidating its hold on the rest
emerges from the wreckage.*

In France, the precipitating political event is usually thought to
have been the convocation of the Estates-General by the King. In
The Coming of the French Revolution, Georges Lefebvre says:
"The immediate cause lay in a government emergency for which
Louis XVI could find no other solution. But the Third Estate
was by no means the first to profit from the emergency, contrary
to the general opinion, taken over from the Revolutionists themselves, who declared *ad nauseam* that 'the people rose up and over-

* This basically was the pattern of the Roman Civil War which ended in 82
B.C. with the victory of Sulla and the oligarchs over the popular party of
Marius. In the 1920s, Germany began splitting along class lines, the workers
going over to Communism, the old soldiers and would-be dictators to the
Freikorps or the Stahlhelm. Having won, the Nazis stamped out Communism
and rid themselves of Freikorps elements in their own ranks (Ernst Roehm,
Kurt von Schleicher, and many rank-and-file S.A. men) in the Night of the
Long Knives in 1934.

threw despotism and aristocracy.' No doubt it did end that way. But the people were not the original motive force. The bourgeoisie . . . was in no position to force the king to appeal to the nation. Still less were the peasants and the working classes. The privileged groups did have the necessary means: the clergy in its Assembly, the nobility in the Parliaments and Provincial Estates . . . 'The patricians began the revolution' wrote Chateaubriand; 'the plebeians finished it.' The first act of the Revolution, in 1788, consisted in a triumph of the aristocracy which, taking advantage of the government crisis, hoped to reassert itself . . . Having paralyzed the royal power which upheld its own social preeminence, the aristocracy opened the way to the bourgeois revolution, then to the popular revolution in the cities, and finally to the revolution of the peasants—and found itself buried under the ruins of the Old Regime."

That the French nobility were the ones to start the Revolution seems from this distance slightly mad; for unless grossly misinformed as to the mood of the country, they must surely have sensed the risks they were taking in challenging the crown when they did. The political ambitions of the Duc d'Orléans in particular were absurd, given the existing state of things. But it is precisely that lack of awareness and reasoned caution which characterizes all classes in a revolutionary epoch.

Preceding the main event, a series of mini revolutions break out,* these being essentially trial solutions through which people are groping toward some explanation of their own rising unease, or some way of relieving it, or both. Young people form a faction whose hate object is parents or "oldies" in general. Workers, almost regardless of their actual treatment, become hardened enemies of management. Among the privileged, some become extreme reactionaries; others turn ostentatiously liberal and "democratic," even subversive (as Whittaker Chambers and other middle-class intellectuals did in the 1930s, or Lafayette and Mirabeau

* As in post-World War I Germany, and including revolutionary art à la Grosz and Brecht as well as the political factions mentioned above. Throughout society, tendentiousness becomes the rule, for in effect what is going on is a choosing up of sides.

in the eighteenth century).* Quacks become more aggressive or revolutionary outright. Women grow suddenly indignant at the oppressions suffered by their sex (as happened before World War I and again in the 1960s). A new class of bomb-throwing intellectuals springs up—men who fulminate in print *à la* Marat and Jerry Rubin or who, like the Weathermen and the Russian anarchist-idealists of circa 1900, literally start blowing things up, sometimes including themselves.†

Everyone in his small way begins to march—where, he has no idea. And when the big event starts, it has the same mindless character. Before Hitler came to power, the Freikorps—small private armies in principle like those of Pompey and Caesar—marched up and down Germany, to what end was not clear. No doctrine, no goal besides power itself is really visible to any of these people. An energy has simply been released upon the world and, *coûte que coûte*, must expend itself.

Of course, there are precipitating causes: in Germany, defeat, inflation, and Versailles; in France, the rise in prices (especially of bread) in 1785–89 and the failure of the grain harvest in 1788. Such causes, however, seem to derive their detonative power from another source—from the systematic progressive undermining of the mental stability of a whole people, the educated and influential as well as the poor and powerless. In France it was the former who, because they had the means to do so, began the Revolution, thereby giving the latter their chance.

Apropos of the idea that revolutions represent explosions essentially of fear, it is interesting that during the first summer of the

---

* Foreign visitors to Paris in the later eighteenth century noted the democratization of manners among the upper classes. Jefferson wrote, in 1787: "In society the *habit habillé* is almost banished and they begin to go even to suppers in frock: the court and diplomatic corps, however, must always be excepted . . ."—as is true today, when full dress survives chiefly in the White House or in such social backwaters as Newport.

† In March, 1970, there was a spectacular incident of this kind in New York. Some young radicals who had been making bombs in a Greenwich Village town house slipped and blew themselves and the building up. As a whole, the bombings of this period, although serious enough in some cases, appear to have been part of a revolution still in its formative, or groping-for-a-rationale, stage —creative political play.

69

French Revolution such an explosion seems literally to have occurred. According to Lefebvre it was known as the Great Fear, and it originated, he says, "in local panics of which two were closely related to the political crisis. . . . Local panics had sometimes in the past spread remarkably far. The characteristic of the Great Fear is that the six panics mentioned above, which may be called the original ones, set up numerous currents of which some can be traced for hundreds of miles. Fugitives explained their fright by enlarging on each other's stories, and these included bourgeois, priests and monks. . . . Even the government subdelegates and mounted constabulary were no exception. . . . In Dauphiné the peasants, already assembled in terror of burning, rose up and themselves burned and devastated the manor houses" —an almost perfect example of the psychological principle mentioned here, the conversion of intense fear into fury.

Local panics had already set in during the spring of 1789, some while before the convocation of the Estates-General by the King. But it is in Lefebvre's account of the Paris Revolution of July 14 and its sequels that one sees most clearly the element of fear-inspired conviction that drove the Revolution as a whole. Both in Paris and across the country, among the peasant and artisan classes, as well as among the bourgeoisie who had reason to know better, the notion of an "aristocratic conspiracy" sprang up, becoming almost overnight a national obsession.

It was supposed that the nobility were organizing France's considerable population of beggars into troops of "brigands" who would be let loose upon the common citizenry. Even madder projects were attributed to the upper classes. According to Lefebvre, "French Guards thought they had been poisoned. A rumor spread at Versailles that an underground passage had been dug from the stables of the Comte d'Artois to blow up the Assembly. In Paris the committee met with the greatest difficulties in procuring grain. These were attributed to malevolence; riots broke out everywhere . . . on the seventeenth [of July, 1789] a miller was massacred at Saint-Germain-en-Laye, and on the eighteenth a farmer barely escaped the same fate.

"Destruction of standing crops was daily expected, and on July 26, the Assembly was informed, mistakenly, that in Picardy it had already begun."

Just before the fall of the Bastille on July 14, the Parisian populace, led and to some extent controlled by elements of the bourgeoisie, began frantically arming themselves. The King's troops were converging on the city, with what in mind everyone knew. "Attacked and bombarded from all sides, the capital would be taken by assault and turned over to pillage. . . . Panic was continuous. . . . These days in Paris were simply the first act of the Great Fear."

It is unnecessary to point out that really these were mass fantasies; far from being bent upon pillage and massacre, the armies of the King did nothing at all—partly for want of clear orders, partly because their commanders were none too sure of the loyalty of the men. The Marquis de Launay, in charge of the Bastille, had only eighty old soldiers under his command, plus an additional thirty Swiss. The sympathy of the old soldiers was more with the people out front than with the Swiss, whom they disliked as foreigners if not as younger men; when the attack on the Bastille began "they were persuaded with difficulty to fire." Thanks to their reluctance and the utter incapacity of Launay himself, a fortress that should have been impregnable to the ill-armed mob assaulting it fell rather easily.

Perhaps better than any single episode, the fall of the Bastille illustrates the element of pure delusion essential to any great revolutionary movement. In the popular mind, then and since, the Bastille was *the* symbol of oppression—notwithstanding the fact that it had years before become a prison for special offenders and the well-to-do, and as a fortress was garrisoned and equipped neither to dominate the city nor even, as it turned out, to withstand much of a siege.* But these facts were entirely beside the point. The Bastille stood for a king and aristocracy now so de-

* At the time of its fall, the Bastille held no political prisoners. The detained consisted of two mental cases, one "abnormal young man," and four persons accused of forgery. Despite the threatening situation, Launay had laid in no supplies for his troops.

mented that they would, at a moment's notice, decimate the populace of the nation's chief city, cut down standing grain in a time of general need or sell precious surpluses abroad,* set "brigands" to looting and devastating the country at large, poison their own troops, or blow up the Assembly which the King himself had called as an emergency measure. (And if these notions seem extravagant, consider some of the things of which student revolutionaries and black militants accused the American Establishment during the late 1960s and early '70s. One theory I heard several times from blacks was that the war in Vietnam was really intended to reduce their numbers—a domestic massacre exported and called something else. To Jerry Rubin, Amerika was a vast concentration camp.)

It never matters that the evidence for these *idées fixes* may not exist or may run contrary to them. From the start of the French Revolution, the evidence was that tyranny in that country was far feebler than anyone had thought. As in the case of the Bastille, the old order collapsed often with hardly a fight. "In many cities," Lefebvre reports, "the municipal revolution proceeded without violence. The municipality . . . simply caved in before the demonstrators. The old municipal authorities merely took a number of notables into their organization or, as at Bordeaux, disappeared before the electors."

Many will argue that the French Revolution was anything but mindless, pointing out the immense amount of effort and contention which the new regime put into drafting constitutions and the Declaration of the Rights of Man and Citizen. But as Lefebvre remarks, the Declaration, in the eyes of its framers, "had an especially great *negative* value, in the sense that it condemned the practices of the Old Regime and prevented their revival. . . . As the historian Aulard put it, the Declaration is essentially *the death certificate of the Old Regime.*" The Declaration, in short, did not correspond to a set of beliefs, radiant in the minds of all, on whose

* In this period, no more than 2 percent of France's annual harvest of grain was ever exported, says Lefebvre. Nevertheless, it became a fixed idea with millions of Frenchmen, apparently, that the nobles were buying up grain, hoarding it, and spiriting it away for sale abroad.

principles everyone was prepared to act. It was a gesture of rejection, like the Revolution itself.

Unlike the Russian Revolution, the French was not carefully planned (e.g., in the safety of exile), nor could it achieve a stable orthodoxy and hence a successful counterrevolution until Napoleon, who subverted the whole effort. Even before it occurred, the Revolution was without a foreseeable rational structure; it was simply not in the revolutionists, then or later, to give it one. The times had become too volatile, the influence of the Id too great. Except at the level of feeling (and sometimes even there), consensus had become impossible. The pragmatic problem of making government work remained unsolved until after the Directory, and the ideas that supposedly underlay the Revolution itself hardly took at all, for Napoleon was able to set them aside with no trouble. Whatever they contained of political truth or ultimate usefulness was incidental; their real purpose was apparently the one Lefebvre describes—to provide a death warrant for the Old Order; to justify men in the excesses of the moment.

This may be the answer to a question raised by Darnton in his study of mesmerism: "The crashing failure of the *Social Contract*, Rousseau's least popular book, raises a problem for scholars searching for the radical spirit in the 1780s: if the greatest political treatise of the age failed to interest many literate Frenchmen, what form of radical ideas *did* suit their taste? One such form appeared in the unlikely guise of animal magnetism or mesmerism."

Actually, there was nothing at all "unlikely" about mesmerism. In the character of its membership and the course of its evolution, it foretold that passionate vacuity which was to be the real spirit of the Revolution. Rousseau's Social Contract was an irrelevance— a survival from the more rational past. The true man of the moment was Saint-Just, who said, "What constitutes the Republic is the complete destruction of everything that is opposed to it."

Likewise, the clearest sign that the Revolution was at hand was not the economically straitened condition of the peasantry, the failure of His Majesty's various finance ministers, the gathering ambition of the middle class, or the spread of Jansenism. What

73

announced the Revolution was a new crisis of feeling which events over a period of fifty years had conspired to create—events not so much in the external world as in men's heads, and concerned not so much with intolerable facts as with an intolerable loss of certainties.

Buckle noted as "well worthy of remark" that French revolutionary literature "was first directed against those [institutions] which were religious." Then, as the *philosophes* turned their attack on the government, the government, in the 1760s, turned its attack on religion—a move that had the appearance of sectarian rivalry but was in reality, perhaps, an expression of official impatience with religion as such.*

A decade later the churches began to be empty, and at the same time the intellectual interests of Parisians underwent a change. Instead of genuine science or the classics, they now inclined toward "amusing physics." Instead of conventional cures, they seemed more and more to need relief from psychic pressure—just as Freud's patients did in the period prior to World War I. From contemporary accounts, it seems clear that many of Mesmer's clients were hysterical cases. Nor is it likely that in that day such disorders were mainly due to sexual repression, as Freud at first maintained his patients' were.

Then as now, the basic cause of the worsening in the emotional climate was not, I believe, social or economic. The change arose out of a growing suspicion, especially among the better educated, that God was dead—that actually He had never lived, so our own lives were briefly pleasurable at best, and at worst a succession of tribulations made hideous by their utter meaninglessness. It was that discovery which made "conditions" suddenly intolerable, even to the upper classes.† As a result, public restlessness and suggestibility rapidly increased, calling forth that astonishing rabble

---

* In admitting the Jansenists (whom Louis XIV had suppressed), the government was in effect using one religious faction to rid itself of the too-pervasive influence of another.

† In the 1960s, most of the hippie extremists came from "good homes" and seemed, to real proletarians, to have little enough to complain about. It was the hippies who announced the death of God.

of quacks and angry cosmologists who descended upon Paris in the last days of the *ancien régime*. In turning spiritualistic, mesmerism was simply meeting a last-minute demand for some sort of otherworldly hope or reassurance, but by then the general agitation had become too intense. Magic no longer sufficed. The only solution to the anxiety problem now lay through rage. So the pamphleteers and fake scientists—not to mention a few real ones—laid aside their usual tools and took up the sword, the first class to make this decisive move being the one that obviously had the most to lose by it. No matter. It was too late. The compulsion was upon everyone, and the quickest to act were those to whom the means lay handiest—the descendants of the old fighting nobility, France's fossil knighthood.

This, in principle, is how many revolutions may come about; and if so, it is clear enough why Reigns of Terror tend to be preceded by Reigns of Nonsense, for they represent successive stages in the same basic process. Eric Hoffer's True Believer is a man determined to drag the supernatural back to life by the sheer power of wishing or, failing that, to vent his desolation on those around him—on reality itself for being such a cheat. And in either undertaking there are entrepreneurs or leaders, "sincere" men of his own sort, ready to help him—Mesmers and L. Ron Hubbards to "cure" him and readmit him to a realm of infantile wonders; quack philosophers *à la* Marcuse to debunk the system for him; Mirabeaus and Robespierres to turn his energies to dismantling it; Napoleons and Hitlers to redirect the same energies outward and dismantle the world—all in the name of evils which may or may not be as bad as they will become; all in the name of utopias which as yet have never materialized.

In the end, as Camus said, atheism breeds not mere disappointment and backsliding but, out of disappointment, revenge, in particular upon whatever remains of decency and real goodness. Anything that smacks of the virtues or ideals once supposedly derived from God is fair game to be degraded and ridiculed*—the

* As for instance "do-goodism," so often ridiculed in American movies, whose creators know better than most what life is really about.

more so because the virtuous and idealistic are so vulnerable. In their silly pretensions, their resolve to be something besides talking animals, their insistence on meaning and dignity in a world we know to be without either, they make the rest of us feel guilty in our degradation, and part of the fun of revolution is that it gives us a chance to get even—to punish excellence along with injustice —to level everything.

It is consequently no paradox that even revolutions of the Far Right, such as Nazism, are egalitarian at least in the beginning. A true revolutionist is a simplifier, resolved to cut the world down to fit his own shrunken self—to bestialize it in the name of the new Word.* Whatever is not "relevant" must go—books, distinctions, qualities of mind or character, persons, if necessary *en bloc* (in Nazi Germany, six million Jews; in France, thousands of the no- bility, then of Girondists or other deviants-of-the-moment; in Rus- sia, holocausts, renewed by Stalin for decades after those of the revolution itself).

This element of the diabolic, which we tend to think of as inci- dental to great social upheavals—a matter of a few psychopaths' "coming out of the woodwork" at the critical moment—is in real- ity fundamental to them. In their antiphilosophies, in the indig- nant nonsense of crank politics or crank medicine, in every sort of paranoid sectarianism, the majority are groping toward what the Saint-Justs and Himmlers finally do.

Having been the most intellectual of nations in 1750, France a generation later was deluged with nonsense, much of it quite ex- plicitly embattled. Medicine and the Academy of Sciences were on the defensive, psychic ailments on the increase. In Germany, the most scientific of modern nations, a quack scientific doctrine, the World Ice Movement (see below, pages 184–85), became the rage in the 1920s, and like mesmerism was swept away by the revolu- tion (which replaced it with the nonsense of Alfred Rosenberg). In present-day America, the nation most dedicated to mass en- lightenment, "reading skills" are mysteriously declining; the cur-

* The more senseless, needless to say, the better. Hence the Russian Revolution, with its intricate doctrines, was much more cheerless than the simpleminded Strength-Through-Joy *Weltanschauung* of the Nazis.

ricula of schools and universities are under attack as no longer "relevant"; and since the 1950s the medical and scientific establishments have been forced onto the defensive by the popular enthusiasm for such things as orgone therapy, Ohsawa dieting, UFOs, psi phenomena, scientology, and the cosmological theories of Dr. Velikovsky (himself a simplifier *par excellence*; see Chapter VIII).

As Edmund Wilson reported in *To the Finland Station*, similar perturbations in the beliefs and behavior of most classes became noticeable in Russia from about 1890 on. (The gloom of Russian plays and the strange, almost monklike fervor of Russian atheists became something of a joke among Europeans of the period, who obviously failed to see what these portended and would have found them anything but funny if they had.)

What distinguishes the French Revolution from its twentieth-century sequels is essentially that it came too soon. The spectacular violence of events in Paris and the scattered horrors that occurred across the countryside have tended to obscure the fact that a really broad base in unbelief did not yet exist in that nation; nor did it anywhere else in Europe. Certain classes in France had become agnostic, and many, for good reason, were anticlerical or down on the monarchy, or both; and that was sufficient. The critical psychological mass needed to touch off an explosion was available. And when the first detonations occurred, the existing apparatus of state was simply too dilapidated to contain them; the whole system blew up, in the order Lefebvre described.

The American uprising of 1776 was not a true revolution but a sort of Fronde. The European revolutions of 1848 were truly that, but by then the apparatus of state was better able to contain them and they ended as merely bloody episodes, as did the Paris Commune of 1871. Again, conditions were not right; a sufficient psychological base was lacking. While agnosticism was apparently spreading during the nineteenth century, the maintenance of forms (churchgoing, manners, etc.), along with religious revivals such as Wesleyanism, served to slow down the drift into outright nonbelief. Hypocrisy, for a while longer, would hold things together. And in the meantime, the mechanical efficiency of government had improved to such a degree that Mommsen declared that successful revolt in a modern nation had become impossible. (He died in 1903.)

In the present era the situation is quite different. In retrospect, World War I looks not like the disastrous accident we once thought it, but rather like the first of a series of great social explosions which, for reasons I have described, are almost fated to occur, in one form or another, throughout the Western world.

For more than a century, the Germans appear to have had the Napoleonic gift of exporting their revolutions. Even as late as the 1930s, their impulse to obey the constituted authorities, to organize and make orderly the most wasteful sorts of cruelty and murder, made them a tyrant's dream. These were no riotous French, but a people ready from the first to direct the bulk of their nihilistic spite against legally assigned victims—Jews or Communists at home and any external power within reach, including those such as Russia and the United States which they hadn't a hope of conquering.

The effect of World War I was to speed up, in other Western nations, the same psychological changes that had driven Germany herself into a suicidal expansionism. Hence, after an orgy of the most ferocious chauvinism on both sides, the Western nations emerged into the so-called Moral Revolution of the 1920s*—the period when astrology, after a long decline, began its comeback in the United States; when divorce became the fashion; when Protestants ceased to go to church; when debunking, from Dada to Mencken, became the going art form; when manners suddenly became more "democratic" or slam-bang; when willful personal belief in moral matters and gradually in everything else began to be thought Everyman's right. (Later this would come to be known as doing one's "thing," and would include tripping on drugs, ad lib promiscuity, and every variety of nonsense from Steppenwolf, Do It!, and the I Ching to guerrilla handbooks and make-believe Marxism.)

---

* Quite chillingly portrayed in the diaries of Evelyn Waugh, currently (1973) running in the Observer.

In Germany, the revolution which the Kaiser had failed to export continued in the shape of the Freikorps and Communist movements, and finally in the person of Hitler, who immediately set about reexporting it. However Der Führer, like Robespierre and Saint-Just before him, had to find some more direct outlet for the immense tides of destructive energy being released in his subjects.* For the Germans then were the France of 1789 raised by many powers of ten.

So the mass extermination of Jews, while it must have interfered with the German war effort† and certainly cost that ever-thrifty nation millions in money, was nonetheless a necessity—as was the subtler, more pervasive ideology of evil which the Nazis worked out to the smallest detail. In effect they were organizing that revenge upon all decency I spoke of—a Wagnerian finale which would leave nothing behind it: books, virtues, *Untermenschen;* even, as it turned out, Superman himself.

Indeed, the more inspired Nazis seem to have felt that in *Götterdämmerung,* one way or another, they would win. The world might combine to crush them, but in the horrifying example they left it they would still have their revenge. The mere fact of all they had done, and not on impulse only but by calculation,‡ would be a last booby trap, lingering on in memory to poison whatever hopes man might yet have for himself. (And sure enough, writers such as Robert Ardrey have picked up the message, making us out, on ethological grounds, to be just the sort of heartless, blindly

* And quickly, too, or he might well have gone the way of those mentioned. Since Hitler was himself a ferocious anti-Semite, this problem was self-solving. Instead of killing his own people—a far more dangerous course—he could kill domestic aliens. As befitted the time he arose in, Hitler was more primitive than Napoleon, supposing that the energies released in his people were, in some sense, his own. Napoleon knew better, once saying: "My son cannot replace me. I could not replace myself. I am a creature of circumstances."
† Merely to transport six million people to liquidation centers must have taken an immense amount of rolling stock and tied up rail lines needed for more productive effort—e.g., supplying the troops in Russia.
‡ Which was yet another way of debasing mind—by showing what it was capable of when in the grip of the beast-self, the Id. And even George Steiner, in *Language and Silence,* was impressed and shaken by the fact that "the cry of the murdered sounded in earshot of the universities"—as though somehow culture and ideals of a humane rationality *had* been shown up. Der Führer could not have wished for more. Carthage, destroyed, was sowing Rome with salt.

adaptive creatures the Nazis said—said and proved, with their techniques for degrading master and slave alike.)

In the outside world, we pretended not to understand. The hideous systematic murders in Poland which so shocked Il Duce that he ordered Count Ciano to leak them to the enemy press, saying, "The world must know"; the death camps; the casual slaughters of prisoners or of Russian and French civilians by the SS; the grotesque tortures inflicted in Gestapo jails; the films which Hitler is said to have watched of the bomb-plot conspirators being hung from butcher's hooks—these, we assured each other, were the work of lunatics and gangsters. But they were not. They were done by men like ourselves, in an extremity of vindictive despair, and on a scale that makes the excesses of the Terror in France seem trivial by comparison. While certain German characteristics perhaps favored that disproportion, the basic difference was not one between Frenchmen and Germans but between that era and this—between the extent and consequences of radical unbelief in the two.

I have in this chapter given special attention to the French Revolution because it exhibits, as it were in miniature, all the features of the more total revolutions of today. Indeed, the word "totalitarian" implies that when such political systems come into being, it is because everybody is ready for them. In France (as one can see for instance from Stendhal's memoir *The Life of Henri Brulard*), that was not yet the case. Frenchmen who lived far from the centers of power were often little affected by either the events of the Revolution or its spirit. And in the 1820s and '30s, religion was back in favor—if not the power it had once been, not the total irrelevance it would become.

Robespierre's decision, during the Terror, to declare a feast-day in honor of the Almighty would have struck Hitler as absurd.* So it does us, for somewhat different reasons; but in fact it was a piece of political realism—Robespierre's way of admitting that his regime had after all come too soon. The French agreed and cut off his head.

---

* Just as Himmler would have looked down on Saint-Just as an amateur. George Washington would not have understood either.

Trouble in Cloud-Cuckooland

The question is, since the failure of the German revolution during its latest export phase (1939–1945) and of the American student dissident movement in the 1960s, where has the revolution gone? The answer is nowhere; the center of revolution in the Western world is still right here.

My object in this chapter will be to convince you of three things. The first is that the New Nonsense, like its predecessor mesmerism, is part of a clearly definable historical process. Because certain features of American life are uniquely favorable to it, that process may have gone further here than elsewhere, with the result that we now lead the world in the production of intellectual rubbish.*

The second point is that a good deal in our supposedly serious intellectual life, from Mencken and Watson and Loeb to Lewis Mumford and Marcuse and Reich (Charles, not Wilhelm), is in fact cryptononsense. Writers and conversationalists in this genre either use science to debunk reason (as the behaviorists did) or reason to debunk science (as Mumford *et al.* are now doing). In the latter case, since science is the embodiment of certain ideals of reason, the literary attacks on it (by Mumford and Reich) or the neo-Marxist (by Marcuse) might appear odd—in a sense even suicidal, since one form of anti-intellectualism so easily leads to

---

* The Communist countries, in which nonsense remains state-controlled, obviously cannot compete with us, at least in sheer diversity. Some of their work in parapsychology, however, shows great promise.

THE NEW NONSENSE

others. The phenomenon is perhaps simply a part of the spirit of the time, and as such unconscious. In putting reason to the task of discrediting itself, our *littérateurs*, like the pamphleteers of Marat's and Mesmer's day, are getting on with something the rest of us seem increasingly to want done.

The feeling now is that it is time to dump the ideal baggage of the past and move on into some (as yet unspecified) better existence, to Consciousness III, whatever that is. No one apparently knew, so the idea died fairly quickly, to be replaced by others no less vague.* Since writers such as Charles Reich are sincere in the political meaning of the term, it follows that the arguments they have used against science, though often silly or grossly unfair, have had a popularity exactly proportioned to those defects.

The ostensible aim of Science for the People is to make research more "relevant"; its actual one, to dynamite the Ivory Tower—to have done once and for all with the "myth" of pure science, of pure anything, of *purity*, as it works out. (The whole hippie life-style can be read as a gesture of this kind—a rejection of sexual purity, of intellect unclouded by drugs or erotic excitement, of bodily cleanliness, of bourgeois scruples about stealing.)

There never *was* pure science, according to Marcuse; according to Mumford, there may once have been, but science from the outset contained the seeds of its own corruption. Interestingly enough, the work that earned Rousseau the Dijon Prize in 1749 and first established him in the French literary world was an essay in which he undertook to prove that the arts and sciences had been a detriment to man.[4] It deserved its success, since it was far more revolutionary than his *Contrat social*.

Thirdly, I will try to convince you that a variety of other changes that have been occurring in this country since World War I have more coherence than might appear on the surface. What looks

* For instance, Jean-François Revel's *Without Marx or Jesus*, which saw our society as a sort of political Second Coming. In the 1960s Marshall McLuhan electrified us with his discovery of "hot" and "cold" media and the obsolescence of print. His notion of the "mosaic" mode of perception, engendered by television, was a kind of Consciousness III; and his disparagement of the old "linear" mode of taking things in (reading) was a form of New Wave anti-intellectualism, a celebration of the viewer mentality.

to be a loosely related assortment of fads, social lapses, reforms, revivals, explorations of New Frontiers, or attacks of plain craziness may in fact represent a definite progression, of the kind that seems quite evident in the history of eighteenth-century France.

That is not to say that the two eras are comparable in any respect, really, but this one. For while France then was "modern" in that the politically decisive parts of the nation had become scientifically minded, agnostic, and at last distracted and unstable, the structure of French society was still almost feudal and the whole system, to that degree, vulnerable. Having lost his aptitude for arms, or having delegated the maintenance of his privileges to armed professionals who were not, in a pinch, to be trusted, the French landed magnate of the period had unwittingly made himself a sitting duck.

The same is not true of the propertied classes in modern America, who are nothing if not security-conscious, expending millions and much ingenuity on their own protection. Here the looting of them has taken rather different forms, notably crushing taxation and a steady increase in spontaneous seizure—muggings, burglary, etc.—often accompanied by a gratuitous violence equivalent to revenge (e.g., on the victim as a caste object*). Partly because they still feel that their interests lie with the Establishment, our police are more efficient than were the constabulary of Louis XVI, but not very effective nonetheless; as in that earlier day, the tide is running too strongly against them. Indeed, some of the newer forms in which the revolutionary spirit has been expressing itself —the hippie movement, for example—do not lend themselves to police control except by an extreme stretch of certain concepts of the legally justifiable. (A case in point, reported in the press in 1973, is the series of break-ins made by Federal narcotics agents, who allegedly browbeat and knocked around suspects or, in a West Coast raid, killed one.)

A third form which class war, or the looting of the *de facto* no-

---

* A description including not only prosperous whites robbed by "rat packs" from black ghettoes, but "oldies" mugged and roughed up by teen-agers. A similarly exaggerated defiance or aggression, without theft, shows up in many father–son or student–professor relationships.

bility, has taken in this century is inflation. An important factor here has been the emergence of labor as an organized estate since the 1930s. While labor itself has contributed to inflation by the demoralization and falling per capita production of the rank-and-file, it has also, as a power bloc, been able to exact successive wage hikes which temporarily at least adjust earnings to rises in production costs and hence in the cost of living. Consequently modern labor, unlike people living on pensions, annuities, or Social Security, has some power to protect itself from inflation;* nor is government, for the moment, likely to try the politically dangerous move of taking that power away. The French laboring class in the eighteenth century had no such power.† According to Lefebvre, "In the best of times wage rises were hard to get; it has been calculated that between 1726–1741 and 1785–1789, prices rose by 65% while wages went up only 22%."

One would have supposed that this recent improvement in the status of labor might be accompanied by some improvement in relations between classes, but that has not, on the whole, taken place. The old suspicions remain—of money as theft, of education and manners as ways of flaunting privilege, of professors and other intellectuals as Commies or potential traitors. If anything, the modern laboring man is more alienated, more devoid of respect for anything but sheer material advantage, than he was in the days of paternalism.

The trend of most current analyses is that worker output con-

---

* In effect, labor is compensating itself for decreases in the purchasing power of the dollar it has helped to bring about—essentially by a revolutionary non-compliance, an underperformance amounting to sabotage. But since large arms budgets greatly aggravate the situation by producing salaries and wages without the corresponding goods to buy with them, neither labor nor the executive class ever quite catches up. Pensioners and poorly organized producers such as the farmer fall farther and farther behind. And between them, inflation and taxes are wiping out all but the largest inherited estates, so that in time we may divide into two classes: a very small one with enormous capital (partly exported) and a very large one with no capital at all—a type of social structure found throughout Latin America.
† The grain trade in France, until the last days of the *ancien régime*, was strictly regulated. And when the restraints were removed, it was the merchants rather than the prime producers who profited—with the result that many peasant revolutionists had as their objective the restoration of centralized controls, in contrast to the urban bourgeoisie who wanted to be free of them.

tinues to drop and boredom, even—or perhaps especially—in large
environmentally engineered plants, is a greater problem than
ever.* The army has essentially the same problem: how to maintain discipline notwithstanding the tedium of life in the ranks and
the absence of any general sense of purpose. And without discipline, how are certain things to get done? Mossberg sees no ready
solution.

For really, worker refractoriness comes down to an attitude also
quite common in middle-class youth—a form of obstinate blind-
ness, a refusal to distinguish demands which are fair and to everyone's advantage from those which are arbitrary and exploitative.
Consequently, good treatment by management, improvement of
working conditions, and reasonable attention to individual or collective grievances may have no effect on morale—any more than
good parental treatment, an expensive education, a car of his own,
and considerable personal freedom may produce a son who is prepared to meet the world as fairly as, in his beginnings, it has met
him. In both cases, it is a question of how far willful personal
belief has gone, and how far, in turn, that habit has elaborated
itself into certain useful prejudices.

It is this inaccessibility, minimizing all commitment, which un-
derlies the spectatorism that has grown on us in the past decades
—to the point that we will watch a murder committed on the
street outside our window as detachedly as we watch similar events
on TV. The same attitude, spreading from leisure into productive
work, gives rise to the odd phenomenon of Man as Bystander at
what he himself is supposedly doing.† At bottom, the slowdown

* See for instance, "The New Steelworkers" by Bennett Kremen, himself a
former steelworker, in The New York Times, Financial Section, Sunday, January 7, 1973. Also "Factory Boredom: How Vital an Issue?" by Walter Mossberg, in The Wall Street Journal, Friday, March 25, 1973.
† In an automobile repair shop I visited recently there was a sign reading:

NOTICE TO EMPLOYEES

*Somewhere between starting and quitting time, and without infringing too
much on lunch period, coffee breaks, rest periods, story-telling, ticket-
selling and vacation-planning, it is requested that each employee find some
time that he can set aside, to be known as the "Work Break."*
—*The Management*

in the work force is simply a variant of what, among white-collar workers, university students, executives, and professional people, is known as alienation—essentially an incapacity to do almost anything with a whole heart.

And it is of course the alienated who incline to radical egoism and finally to radical subjectivity. (Why work hard if it's just for The Man? Why stick to reason if fantasy is more fun?) In a world seen as purely mechanical and pro tem, Me for Me begins to seem the only irreducible proposition, because it has the authority both of reason and of the instincts behind it.

When skepticism comes to include a profound doubt of reason itself, radical subjectivity becomes perfectly permissible—indeed, almost unavoidable, since an important check on sheer fantasy is now being removed. Educated or not, the radical subjectivist feels free to believe whatever his more primitive self demands. He *feels* free, but increasingly is not—is more and more driven to think and do what his Id and his conditioning tell him, and in proportion becomes contemptuous of himself. Sensing his inner bondage, he pretends it is external and blames The System.* His secret knowledge of his own limits makes him mistrust the ideas and character of others. He begrudges them an identity he himself does not have, and reason a freedom and power that his own lacks. He becomes, as it were, committed to disrespect—an attitude today as prevalent among the privileged as among our organized and largely bourgeois *sans-culottes.*†

If reason, understood as a kind of inner freedom, is out, reason as "brains" or shrewdness is definitely not. It is a matter of what, in the individual, the instinct for survival demands—if worldly success, then he, the radical subjectivist, will make an exception, using reason in his "specialty" while continuing to believe pretty much what he likes outside of it. Because of the prodigies of

---

* Regardless, that is, of how much literal freedom or leisure it may grant him.
† Whose leadership, if they understood the position better, would be demanding stock options in lieu of wage increases, since only in that way can the laboring man, who finally becomes a pensioner himself, obtain some protection against inflation. But he is still suspicious of stock and would rather play the horses; and management is glad to leave it that way.

TROUBLE IN CLOUD-CUCKOOLAND

shrewdness by which we have turned the discoveries of science to military or commercial advantage—because of the consistency and cold-bloodedness with which each of us calculates his own—we imagine we live in an age tyrannized by reason. What makes it seem one, and increasingly turns our young people against it, is that increasingly these are the *only* uses to which reason is being put.

In the realm of pure ideas—imaginative reason—we are drifting into a chaos of eccentric private notions amounting almost to superstition. Whether as specialists in professional life or as cultists in private, we can scarcely talk to each other;* and along with that, we have slipped into a more and more unsettled emotional state. The latter first became apparent after World War I and by the mid-1960s had grown into a national emergency.

In that decade, it was as though all our troubles were coming to a head at once. The gathering hatred of young people for "oldies" found a cause, and a good one, in the Vietnam war. Even our superspecialists—General Westmoreland, Walt Rostow, the Bundy brothers—failed us, thereby nearly turning our protorevolution into the real one. It was then, too, that the boom in the occult, in quack therapies, in porn, drug use, neoprimitive life-styles, "guru babble,"† satanism, the rip-off, hedonism in Suburbia (*Couples*), mystic dieting, and the alienation of practically everyone began in earnest. Compared with those psychedelic days, when every group one could think of took to the streets, often to do nothing more creative than wreck its own neighborhood or pelt the police with plastic bags full of feces, the goings-on of the 1920s—the flappers and Red scares and Sacco-Vanzetti, the Joe Colleges out drinking bootleg booze and necking in their Stutzes, even the market manipulators and Teapot Dome and the crude precorporate Mafia

---

* A trend so pronounced in the sciences that it produced the interdisciplinary movement in reaction. I participated for a year in one of these attempts at cross-cultural interchange (at M.I.T. in 1964–65) and found the results discouraging. It was a little like show business; at one "interdisciplinary" meeting after another, one saw the same men get up and run through their latest findings, each keeping to his *shtick* and going home apparently as un-crossfertilized as he had come.
† A phrase lifted from Ed Sanders, a biographer of Charles Manson.

of that time—seem rather innocent. In the ten years between the Cuban missile crisis and Nixon's tainted campaign for reelection, there were more bombings and political assassinations than we had had during the whole preceding century.

In *Future Shock*, Alvin Toffler quotes Daniel P. Moynihan, then (circa 1970) chief White House adviser on urban affairs, as saying that present-day America "exhibits the qualities of an individual going through a nervous breakdown." Elsewhere, Toffler cites a passage from *Newsweek* which describes us as "a society that has lost its consensus . . . a society that cannot agree on standards of conduct, language and manners, on what can be seen and heard." Finally he mentions "the findings of Walter Gruen, social science research coordinator at Rhode Island Hospital, who has conducted a series of statistical studies of what he terms 'the American core culture.' Rather than the monolithic system of beliefs attributed to the middle class by earlier investigators, Gruen found—to his own surprise—that 'diversity in beliefs was more striking than the statistically supported uniformities. It is,' he concluded, 'perhaps already misleading to talk of an American culture complex.' "*

Radical subjectivity, in short, is here, and with it, emotional symptoms which to Moynihan suggest a collective nervous breakdown. What *Newsweek* seems to say and Gruen to confirm is that "American core culture" is disintegrating into the chaos of willful personal beliefs I spoke of.

If so, how grave a development is that? Will our views reorganize and stabilize themselves again shortly? We do tend to think of such things as Mind Control, the hippie movement, and Fem Lib as fads, even if fads with a purpose. And there is nothing in our present theories of human nature which makes it immediately ap-

---

* Our complex, back in the '20s, being that we had none; so culture here had to be created overnight, and the more sensitive fled to places such as Paris where it reportedly existed.

It might be thought that Gruen's findings are really a good sign, showing that we have put the conformism of our earlier days behind us and emerged into a fruitful diversity. The trouble is the diversity may not be fruitful. What looks like a renaissance of the individual may just be Babel revisited.

parent why reigns of nonsense should lead to reigns of terror, rather than dying harmlessly away, as most vogues do. We continually say that we live in an Age of Anxiety, that a great many of us are "neurotic," but really these are just names for a condition no one quite understands. The root of the difficulty may lie in our concepts of the self—of what causes psychic illness and what constitutes psychic health.

What, for instance, is a neurotic? Someone, we would be apt to say, who had been emotionally traumatized in childhood to such a degree that as an adult he has remained incapable of shaking off his "bad" early experiences. Having "conflicts" too severe and deeply buried to be manageable, he handles them indirectly, through a system of "defenses" (rationalizations and maneuvers) which may enormously impede him in his personal relations and cause him some degree of psychosomatic illness, but which do, after a fashion, keep the emotional peace.

A neurotic, in a word, is unfree in the basic sense of having far less latitude of rational choice, less imaginative scope,* than he might. His power to act on what he knows, either in everyday fact or in his thoughts, is excessively limited, as is the range of his interests or affections. What does not, in some way, serve his peculiar purposes is apt not to move him at all. He is, in short, a specialist by temperament—the ultimate utilitarian who owes his success, if any, to an enforced concentration upon certain things. His sympathies tend to be abstract and symbolic and distantly self-serving, rather than immediate and human and spontaneously generous. He is often a great one for causes, a natural ideologue, but seldom the warmest of friends. Whether successful by the world's standards or just a "neurotic," he lives according to a set of imperatives which, even when he comes to understand them (as in psychoanalysis), may still dominate him.†

Rather than imagination, a faculty of active construction in-

---

* Because much that he might freely have thought about becomes, for subliminal reasons, off limits to him.
† If analysis has taught us anything it is that to know thyself may not be enough.

volving reason in the fullest sense, he tends to have fantasies—dramas of which he is merely the watcher and mind merely the instrument. The same passivity or malleability of the waking self figures in rationalization, a form of pseudo thinking in which mind is driven to bend the rationally perceived truth into a shape that more nearly conforms to some primitive wish or "drive" generated outside mind itself, often by forces wholly invisible to it.

This description fits what I have called the radical subjectivist, the man who believes not what reason but what other forces inside him dictate. And since a variety of evidence* suggests that large numbers of us are becoming radically subjective or "neurotic," it follows, I think, that something may be wrong with our conventional view of the nature and origins of neurosis. If early traumata such as deprivation of love; exposure to cruel, capricious, manipulative parents; or inflexibly harsh training in bowel control, sexual self-restraint, etc., actually are the main causes of neurosis, is it reasonable to suppose that a sizable percentage of our population—including many among the more privileged—has had such terrible beginnings? It is fashionable to say that of course that is so—The System, and especially parents and educators, have been the ruin of us.

In reality, the trend in this century has been away from the more gross, and even the subtler, abuses of the past. True, our prisons are still nightmarish, and some of our mental hospitals and urban public schools likewise. But *on the whole*, the move has steadily been toward greater lenience, toward better understanding and at least an institutionalized sort of decency, in everything from child rearing and education to the treatment of criminals in our courts. We have made large-scale experiments in permissiveness, have greatly reduced the amount of corporal punishment administered to children,† have all but abolished the death penalty, have tried

* Including, of course, the present boom in nonsense.
† It is true that recently published statistics on child abuse show a trend in the other direction. But official beatings in schools, and the caning or whipping of children so widely practiced into late Victorian times, have been going out since 1900.
The phenomenon we need to explain is that, while institutional or official decency was still improving, individual decency began to deteriorate.

the greatest assortment of techniques for progressive education (in public schools as well as private), and have produced what is probably the world's largest literature of help and guidance for anxious parents.

We have undertaken to care for our sick and aged and unemployed on a scale not even approached by civilizations of the past (and equaled in only a few countries such as Britain and Sweden today). Counseling and social work have become major enterprises here; and there is, moreover, continual agitation for prison reform, for better legal protection for the poor, for more low-cost housing. And bit by bit, some amelioration of our worst evils, even of white prejudice against blacks (though not, as yet, conversely) is coming about.

Does none of this count? *Has* The System been the ruin of us? Is it really sensible to describe Amerika (to use Jerry Rubin's habitual spelling) as a tyranny more vile than Adolf Hitler's? It is if one knows nothing about history, including that of only thirty years ago. But the more important question is why these quite tangible improvements have not worked. In the period in which most of them were being made, social unrest has been rapidly increasing, and with it, crime, "anomie," and an almost universal sense of grievance, as though Everyman, far from feeling he had made headway in matters of fundamental right, considered himself more defeated and put upon than ever. Thanks to forms of liberalism and technology now ritually damned, he can enjoy a degree of luxury, a mobility, even a share in the management of his community, which in times past were the privilege of only a few men at the top of the social order. And with that, he has become possessed, it seems, by a rage to ruin his luck, the first step being to deny that he has any: things are no better, they are worse.

More absurdly still, the leaders in that movement have mostly not been *sans-culottes*. Black militants excepted, the majority of extreme dissidents in the 1960s were middle- or upper-middle-class white young people whose parents sent them to college and often supported their revolutionary activities on allowances from home. Whereas the laboring man may merely sabotage the economic system by soldiering on the job, or blacks threaten it by riots and muggings, the youthful radicals of the past decade wanted to destroy it *in toto*, including the allowances, welfare checks, and food stamps that were the practical base from which they operated. They had reason to fear their own success, for in contrast to the leftists of the 1930s, they had no plan for a social order to replace the one they intended to bring down. Lenin, Trotsky, *et al.* were doctrines personified; Ché was a slogan. The *Contrat social* would never have made it with the Weathermen.*

The point is that one could describe these as signs of a mass neurosis or regression of some kind, but of what kind no one has as yet satisfactorily explained. The reason may be that our concept of neurosis is based upon theories of the self which, from Freud on, have been too tainted with the modern prejudice against intellect to be reliable.

In the Freudian psychic trinity—Ego, Superego, and Id—the weakest member was, and still is, conceived to be Ego. Superego (roughly conscience) and Id (the instincts) held the real power and Ego (roughly the waking conscious "I") had much the same role as the early behaviorists and Skinner assigned it. It was at best a diplomat, smoothing out relations between instinct and conscience; at worst, the servant of these other two. In the extreme it became a mere onlooker, the role it is assuming today.† And just in that conceptual scheme, in the assumption of the near-powerlessness of the Ego, may lie the critical mistake.

In reality, the three major divisions of the psyche may be organized to work on a balance-of-power principle, an equilibrium in which the waking conscious self not only may play as active a part as the other two but, in man, *must* do so, if he is to be truly sane or in possession of himself. The difficulty, for us, is that the

---

* Indeed, had their revolution caught on, it would have gone directly into the Terror, having no rationale even for such confused attempts at government as the National and Constituent Assemblies.

† See above—Man as bystander at what he himself is supposedly doing. Drug taking is likewise a form of spectatorism—going to the mental movies—as are various forms of meditation which aim to release a self other (and more "real") than the thinking one.

instincts are simply there. So too is conscience, which, along with other forms of conditioning, we acquire willy-nilly during childhood. More than either of these, the waking "I" needs to be developed, actively by its possessor as well as passively through external influence. Its strengths are not only the least given but the last to come into effect.

Unlike conscience, which can arise from blows and kicks, the waking self in its feeble formative stage needs the most extensive and detailed encouragement if it is really to take shape. Whereas conscience involves acquiescence, mind involves learning to think —which means in the end to be nonacquiescent, to move about freely in one's head regardless of internalized prohibitions. And just as conscience or conditioning greatly depends upon things which happen to us in the first five to ten years of life, so the waking self may or may not get the early start needed to make it more than a bystander in the psyche later on.

Ideally, its task, during the upheavals of adolescence, is to make the contents of conscience conscious, revise them in the light of reason, and retain the result as part of its own repertoire of devices for thinking. During that massive "return of the repressed," when we begin to examine and indignantly throw out many of the rules by which we have been raised, the "I" is performing a most vital task; it is deautomatizing or bringing under its own control a rival division of the self—the Superego. If the "I" fails in that task,* Superego and Id thenceforth remain allies in the sense that each, acting through the same machinery of feeling, can manipulate reason while being largely proof against control or manipulation *by* it. Faced with this combination of forces the "I," in short, is decisively defeated; from which arises the apparent paradox that the automatically moral man, the perfect conformist, is often not moral at all but merely one obedient to internal *force majeure* and as such a tireless rationalizer.[5] If the tics of instinct prove

* That is, if it does not rework the contents of conscience but allows these to lapse, unchanged, into unconsciousness. The parallel in life is an adolescence which comes to nothing—which peters out in sporadic rebellion or overt violence, leaving an adult automatized still, with no shape or convictions he can properly call his own.

stronger than those of conscience, causing him to do something bad, his guilt will at once ease itself through the agency of his subjugated intelligence: i.e., he will allow his thoughts to be falsified by his wish to feel less emotionally uncomfortable; nor will he be troubled by an awareness that there is something subnormal, not to say subhuman, about the whole process. Guilt of that sort, or what one might call true responsibility, is quite beyond him.

Superficially it would seem that the opposite psychic type—the man whose conscience has become conscious and controlled accordingly—might be the one to turn into a Machiavellian monster. Actually, however, reason alone would never lead to Machiavellianism; it is reason surrendered to the instincts for survival and self-promotion that does so—reason as it is understood by "good competitors" and men of the success mentality generally.

Reason alone has its own aesthetic and interests, in contrast to which those of the Id seem ugly and rather foolish. Men in whom reason proper is dominant are more apt to have the moral views of Kant and Einstein and Russell and Linus Pauling.

To an extent, the same control which the waking conscious self can establish over Superego it may also establish over Id. In the nature of the case, however, Id is the more intractable of the two. Conditioning is a matter of chance, but the instincts are a sure thing, many of them operative from infancy on, and all of them hidden from direct conscious view, manifesting themselves in feeling states and "urges" whose meanings we have to learn as we go along—just as we learn the techniques of fighting or lovemaking, by modifying various reflexes and putting them together into suitable patterns.

Conscience involves ideas; the "ideas" of instinct are external to mind and inferred by it, exactly as the laws governing events in the external world have to be inferred. Nevertheless, with Superego on its side, Ego can attain a considerable control even over the most violent drives or emotions arising in the Id. It is just that control—that acquired strength of the conscious self—which distinguishes a man of high civilization from one who is tribal or part of a culture (such as Islam) that has been in a state of regression for centuries. The difference is not merely in passive control—in endurance—but in the power of active understanding—of initiation.* Many tribal peoples are noted for their stoicism. It was not for want of that quality but because he could not change fast enough—because he lacked initiative in the most basic sense —that the American Indian was so totally defeated by the white man.

We know now that that was probably not due to the Indian's native stupidity.† Essentially what crippled him was his intangible heritage—his tradition. Because that had not sufficiently evolved, the rational "I" in him remained weak. He was incapable of radical innovation, for the reason that his conscious mental processes were too much under the control of Superego and Id—were too much dominated by a conscience of the totem and taboo type, and by a primitive *machismo*. He could not, therefore, break the mold of his own customs even when his very survival depended on it— and in fact today, living on his reservations, neglected and in danger of total dispossession, he is still half a captive of his past, still hoping some sort of restoration of the old ways may yet be possible.‡ The recent siege at Wounded Knee reads like a page out of Cervantes.

The fundamental point is that man's psyche is not given but to a large extent built, and not merely by conditioning or elaboration of the Superego (Skinner's thesis) but by the encouragement or in-formation (*sic*) of the Ego—by the construction of a waking conscious self to the point that it is not a mere problem solver but a psychological power in its own right. This indeed is our distinctively human feature, however few of us in fact develop it.

A "neurotic," consequently, may either suffer from a kind of

---

* In the realm of ideas, known as "creativity"; in practical matters, as "competence."
† When I was a schoolboy we read, as I recall in our civics books, that American Indians were stupider and had smaller brains than whites, but were not as stupid or small-brained as black Africans. In those days, no one thought of weighting I.Q. tests to compensate for environmental differences in the testees; but it wouldn't have mattered, since we all believed whites had the biggest and best brains anyway. The Indian's reported vulnerability to alcohol may, incidentally, have had the same origin as his lower I.Q. scores—namely, his tradition and relatively underdeveloped "I."
‡ Compare this situation with that of the Nisei, themselves a people of high tradition, who had no trouble at all becoming modern Americans.

conditioning too intensive or too damaging for the "I" to overcome in the critical period of adolescence or later, or may, without any excess of "bad" conditioning, succumb to the combined forces of Superego and Id simply because the "I" itself was not sufficiently encouraged or in-formed (*sic*) during his earlier years. In the latter case (probably the more common today) one can say he became neurotic by default—through a mere want of the intangibles the "I" needed to grow on.

The American Indian, whose "neurotic rigidity" cost him his battle against the whites, is a casualty of the latter type. So, ironically enough, are the people who displaced him coming to be, by a process of regression which I will now try to describe in outline.

If the psyche is organized as I have suggested, it is clear why great civilizations in their rising phase produce at least minorities of men whose intellect and force of character make them appear to be almost of another race. Thanks to the accumulations of ideas we call tradition, development of the "I" has gone far enough in them so that they have become free to act to the limit of their own highest capacities. It was from an intuitive awareness of that principle of self-realization that the men of the Renaissance made an ideal of *l'uomo universale*—the all-sided man. They sensed, correctly, that education is more than a matter of direct utility and culture more than an ornament. Both, they seem to have felt, were ways in which man became human in the fullest sense—a creature able to escape from the trap of innate or acquired habit in which all other creatures (and most men) are condemned to live. Through the "humanities" he in-formed himself to such a degree that instead of fantasy and rationalization—captive reason—he developed thought and imagination—reason proper. It was essentially this potential in ourselves that we expressed in the notion of Free Will.

It happens that most great traditions were in their origins religious. Their strength lay not only in the fact that the promises of religion gave men a powerful instrument for controlling the Id, but also in the systems of moral principles which most religions, no matter how maladministered, have taught. For to Man the primitive, a set of moral precepts such as the Christian provided the first step toward a wider awareness. They gave him a way of looking at all behavior in a sense objectively, in the light of certain general principles. Later, as the civilization itself matured, this same sort of widened awareness went on to become artistic or philosophic or literary or scientific ways of looking at the world. Basically, then, the moral teachings of religion start the formation of the "I," whose ultimate capability is to apprehend reality not in the narrow way enforced by the instincts or blind conscience, but in the light of imaginative understanding and *sub specie aeternitatis*.

One can easily trace this progress—the slow emergence of the "I" and an accompanying slow mitigation of certain social evils—in the history of our own civilization from Charlemagne's day to Lincoln's or FDR's. If one compares life in the Western world in this century with that in England and Europe in the reign, say, of Edward III, or during the sixteenth century,* it is obvious that however deplorable our behavior, customs, and institutions may still be, certain gains have undeniably been made. And during the same period, in particular since the seventeenth century, there has been virtually an explosion of achievement in the arts, literature, and science—even (pollution and the Bomb notwithstanding) in the practical management of life.

I bring up these points for two reasons. One is that we talk so incessantly about the injustice, inefficiency, and corruption of our own society, are so insistent that progress is really an illusion, that a commonsense reminder seemed necessary. No matter *how* bad our world appears, no one in his senses who knew even the rudiments of history would exchange his present existence for life, say, as a commoner in the reign of Louis the Fat. The second, and main, reason is that the process by which our tradition has slowly expanded in the centuries since, bringing increasing (if never very large) numbers of fully developed rationally self-possessed individuals in its train, may now have begun to reverse itself.

* When savage punishments, even for trivial offenses, were common; when witch persecutions of extraordinary ferocity were practiced in many countries; when France was devastated by the Wars of Religion, etc., etc.

Instead of continuing the gradual conquest of the irrational—of Superego and Id—we may have started losing and giving up the fight. The consequence is that we live in an age in which millions of us are becoming "neurotic" merely through a kind of neglect —as a result of a drastic skinning down of our notion of ourselves to the point that even according to purely functional standards we are ceasing to function very well. The key to this phenomenon is to be found in the omissions that are so essential a part of modern skeptical materialism.

It is clear that traditions greatly differ (in the range and effectiveness of their ideas) and may be in any one of three states: growing (as ours was from about A.D. 800 into the nineteenth century), static (as that of many tribal societies is), or shrinking (as happens when civilizations begin to decline but before they have reached the "fossil" stage equivalent to a renewed tribalism).

In the first case, the fathers are passing on more to their sons than they themselves received; in the second, there is little change from generation to generation. In the third case, the fathers may be rejecting more of their own heritage than they can replace, with the result that they pass on less to their sons than they received. Most commonly, of course, ideals or principles about to be dropped from the collective repertoire are not explicitly dismissed. On the contrary, they may be spoken of with greater reverence than ever, which only underscores the increasing contrast between official belief and reality. In calling the later Victorians hypocrites, that is basically what we mean: while maintaining many of the old forms, they were, by the *fin-de-siècle* period, obviously ceasing to believe in the ideas behind them, it being just a question of time before the forms themselves were given up.

This latter process began after World War I with the so-called Moral Revolution of the 1920s, and has continued at a gradually accelerating pace ever since. The old forms, even as such, ceased to be maintained—in particular those relating to God and right conduct. Along with the notion of the immortal soul, a whole structure of moral convictions commenced to crumble, to the point that no matter what the fathers said, no matter how they tried to keep up some semblance of the former state of things,* the sons got the message, leaving out their own beliefs, and so out of the repertoire of the "I," what the example of their elders told them was no longer real.

In the way of thinking devices—principles capable of producing men with a large view of themselves and the world—we were dropping more than we added. In effect our tradition, whose growth had perhaps somewhat slowed in later Victorian times, had passed its zenith and was now starting to shrink. And just as civilizations pick up momentum during their upward movement, so they show a similarly dramatic acceleration when they first turn downward.

For it is just in such epochs, as the doubts of the fathers begin appearing as deficits in the sons, that the civilization itself is reaching a climactic complexity, becoming more urban and sophisticated and technologically advanced than it may ever be again.† In a world in which the "I" needs more than ever to be fully developed, it increasingly fails to become so. Given too little to start on, it cannot, at adolescence or later, win the battle for its own freedom and assume its proper role as the dominant part of the self. Instead, Id and Superego combine against it, the psychological type that results being the revolutionary mass man of today—the man who, regardless of his actual class, finds he is not up to the intricacies of the world he has inherited and so starts yearning for a simpler one.

Unable to resist his own instincts, he becomes a radical egoist, finally a radical subjectivist. He abandons the moral constraints of the past not by choice, as he imagines, but because he is inwardly driven to do so; and so rapid and general is this change that sexual mores and institutions, such as marriage, that have lasted for centuries begin to weaken or disappear overnight. From the same want of self, he is driven to believe in mystical nonsense because

* For instance, in the upper middle class, by sending their sons to private schools such as St. Paul's in which religion was given an emphasis it no longer had at home.
† This seems to have been true of the Rome of Sulla's or Cicero's time, and may have been true of China in the Age of the Hundred Schools (of philosophy). The zenith of Egyptian culture appears to have been in the XII Dynasty, before the revolutionary Hyksos period and the Empire.

it allays his instinctive fear of death, or in ideological nonsense because it promises (at the cost of a freedom he will never miss, since he has already lost it) to simplify his earthly life for him, relieving him at last of his "anomie" by giving him clear brutal objectives and a new togetherness in the Movement.

An alternative solution—the American, of the 1960s—is for him to drop out, forming with others like himself a spontaneous new proletariat, an enclave society in which he can play at going back to the soil; can give rein to his now-compulsive sexuality or manage his now-unmanageable feelings with drugs; can convert his anxiety into rage by pouring hatred on the "straights" and playing at revolution; can indulge in "rip-offs" on the rationalization that in doing so he is really being a brave guerrilla; can develop a primitive creativity (rock; leathercraft; pottery) and an impoverished "in" language of his own* because they are "now," are his "thing"; eat brown rice diets because they promise long life and allow him, in the meantime, to "trip" on ketosis;† and talk "guru babble" because it reassures him that there is another spirit world in which he may live on forever.

As already mentioned, the trend of many psychological theories especially in America (which gave us behaviorism, Skinner, the James-Lange theory of emotion, and psychoanalysis in its most monumental form) has been toward the conclusion that mind or the waking "I" is a sort of fiction. The Real You lies elsewhere—in the Unconscious, in reflexes, hormones, the Id. According to the James-Lange theory, even our emotions, which we had thought of as arising in our heads and reflected in our bodies, actually arose in our bodies and were reflected in our heads—a rather extreme statement of the self-as-spectator idea.‡ John Dewey (as

* Actually not his own, but adapted from the jazz argot of the 1950s.
† In the later stages of the Ohsawa ("Zen") diet, the body becomes so starved it begins using up its reserves of fat. Compounds known as ketones are a metabolic by-product of this process, and some can evidently pass the blood–brain barrier, causing the mild intoxication or illumined states experienced for instance by mystics during fasting.
‡ Lange was Danish. He and James announced the same idea, independently, in about 1880. Their theory was incorrect, as it turns out. If the body is made "anxious" by injections of adrenaline or noradrenaline, the subject does not necessarily become so.

Santayana remarked) dissolved us into our social relations decades before Skinner, in a somewhat different way, started doing the same thing. For over fifty years, before the radically enfeebled, automatized self had become a general phenomenon, the prophets of the age were foretelling it, in the shape of theories as intellectually impoverished as twentieth-century man himself was soon to be.

The progress of our hollowing out is likewise easy to follow in literature, from Eliot and Céline to Beckett and the Black Comedians. Around 1930, Ortega y Gasset wrote (in *The Revolt of the Masses*): "The average type of European at present possesses a soul healthier and stronger, it is true, than those of the last century, but much more simple. Hence at times he leaves the impression of a primitive man suddenly risen in the midst of a very old civilization." Two decades later, in the 1950s, David Riesman discovered what he took to be a basic change in the American psyche. Instead of the "inner-directed" type of man, prevalent during the nineteenth and early twentieth centuries, we now mostly consisted of "other-directeds."

One might describe an "other-directed" as a psychic-starvation case, someone who has reached adulthood still formless and therefore excessively dependent, as a child is, on models which he can imitate. Having almost no real self, he may, however, with a little sophistication, learn to fake one. And gradually, as everybody comes to understand what the game is, it is taken for granted that we are all faking—that the self each of us displays is a contrivance.* (See Chapter X.) Historically this is a development that seems to have begun about 1960, or during Richard Nixon's first Presidential campaign. So, ten years after Riesman's discovery of "other-directedness" or Man-as-Amorph, we have its logical sequel —the "image" or Man-as-Pure-Persona (and eight years after that, elect Mr. Nixon himself).

In the "straight" and "hip" worlds both, a strong element of

* And in this century, understandably enough, the social status of actors has enormously improved. In the Middle Ages, I have read, it was thought that actors had no souls; and in Victorian times, their ability to simulate emotions was considered a mark of bad character or of none. Today they are seen as simply doing better what everyone does.

"camp" developed in the later '60s. Originally a homosexual way of satirizing oneself and those who thought themselves normal and sincere, camp became the natural art form for men who knew that all normality and sincerity were false. In the same period, movies began to replace literature as *the* "in" thing and mirror of our times; and Marshall McLuhan suddenly appeared, to tell us that print was out, that a whole new perceptual world was shaping up, much richer than the old one based upon a "linear" plodding, as through books or inventories.* Another school offered us "soft architecture"—perfect for those whose own vague outlines were continually changing.

The formal discovery of this psychic type—the next stage on from the empty conformism of Riesman's "other-directeds"—must be credited to Robert Jay Lifton, who called him Protean Man.† As Lifton describes him, Protean Man will try any number of roles the way ordinary man tries on suits. It is of no consequence if these involve him in a succession of contradictions; for in his case it is not even (to paraphrase a Nixon aide) a question of what works. Protean Man believes in what, at the moment, *feels* good— what works subjectively. His roles do for him what "defenses" did for the old-fashioned neurotic, and at a far smaller cost in mental effort.

Hence the American student leftists of the '60s, unlike their predecessors of a generation earlier, felt no need to load up their minds with facts and figures and elaborately detailed social schemes. A few watchwords were sufficient; and as the danger of being drafted to go to Vietnam passed, half of the *raison d'être* of the New Left passed with it. It began to feel better to be a Jesus Freak or a member of the Process Church, or just to sit out in the

* McLuhan's concept of the "mosaic" was a sort of take-it-at-a-gulp theory of perception. There is some question as to whether perception really can work like that—whether a holistic way of seeing things isn't in fact built up by much "linear" effort of the old sort. But these questions were of no concern to his readers; if he said the "mosaic" method worked and they, staring at their TV sets, felt that it did, that was enough.
† Interestingly enough, Lifton's chief subject was a young Japanese who had grown up in the chaotic post–War II world of his own country, a period when the older Japanese tradition was in some disorder.

sun digging God and nature.* Protean Man may have problems, but intellectualizing, and the obstinacy of conviction that often goes with it, are not among them.

It is a truism that the earlier in life we are traumatized, the more lasting the effects are apt to be. The same principle may apply to starvation of the "I." Some ethologists believe that man, like other creatures, passes through critical learning periods. As a practical matter we know that to be true of muscular skills such as ballet dancing or playing a musical instrument. There may be reason to suppose it is true for learning motions of the mind as well. The first five to seven years of life are perhaps as important to the future powers and autonomy of the waking conscious self as they are to the nature and intensity of our future emotional re-actions or to the eventual organization of our motor patterns. If so, what that means is that by a process of entirely inadvertent neglect—through having been starved of certain kinds of mental stimulation and example—many of our children may be reaching school already half ineducable, like the virtuoso-never-to-be who may have had real talent but whose hands simply weren't started soon enough.

Indeed, it may be for that reason that we have had so little suc-cess with our recent attempts to improve education. On the con-trary, one might say that since the '50s education has been forced into making more and more concessions just to hold its own, low-ering its standards and trying every possible gimmick to recapture its audience's attention—brighter schoolrooms and better "facili-ties" generally, more attractive texts, the New Math, emphasis on "relevance," negative emphasis on memory work (dates, spelling, English grammar, Latin in any form). If grades make you nervous,

* "Rennie C. Davis, the antiwar activist, held a news conference the other day to explain the new focus of his life, a 15-year-old guru in India called the Maharaj Ji. 'My main message is that there is now a practical way to fulfill all the dreams of the movement of the early sixties and seventies,' Mr. Davis de-clared. . . . That method he said, involved 'receiving knowledge.' . . . The guru, whose followers are said to total several millions . . . received public at-tention last November when it was reported that he had tried to smuggle money, jewels and watches into the country, and that the Indian government was investigating his finances." (*The New York Times*, Sunday, May 6, 1973)

we will abolish them. If History sounds dry and forbidding to you, we'll give it a "now" name—Social Studies. If your memory is so resistant to details, well then, just show us you know a few principles—show us you know *something*.

In the same period there was a flurry of articles (by Oliver La Farge, President Griswold of Yale, Professor Willard Thorp of Princeton and others) complaining that our students couldn't seem to write clear English anymore. The students they were talking about were not from the ghetto but from "good homes," meaning families of the middle to upper class. Reports of further declines in "reading skills" (and not only in urban schools flooded with blacks, Puerto Ricans, and other deprived minorities) have been appearing intermittently in the press ever since. Assuming that this is really a trend, we may be seeing in it a quite concrete example of the principle mentioned earlier—the shrinkage of our tradition to the point that the doubts of the fathers are turning up as clearly measurable deficits in the sons.* Nor is this particular one trivial. As an index of the order, power, and range of mind, the state of a people's language is probably as good as any.

In parallel with these signs that the "I" is critically failing to take shape, there are others which indicate a corresponding release of the Id. It was in the 1950s that juvenile delinquency hove suddenly into public view—when teen-age violence, including gang wars, savage beatings of teachers or of old people in city parks,† "biker" hoodlumism and shakedown rackets in public

* *The New York Times* (December 16, 1973) reports "a steady 10-year decline in high school students' scores on the Scholastic Aptitude Test." The S.A.T. is the principal admissions test used by colleges or universities, "especially private ones," and the decline may not be due to democratization, since "the number of students taking the S.A.T. had leveled off at about one million several years ago." Interestingly enough, the average annual drop in language-ability scores was far greater in this latter period—5.2 points per year for 1968–73 as compared with 2.4 points per year for 1962–67. The decline in mathematical scores was less than in the verbal (4.2 percent versus 6.9 percent for the whole period), but the trend in both was clear and showed no reversals. "'The question of what is causing the drop is something none of us can answer,' said Dr. William Angoff, executive director of College Board programs for the Educational Testing Service of Princeton, New Jersey . . .'"
† One also read of more exotic crimes, such as the burning alive of "alkies" on the Bowery. Lately arson, by teen-agers and subteens, has become quite popular

schools, became so noticeable a feature of our national life that psychiatrists such as Robert Lindner declared our youth to be in "active mutiny"; and in 1954, the Senate held hearings to see if possibly the comic-book industry mightn't be to blame. (With the same idea, numerous studies have since been made of violence on TV.)

In the '50s, drug use—if one excepts tranquilizers—was chiefly a ghetto phenomenon. By the mid-1960s it had spread to the privileged classes, invading virtually every prep school and college in the country. How was it that we had suddenly developed such a huge number of "addictive personalities"? The answer is suggested by the kinds of society in which the "addictive personality" seems to be perennial—small bored ones in which men are trapped by their own tribalism or old fossilized civilizations (Islam; India; Manchu China) whose centuries of growth lie far behind them and whose traditions survive as corrupted remnants in the minds of their inheritors. For men of these psychic types, drugs do what the waking conscious self cannot, either because it has lost the ability (in fossil civilizations) or never properly developed it (in tribal ones): they alter feelings and subdue or manipulate the Id; and in the case of hallucinogens, they provide mental movies for Man-the-Spectator to watch.

Typically, many hippies used both basic solutions to the problem of floating anxiety: converting it into anger and becoming intransigents; and converting it into other things (sometimes psychoses) by taking drugs. It is obvious that drug users make inefficient revolutionaries, not merely because some of the effects of drugs—mystical elation in the case of LSD or mescaline, silly good humor or sexiness in the case of marijuana—have negative political value. Although everyone complained of them, the drug taking and indiscipline of groups such as the Weathermen were a godsend, since they guaranteed that the young revolution would never

<hr>

in New York and elsewhere. *The New York Times* for Sunday, April 19, 1970, reported that in Manhattan and surrounding boroughs, vandalism, including arson, destruction of laboratories and classrooms, etc., was up 20 percent in 1969 from the year before, the estimated losses amounting to $3.2 million.

get anywhere. And aside from a few bombings, it never did.*

What I have just described are, in effect, avant-garde forms of our disorder. But the Young Revolution of the '60s was more than a minority phenomenon, in that the basic attitudes and life-style of the dissidents were adopted, in milder form, by a sizable silent majority. What began as the small Beatnik movement of the 1950s had spread to involve a whole generation ten years later. Drug use and the sexual revolution, by the end of the '60s, were anything but minority phenomena. Long hair, according to Jerry Rubin, was the liberty cap of the revolution, and in 1972 almost everyone, including crane operators, ballplayers, and middle-aged voluptuaries, was wearing it.

In the realm of intellect—Serious Writing—there was a simultaneous drift into anti-intellectualism, with particular emphasis on the debunking of science. C. P. Snow's Two Cultures being unfortunately a reality, most literary men have never much liked science anyway. It seems to strike them as a cold, opaque way of doing things, and in many doubtless stirs up memories of classrooms in which they once struggled to grasp concepts or solve equations that certain boys around them mastered with humiliating ease. Now, as grown-ups, they have their innings, holding

* In *Science* (March 12, 1971; 171:977–85), J. L. Horn and P. D. Knott reviewed a number of studies of activist youth made by Bettelheim, Keniston, and others. These showed that activists and hippies—although both groups came from the middle or upper middle class—had somewhat different family backgrounds. Activists were more apt to be children of academics or Ph.D.s and, rather than rebelling against "straight" parents, were often going the militancy of their parents one better. Unlike the hippies, the activists were not dropouts but B-average college students who tended to be well organized and to do rather demanding things such as teaching in ghetto schools.

The hippies, by contrast, were "tragically estranged from their families, most of which, in outward appearance, seem to have represented the Establishment." The hippies' religious beliefs differed from those of other students and also from those of their own parents. ". . . The parents of activists, when compared with the parents of non-activists, were more frequently reported to be atheists, agnostics, Jews, Unitarians and Friends."

Finally—"the studies suggest that young activists lacked the academicians' enchantment with ideas in the abstract and were in fact . . . sometimes rather contemptuous of well-educated people. . . . In this regard, the activist could be characterized as pragmatic. . . . He was apt to be critical of education . . . premised upon a belief that it is worthwhile to know just for the sake of knowing."

science responsible for everything from the Bomb and pollution to the death of God. Anything you care to name—anomie, the horrors of the factory system, germ warfare, thalidomide, Auschwitz—is traceable to it, is the stepchild of our natural knowledge—as though all of us were being punished for the Promethean folly of a few.*

But behind these complaints—many of them quite absurd—one finds another, more significant theme. In essence it is that the detachment or pure reason which science supposedly represents—a form, as it were, of mental virtue of which the successes of science might be thought the best possible proof—*really does not exist.* Pure science is therefore in no way distinguishable from applied, or from technics, and so deserves no special respect. The disinterested curiosity, the lifelong preoccupation with knowledge or understanding as such, which seemed to set off such obscure, dedicated, underrewarded men as Willard Gibbs† from the run of their fellows, have suddenly become human attributes we cannot and will not believe in any longer. It is pure science—not just technology, its "interested" by-product—that must be brought down. Like the rest of us, "pure" science is after all corrupt, subjective, eager for power and advantage; a hypocritical tyrant who works hand in glove with the Establishment and always has. In "The Megamachine,"‡ this is how Lewis Mumford puts it:

> Beneath Descartes's equation of thought with existence another idea was implicit, which derived from the social style of the Baroque period: Under a rational system of ideas, all minds would be forced to submit to scientific "laws" *as though*

* And in this view Rousseau anticipated us, as did McLuhan's crusade against print.
† Gibbs taught theoretical physics at Yale for nine years at no salary. When Johns Hopkins offered him $3,000 a year, Yale countered with an offer of $2,000 and he stayed. He was touched, as he said, by "a very unexpected opposition to my departure." Gibbs himself was not a rich man, having inherited $23,500 and a house which he shared with his two sisters. He won the respect of Clerk Maxwell, but otherwise little acclaim. He simply loved his work and did it. He was perhaps the greatest scientist we have produced, but hardly one American in ten thousand today has ever heard of him.
‡ *The New Yorker,* October 17, 1970, pp. 51–52.

they were subjects of an absolute ruler. Such laws, as Wilhelm Ostwald was later to point out, established the realm of predictable behavior; this simplified choices and economized effort. . . . If scientific determinism operated everywhere, then human lives too might eventually be brought under control. *This naturally assumed that, as in any absolute system of government, there were no unruly elements that were not known to the police or could not be rounded up and imprisoned indefinitely.* . . . [Italics added.]

For all its reasonable air, this passage is surely a little insane. In proceeding from Descartes' *cogito* to the last sentence, Mumford seems to have lumped natural with juridical law. Thinking in terms of the former was apparently not an act of obedience to (given, physical) fact, but a habit "derived from the social style of the Baroque," and one, moreover, aimed at clamping a tyranny of reason on everyone, the new "absolute ruler" being ostensibly Nature herself (but really just scientific "laws"). The confusion is increased when he suggests that these same "laws" can actually make men's behavior predictable and hence vulnerable to state control; so scientific "laws" are *not* just a reflection of the "style of the Baroque" after all but principles valid in themselves and much to be feared for the use likely to be made of them, presumably by scientists working in collaboration with the police.

The message underlying this pretentious muddle is the one available in any issue of the *National Enquirer,* or in countless popular works about "brain science." A few years ago the fantasy was that the machines were about to rebel and take over; now it is that Big Brother will soon be implanting brain electrodes in us all, so as to manipulate us by remote control.*

GIANT U.S. COMPUTER WILL SNOOP INTO YOUR PRIVATE LIFE . . . *And if a Wrong Button Is Pushed You Could Be Ruined,* says the *National Enquirer* (February 25, 1968). You can bet no "unruly elements" are going to escape *that* kind of surveillance.

* A project at the moment not feasible, the amazing thing being that anyone with better than a grade-school education would think that it was.

If scientists are actually at work on any such sinister program—if despotism is, as Mumford suggests, somehow inherent in the very structure of science—the odd thing is that many scientists seem unaware of the fact. If anything, they feel socially rather out of it, as is shown by some remarks made by the astronomer Fred Hoyle before the American Physical Society in 1968: "Is it really true that we can do nothing about society, or are we simply suffering from a kind of mental blockage? Isn't it really that in the past scientists just haven't dared to allow themselves to think openly of taking society by the scruff of the neck?"

To men such as Clerk Maxwell and Willard Gibbs—to John Tyndall, who a century ago made a lecture tour in this country, as he said "to present science to the world as an intellectual good" (and in proof of his sincerity gave the proceeds from this tour, several thousand pounds, to an American society for the advancement of science)—the idea of "taking society by the scruff of the neck" would have seemed ridiculous. Even in Nazi Germany, where they had a rare opportunity to do so, few first-rate scientists appear to have availed themselves of it. And men such as Einstein, Pauling, and Russell have been liberal to the point of being almost antipolitical. It doesn't matter; the comic-book Mad Scientist idea is too deeply rooted. Because scientists have made such vast powers available, they must *want* power. Control, not knowledge, is the object. Professor Marcuse tells us so, straight out; pure science is bunk:

> We may now try to identify more clearly the hidden subject of scientific rationality and the hidden ends in its pure form. . . . In this form the object-world entered the construction of a technological universe—a universe of mental and physical instrumentalities, means in themselves. . . . In the construction of the technological reality, there is no such thing as a purely rational scientific order; the process of technological rationality is a political process.

(If I understand him, Marcuse means that the "hidden ends" of science are the real ones; "there is no such thing as a purely rational order" at all.)

Whatever in this century science may be becoming, the truth is that pure science was not a fiction, and exactly in its purity lay its strength. Scientific detachment—repugnant as some scientists may find the idea—is a descendant of certain religious ideals. The Christian notion of forgiveness implies a giving up of bias—means disciplining ourselves to see and accept others not as we would wish them to be but as they are. Transferred to the processes of nature, the same notion became the ideal of objectivity. Instead of trying, as they had always done, to wring some tangible benefit from the material world, men began to "forgive" it and study it for what it is. The basic theorem is: Keep yourself out of your own calculations, set aside your instinctive wishes and the illusions that go with them, and all will open unto you. And indeed it has.

While a few men before the Christian era had experimented in the modern sense, experiment as a consistent method of approaching nature developed only in the seventeenth century. For by then our tradition had evolved to the point at which mind or the rational "I" was ready to set off in pursuit of its own objects—which were not "fruit," as Bacon remarked, but "light"; not practical rewards and gimmicks but understanding—and at the risk of having to face an Inquisition, many minds did so.

The power which they acquired in this way may be judged from the result. Whereas alchemy (whose object was transmutation, hence wealth)* and various more useful technologies had fumbled along for centuries, producing recipes that worked, if at all, for reasons no one understood, science transformed our understanding of the physical world, and that with such rapidity and on such a scale that 98 percent of what we now know of its (Nature's) workings has been accumulated in the three hundred years or so since Bacon, Kepler, and Galileo. The fact remains that the modern "technological universe" was not the direct creation of scientists but largely a by-product, the result of their discoveries' being

* It is regarded as the ancestor of chemistry but as practiced in medieval Europe was really a form of magic or wishful science in which the element of disinterested curiosity hardly figured. Some of its discoveries were of use to chemists, but its basic approach was not.

put to use by manufacturers bent upon making money or heads of state bent upon making war. The conflicts and emotional torments suffered by men like J. Robert Oppenheimer were of a kind most of us perhaps cannot now understand, believing as we do, with Marcuse, that such things as the Bomb were part of the "hidden ends" of science all along; or with Lewis Mumford, that science inclined from the first toward a despotism based upon natural law.

A century ago, when Tyndall was making his American lecture tour, A. H. Dupree reports* that Thomas Huxley "worked out many of his most effective essays not in learned journals but before audiences of workingmen."† In those days most of us, Everyman included, seem to have regarded science quite differently. We shared Tyndall's belief that it was an "intellectual good," and in that echoed the conviction of the men of the Renaissance—that to know, to no other end than understanding for its own sake, was the key to our humanity. It turns out that in a most basic psychological sense, we may then have been right; whereas now, from a compulsion we scarcely understand, we may be throwing the key away.

In the fact, moreover, that we seem not merely indifferent but actively hostile to things of the mind—to *purity*, whether of speech or morals or inquiry—there is a suggestion of that revenge upon all excellence I mentioned earlier, a hint of the Nazi approach, which makes this a phenomenon that goes far beyond mere folly or vulgar-mindedness. In it, as much as in such matters as the Watergate affair, may lie the key to our political future. For of course the key to man's humanity and the key to his politics are ultimately the same. When the former is lost, all locks have

* *Science*, 134: 716; 1961.
† Dupree adds: "The audiences of the nineteenth century responded with enthusiasm. The crowd in Boston which broke a plate-glass window trying to get tickets for a Lowell Institute lecture is not easily duplicated today." In 1960, in the preface to their book *Great American Scientists*, the editors of *Fortune* wrote: "Any bright schoolboy can name scores of movie and television personalities . . . But how many can name a dozen living scientists?" It is no wonder we read the *pensées* of Mumford and Marcuse with such evident approval. A people so ignorant of their own intellectual tradition can presumably be told anything about it.

to be changed accordingly; and it is a peculiarity of most ages never to discover that that is happening until too late. The problem is to understand what our prophets true or false, are really telling us.

One would finally like to know why our country, once the Cloud-Cuckooland toward which the whole world yearned, has since become the focus of nonsense and revolutionary unrest in the West.* In fact there are circumstances peculiar to us which may have led to that result. From Colonial times up until the First World War, we had the advantage of being free of direct continuous rivalry with other nations, and of having a political system of a practical Anglo-Saxon kind. Unlike the Continental Europeans, we treated politics and government not as a mystique but as a business—one until recently secondary to most other businesses. So it was not until the Red scares of the '20s, McCarthyism, and the foreign policies of Truman, Eisenhower, and Johnson that political nonsense began to become the bugbear for us that it has perennially been for Frenchmen and Germans.

Our weakness developed from another direction. To expand over the continent, displace the Indian and the buffalo, cut off the forests, and make livable homes for ourselves in what is mostly an atrocious climate, we were forced to put practical matters ahead of "frills" and culture. In doing so, we were unwittingly preparing the psychological undermining of ourselves; that is to say, we began the narrowing and enfeeblement of the "I" which is today such a problem for our educators by confining mind too strictly to the pragmatic—effectively to biological adaptation to our new environment.

The consequences of this process of enforced self-limitation were becoming evident as early as the time of Mrs. Trollope's famous visit† to the States (circa 1830) when she commented on

---

* And an object of some suspicion, not only as a military and economic threat, but as a barbarizing influence upon people who once could not wait to come here.
† De Tocqueville, who visited us about the same time, also, of course, made many prophetic observations, some of which clearly implied we might become anti-intellectual and nonsense-prone as I have described.

the coldness and want of interest, even in their own subjects, that she detected in our intellectuals (in Philadelphia, not Boston, note). She also remarked on the variety of strange religious sects that were springing up among us even then. In the same period, modern spiritualism was born, in Hydesville, New York.* In 1818, an American army officer, John Symmes, rediscovered the Hollow Earth Theory† (also known as Symmes' Hole); and homeopathy, having been originally a European medical cult, migrated like psychoanalysis to establish a far greater following here. (Hydropathy also did well in America, as did something called Eclectic Medicine, based upon herbs.)

A century later, this same vulnerability to snake-oil merchandising was to turn us into the world's greatest market for nonsense, attracting gurus in droves from India, professional witches from England, and quacks from everywhere. Compared with the boom in insane medical cures that was developing in this country by the 1920s, the vogue for mesmerism and fake science in pre-Revolutionary Paris seems tame and rather small potatoes.

To give but one example: In 1861, an American general whom Martin Gardner identifies as Augustus Pleasonton discovered the amazing curative properties of blue light. But it remained for a Colonel Dinshah Ghadiali to cash in on this great discovery sixty years later with his Spectro-chrome Institute, which occupied a fifty-acre estate in Malaga, New Jersey, and was estimated to have had an enrollment of over 10,000 patients, who were charged at the rate of $90 a head for membership, plus $250 for a two-week study course.

It would be impossible, in the space of a few paragraphs, to convey an accurate idea of the variety and mad ingenuity (not to mention the earning power) of the nonsense we have dreamed up or imported in the years since the demands of life on the frontier

---

* In 1848, in the home of a Mr. and Mrs. J. D. Fox.
† Cotton Mather had prediscovered it in the work of the seventeenth-century astronomer Edmund Halley (of Halley's comet). It was rediscovered by one American right after the Civil War, and again by an Illinois corset manufacturer in 1913, neither of whom gave Symmes *et al.* any credit.

first began unballasting our reason, leaving each of us free, after his daily work was done, to float off to whatever loony realm most appealed to him. If you only read the chapter heads in Gardner's *Fads and Fallacies in the Name of Science*—still one of the definitive works in the field—you will find that in most of the subjects he covers we once had, have now, or probably soon will have first place. In dowsing, semantics, sentics, ufology, Atlantis and Lemuria cults, vomit therapy, Scream, healing by radio, antigravity research, writing novels and/or divining the future by Ouija board, pyramidology, naturopathy, PK studies (in which, however, the Russians seem to be gaining on us), Lawsonomy, Rosicrucianism, diet mystiques, Rolfing, numerology, Transactional Analysis, graphotherapeutics, iridiagnosis, and demented one-factor theories of practically anything, we are the number one consumers and the hub of it all. If a Nobel Prize were given in nonsense, we would win it every year.

Moreover, if it *was* the demands of the frontier that unballasted our reason, the place where it is still lightest on its feet should be that part of the nation which we were last to reach and where the old civilization consequently runs thinnest—the West Coast. And who can deny that that is so? Is Los Angeles not a mecca for the Absurd, the magnet which draws seers and healers to us from all over the globe?

In the later nineteenth century, as our pragmatism hardened to become a national characteristic, the New England culture of Hawthorne and Emerson and Thoreau and Melville simply died of inanition; and the new one that replaced it in the 1920s has never had a very broad base. What all of this adds up to is that the specialist mentality, the very opposite of the Renaissance ideal —a waking self stringently restricted in the range of things it can think effectively about, limited from earliest youth and therefore difficult to educate, oriented toward the immediate and the mechanical, intensely competitive and excellent chiefly in the interests of self-protection or self-advancement—this is the psychic type most prevalent in the modern world, and particularly, perhaps, among us. But it is just this type, not in spite of its "realism" but because of it, which is so vulnerable to nonsense and so prone, as we are discovering, to violence and a suicidal self-indulgence.

It is as though history were a sort of parable, a Looking-Glass garden in which, to get where you want to go, you must walk in the opposite direction. No "realist," left to himself, would have created science—or culture either, for that matter; and now, in seizing the opportunities which both have made available to him, he finds them turning to broken glass in his hands. Converted to use, the discoveries of science threaten to destroy him; converted into skepticism and an indulgence of the Id, they are undermining his common sense and making enemies and savages of his children. The garden was not laid out as he thought; he walked the wrong way.

PART TWO

vi

Mind in Flight

For a long time—roughly since the experiments in telepathy carried out by the British Society for Psychical Research in the 1880s —extrasensory perception was a curiosity investigated by a few serious scientists like Dr. J. B. Rhine and accepted as fact by the same sort of lay minority that has perennially supported numerology or Rosicrucianism. Because there have always been a few people who could apparently divine what was going on in the minds of others or "see" distant events, belief in extrasensory perception is very old, as is the related idea that we have an astral body (the ancient Celts called it the co-walker) which can at times detach itself from the physical one and fly off to other places. By the end of the last century it seemed that these notions, along with astrology and witchcraft, were about to die out. One might have foreseen that they would persist a while longer in odd corners of science or the popular press, but a general revival appeared unlikely.

Now, however, one is under way, and scientists as well as lay people are involved in it. How are we to interpret this development? Does it mean there is something to ESP after all? Or is the climate of distraction that has so affected the politics and popular tastes of this century beginning finally to be too much for everyone? Is science at last cracking open its doors to the enemy, and nonsense about to carry the citadel itself? Or are we, as Arthur Koestler and others suggest, entering an exciting new era in which men will add a sixth (telepathic) sense to their other five and learn to project their astral selves along some hidden dimension out to the farthest reaches of space? Anyone familiar with the history of scientific discovery would be unwise to discount such possibilities; but given the present drift of things, it might be well not to jump to the opposite conclusion either.

A skeptic would be inclined to attribute many cases of supposed thought transference to a mechanism of statistical forecasting that all of us appear to have built into our heads. It might be called the odds maker and defined as a faculty or subsystem that works independently of conscious awareness. Like the instincts, it is very old* and essentially subliminal. We do not see how it handles its information; we see only the results.

It is the odds maker that presumably gives us our hunches that a particular event is "due" or that someone is thinking such-and-such—intuitions which are all the more startling in that they seem to come to us from nowhere. The net result is that our minds may more and more reliably anticipate the trend of external events as our experience accumulates—or, in statistical language, as N, the size of the odds maker's samples, grows larger and larger. This amounts to saying that a great many bits of information too trifling for us to take conscious note of are nevertheless added into various running averages which, in turn, provide us with an automatic (and often remarkably accurate) estimate of the turn things are about to take next. The odds maker, one might say, is a special sort of memory system which retains not facts but the weightings to be given them. Whereas in our conscious thinking we may tend to be carried away, the odds maker tries to bring us back by telling

---

* It is, in fact, the basis of conditioned reflexes, these being the result of an automatic computation of the odds that given event A, event B is likely to follow. If a turtle is rewarded with food 70 percent of the time following a green flash and 30 percent of the time following a red one, it will begin to respond in about the same ratios, moving toward the food box 70 percent of the time when shown a green light and 30 percent when shown a red. A monkey, in the same situation, does what is called "maximizing." That is, he will move 90 percent of the time when he sees a green flash and only 10 percent when he sees a red. The odds maker is present in both animals, the difference being that the "higher" one fiddles with the odds maker's figures while the "lower" does not —a significant change, as we shall see.

us in its insistent small voice what the existing probabilities really are.*

Because this ancient faculty works tirelessly and out of sight, hunches or intuitions are common and quite a number prove correct. Moreover, its messages are most apt to get through to us at off moments when we are relaxed and thinking of nothing in particular. Active thinking may override the odds maker, and active wishing may cause us to ignore or grossly falsify its reports; but even at that it is the most reliable logical faculty we have. For unlike those of conscious intelligence, the operations of the odds maker seem little affected by the strong wishes or feeling states arising in the Id. The odds maker itself does not rationalize; it simply runs up its results and forwards them to whomever they may concern.† (Hence perhaps our current preference for "intuition," our belief that we may be better off trusting our hunches than tampering with them and trying to think matters out for ourselves.)

An example of some of these principles occurs to me from my experience of gambling. A man walks up, cold, to a roulette table and studies the play for a while. As he watches, he begins to develop hunches as to where the ball will drop next. Finally he puts down a bet, and perhaps wins. But win or lose, he is now psychologically involved in a way in which he was not before.‡

If he continues to play, his anxiety to recoup or to win more may become so intense that the odds maker's reports no longer get through to him. Instead he starts making conscious calculations which are more and more in the nature of wishful thinking.

Since at the best of times his conscious intelligence is not as good at statistical reckoning as its subconscious assistant, and since

---

* As opposed to what we may hope or wish them to be. The odds maker's estimates, like our hopes, may be in error; but the error is apt to be smaller.

† This being its adaptive value and the reason it has persisted in vertebrate evolution from the fishes to man.

‡ Note that money is the symbol of all instinctive gratifications because it is the means to most of them. Hence the Id is involved in all money matters, to such a degree that we can become passionate over quite small sums. Every year, a number of murders are committed as a result of disputes of this kind, often involving only a few dollars.

in this situation it is under increasing pressure from the Id as well, the gambler begins to lose his feel for what's happening, and with it large amounts of money. Hence runs of good luck may occur early (as has usually happened to me) only to be followed by much longer runs of bad. If one becomes as desperately involved as Dostoevski's gambler (in the short novel of the same name) one can go into a losing streak of indefinite length and be wiped out.

Interestingly enough, a progressive falling off of good hunches has been reported in card-guessing experiments such as those conducted by Dr. Rhine. The controlling factor in these may not be the subject's excessive emotional involvement but his total lack of it. After a series of guesses significantly above chance, he becomes so actively bored that all his systems, including the odds maker, switch off. In some cases his performance then falls significantly *below* chance, which suggests that his conscious intelligence is feebly substituting for subliminal processes which have gone off the air.* In his boredom he is simply trying to keep up appearances, and by doing so making them worse. (In my experience, card-guessing experiments are extremely boring even to read about.)

A skeptic might be inclined to wonder how much the odds maker figures in supposed ESP phenomena in general. The difficulty is that while it is perfectly conceivable that the odds maker could generate plausible random sequences (say, of cards), it is highly unlikely that any such imagined sequence would show a 1-to-1 or even a 30-percent correspondence with a real one being generated at the same time (say, by a dealer in the next room). That is, it is unlikely if our notions of purely chance events aren't mistaken. As an engineer friend of mine puts it, "random" may merely be a word we apply to those events whose regularities or laws of occurrence remain concealed from us—in which case ESP

---

* That is, he may be making guesses according to some nonrandom cut-and-try system which has, in this situation, negative predictive power, giving results counter to chance. Similar results may be gotten by racetrack bettors whose system is to play, on the nose, all horses whose names begin with W.

may be a matter of the odds maker's seeing regularities not yet directly visible to conscious intelligence.

This seems to be the idea Arthur Koestler is getting at in his recent book *The Roots of Coincidence*. In the chapter entitled "Seriality and Synchronicity" he discusses the ideas of the neo-Lamarckian Paul Kammerer and of the late psychiatrist C. G. Jung, both of whom appeared to feel that there is some kind of order hidden in chance events. It is this order, they believe, which gives rise to various amazing coincidences or to "runs" of good and bad luck.

An example given by Koestler, from Jung's writings, involved a young woman patient who had had a dream "in which she was given a golden scarab. While she was telling me this dream I sat with my back to the closed window. Suddenly I heard a noise behind me like a gentle tapping. I . . . saw a flying insect knocking against the window-pane from outside. I . . . caught the creature . . . as it flew in. It was the nearest analogy to a golden scarab that one finds in our latitudes, a scarabaeid beetle . . . which contrary to its usual habits had evidently felt an urge to get into a dark room at this particular moment."

Presumably Dr. Jung would have been even more impressed by the list of "accidental" similarities between the assassinations of Abraham Lincoln and John F. Kennedy noted most recently (November 19, 1972) in the *National Enquirer*:

> The draft riots of the 1860s were matched by the draft resistance movement in the 1960s.
>
> Three presidents were inaugurated in both decades, and the first assassinated in each.
>
> Lincoln's secretary was named Kennedy and Kennedy's secretary was named Lincoln.
>
> On the assassination day, Lincoln was sitting in Ford's Theater and Kennedy was riding in a Lincoln.*

* For these incidents to be perfectly symmetrical, the play in Lincoln's case should have been written, or starred in, by someone named Kennedy, while Kennedy's chauffeur should have been someone named Ford (preferably Henry).

Both were slain on a Friday, with their wives present. Both were shot from behind and . . . in the head.

Booth shot Lincoln in a theater and ran into a warehouse. Oswald shot Kennedy from a warehouse and ran into a theater.

Both assassins were shot before they could be brought to trial.

Booth was born in 1839, Oswald in 1939. Both were southerners.

Both vice presidents were named Johnson, and both were southern Democrats who had been senators. Andrew Johnson was born in 1808, Lydon Johnson in 1908.*

The names Lee Harvey Oswald and John Wilkes Booth each contain fifteen letters.

The last names of Lincoln and Kennedy have the same number of letters—seven. The first names of the two Johnsons have the same number of letters—six. The first, middle and last names of Nixon and Grant . . . the third presidents in the two decades, have the same number of letters, seven, seven and five.

It would be quibbling to point out that the Civil War Draft Riots occurred in 1863, nearly two years *before* Lincoln was shot, whereas ours took place during Lyndon Johnson's administration (nor are the two sets of events comparable in other ways, including casualty figures). Kennedy's first name comes to four letters, Lincoln's to seven. There was a move to impeach Andrew Johnson, who didn't deserve it, and never one to impeach Lyndon Johnson, who did. That the Oswald-Booth and Johnson-Johnson birth dates coincide suggests simply that Presidential assassins tend to fall in the 24–26-year-old range,† while Vice Presidents tend to be in their middle fifties. Since elections come at the same four-year intervals in each century, it follows that certain Presidents elected exactly a century apart may meet the same fate, particularly if war is imminent, under way, or just past in both cases and the times correspondingly disturbed. As for other amazing coincidences, consider these:

* And both, one might add, failed spectacularly in office, although for quite dissimilar reasons.
† Gun toting and shootings also tend to be more prevalent in the South.

Napoleon's real name, Buonaparte, has the same number of
letters as Wellington's—ten. His name in French, Bonaparte, has
the same number of letters—nine—as the Iron Duke's *real* name
(Arthur) Wellesley. Alexander of Macedon also had nine letters
in his name, as did (Benito) Mussolini. Josef Stalin and Adolf
Hitler had the same number of letters in their first and last names
(five and six). Stalin's real name—Josef Visarionovich Dzhu-
gashvili—comes to thirty letters, or appropriately enough the number in Booth's and Oswald's full names put together. My own
name, Charles, has the same number of letters in it as that of the
Roman general Agrippa (not to mention, of course, the second
and third Stuart kings of England). If Jung and Kammerer are to
be believed, there is some deeper significance in all this; we are
seeing "the tip of the iceberg" and can only guess at the extent of
the something lying beneath.*

The idea that good or bad events tend to come in clusters is an
old article of folk belief. We are apt to feel too that we can spot
the omens which tell us another such cluster is coming. We read
in the papers of a plane crash and immediately have a hunch that
there will soon be several more. Are clusters of plane crashes more
likely to occur in February than in June?

On commonsense grounds one might suppose so, the weather
generally being worse in February. The real question, then, is
whether more people get these hunches in February than in June.
If so, it might mean that the odds maker has kept closer track of

* To sort these ideas out a bit, it is obvious that my engineer friend may be
right. There may be classes of "random" events which in fact follow complex
laws of recurrence. To prove this point I devised a system by which, using a
random-number table and a set of complicated rules as to what integers should
follow any randomly drawn one, I was able to generate a graph indistinguish-
able from one produced by a plot of random numbers only. A computer, properly programmed, could doubtless have detected the regularities hidden in my
pseudo-random graph, if it had had a big enough sample to work with. Of
course, the more complicated my selection rules, the bigger the sample would
have to be. On the other hand, the coincidences that Jung and Kammerer collected may have had nothing to do with the problem just described. In their
case, it seems to be a matter of the abstractions one is on the alert for. Thinking "five," I see a five-year-old boy in the park with five dogs, playing next to a
rest house (Number 5), with an older sister five feet tall. The regularity is not
in nature but in my head; I am, as psychiatrists say, "projecting"—in this case,
the abstraction fiveness.

events than they are consciously aware of—which in turn means that our correct hunches are spooky only in that we can't see how we arrived at them.

(Not long after I wrote this passage, a spectacular plane crash occurred in the Canary Islands. Just before takeoff, two passengers, a man and his wife, decided to debark because the wife had a hunch that something was going to go wrong. The question is, did she have a genuine glimpse into the future, or had her odds maker been totting up various small observations she herself was unaware of having made? Did the plane look a bit old or poorly maintained? Did the flight attendants seem slipshod or tired? Was the flight itself one of those quick-turnaround affairs, allowing no time for standard checkout of engines, fuel lines, tires, etc.? Had the woman perhaps overheard something to that effect? An interesting way of investigating cases of this kind might be to hypnotize the person who had had the hunch in order to see what subliminal cues, if any, might have been involved.)

A point to notice is that the odds maker often makes mistakes. Like many people, I have had strong hunches that did not prove out and some that did, my tendency being, of course, to remember the ones that did. Great numbers of us can recall horrifyingly vivid dreams in which we saw a distant loved one in some sort of trouble—only to awaken and have a letter arrive or a neighbor rush in with news of just such an occurrence. But how many dreams or hunches have we had that were *not* subsequently confirmed? And among those that were, how many in fact might have been derived from various small clues which the odds maker took sharper note of than we did? Mother was a touch pale on her last visit; nervous perhaps, lying in bed and smoking cigarettes for an hour or two before going to sleep every night and complaining of her restlessness the next day. One morning several weeks after she has left, we start up in bed, having dreamed she was burned to death, and smelling smoke. In a certain percentage of cases, Mother may, the same night, have fallen asleep in the middle of a cigarette and set fire to herself. The odds maker has hit it on the nose, and the whole thing goes down in family history as an astonishing case of ESP. But if the odds maker was wrong, then the dream was just a dream, which everyone will have forgotten by lunchtime.

Out of the hundreds of dreams dreamed by millions of people every night, it is natural that a few now and then should approximate real events to the point of seeming telepathic or prophetic. A man dreams that the plane he is going to take the next morning crashes. He cancels his reservation or is detained and misses the flight. Sure enough, the plane does crash—on Friday, February 13 —the first big crash in months. Two hypotheses suggest themselves. One supposes that the man has experienced a genuine precognition—for instance, by means of a sixth sense enabling him to look forward along the time dimension. The other hypothesis says that his odds maker might have been running statistics on plane crashes—particularly if the man himself was a habitual air traveler—and concluded (since it was also midwinter) that another cluster of them was due. As the man himself was a busy executive without time to listen to his hunches, this one inserted itself into his dreams, and lo! the prophecy came true. But how many other prophetic dreams, dreamed the same night, failed to come true? One might guess the ratio to be on the order of $1/10^6$ (1:1,000,000), suggesting that prophetic dreaming is a phenomenon rather like hitting the daily double. Nobody does it much, which is why we notice when it does occur (and think nothing of it when it doesn't).

In 1889 the British Society for Psychical Research collected 17,000 reports of "hallucinations" that people had had of distant friends or relatives. These were screened down to some 350 cases in which the person seen in the vision was clearly identified.

"The probability that any person will die on a given day is roughly 1 in 19,000; if therefore chance alone operated, one apparition in 19,000 would coincide with a death; after making all allowances for error the census committee found that 30 . . . apparitions coincided with a death of the person seen, the same day." The conclusion, which I did not quite follow, was that this result was 440 times greater than chance.*

* See *Encyclopaedia Britannica*, 11th Edition, "Telepathy" and "Psychical Research." These two accounts do not entirely agree on details.

Certain factors here have clearly been overlooked. Out of the 30 (one account says 80) "hits," how many involved persons were known to the subject to be in poor or desperate health?—i.e., in how many cases was it the odds maker that produced a result contrary to chance? The psychological mechanism involved is presumably the same as in prophetic dreaming: a hunch breaks through into consciousness as a picture, in this case not dreamed but "projected" as a fleeting vision or hallucination.

The important point is that if we assume functions such as telepathy or precognition, the evidence is that they are highly unreliable—to such a degree that we need statistics to demonstrate them. But if we assume that the odds maker is responsible, then we *expect* probabilistic results such as are actually obtained. It's just that the odds maker is a more tireless and accurate function than we realize, so that some of its forecasts surprise us. And being probabilistic, as well as sometimes based on too-small samples of data, its forecasts are frequently wrong, in which case we ignore them.

Now, however, certain scientists, along with any number of laymen, are coming around to the view that prophetic dreaming is just what medicine men have always said it was. To reconcile this ancient notion with our present scientific concept of things requires, as might be expected, some highly sophisticated reasoning.

Koestler, for example, cites the late Adrian Dobbs, a Cambridge mathematician and physicist, as proposing a universe with two time dimensions. "A five-dimensional universe with three spatial and two temporal dimensions had already been proposed by Eddington and others. . . . However the main interest of Dobbs' hypothesis lies in his attempt to provide a physicalistic explanation of telepathy and precognition. . . . The gist . . . is that the anticipation of future events follows the second time dimension. . . ." Information about them is conveyed to the subject by hypothetical messengers which Dobbs calls "psitrons" and which operate in his second time dimension. The psitron "has imaginary mass (in the mathematical sense) and thus, according to Relativity Theory, can travel faster than light indefinitely, without loss of (imaginary) momentum." Under this hypothesis, the man's dream about the coming plane crash had nothing to do with his odds maker. In his sleep he simply caught a shower of psitrons. But why, one wonders, doesn't that happen more often? If all the machinery for seeing into the future exists, why does it work so erratically?*

Sir John Eccles, a Nobel Laureate in neurophysiology, believes that mind is not merely a by-product of the brain. He proposes an extraneuronal force or "will" which, by acting on a single brain cell, may influence all the rest. Apparently he supposes that this same "will" can reach out to other minds (producing telepathy) or even to inanimate objects (producing PK—psychokinesis).

Heady as these ideas may sound, they are nothing to the Pandora's Box opened by two young women, Lynn Schroeder and Sheila Ostrander, in their *Psychic Discoveries Behind the Iron Curtain*. The book suffers from a tendency to skate over its subject, gliding easily from one marvel to the next and leaving us wondering about certain critical details. (However, the few passages intended as technical description I couldn't follow at all.) The gist of it is that in Russia, controlled experiments performed under the supervision of highly trained scientific personnel have shown the following:

—That one man can by telepathy produce dramatic changes in another's electroencephalogram.

—That a certain Russian lady wills objects to move and they do so, under conditions precluding any possibility of fraud.

—That "Kirlian photography" reveals the auras of living things, and can show the difference between a sick aura and a well one.

—That ESP is a plain fact, like gravitation.

—That the Russians are miles ahead of us in these matters.

The indications are, however, that we may be catching up. For

---

* Koestler gives us a clue when he tells us: ". . . The distance in space which the psitron has to travel is irrelevant, as it is to neutrinos." But that, I believe, is a mistake. Neutrinos can be captured by head-on collision with other particles; so the distance they have to travel, through regions of space containing large amounts of matter, *is* relevant. Presumably the same applies to psitrons; they may hit the wrong brains or end up bumping into a rock or a piece of furniture, this being the reason so many of their messages never get through.

instance, on October 8, 1972, *The New York Times* carried a news item headed PARLEY EXAMINES HEALER METHODS, *Water Treatment and Laying On of Hands Outlined*—but this was not, apparently, the congress of quacks and seers one might have expected a few years ago. Many of the participants were people of high academic standing, and the research they were doing was all along the lines reported in the Ostrander-Schroeder book. A psychologist, Dr. Thelma S. Moss, was taking Kirlian photographs of a "wounded leaf." A number of the conferees described the "healer" personality—the person with good "vibes" who can make plants grow just by being in the room with them. (Water, "treated" by a healer, can have the same effect; and of course there is the "brown thumb" type, whose vibes are bad and kill everything within reach.) A former astronaut who had done experiments in ESP while aloft "urged that inquiries in this area be made a serious scientific enterprise." And so on.

A friend of mine who was with NASA at the time wrote to say that experiments in psychokinesis, in the alteration of magnetic fields by thought projection, and in "egg recording"* were going on in a number of laboratories—so many, he said, "I can't keep track any more." He had tried to duplicate some of their results in his own lab, with no success. It may be that in these events we are seeing the start of another Space Race, though one understandably less publicized than the last.

Ostrander and Schroeder mentioned some of the military uses to which ESP might be put—and indeed, in that role it should be very valuable. If one can "project" one's thoughts into the seats of the enemy's power and discover what his top men are up to, the whole dangerous, expensive business of spying might become obsolete overnight. There may even be other possibilities, which the popular press, anticipating science, is already talking about. In the October, 1971, issue of *SAGA* there is an article by Otto O. Binder whose lead caption reads:

* This line of inquiry seems to have started with Cleve Backster. It involves recording the electrical activity, or "EEG," of eggs, while doing things that are supposed to influence the chick embryo telepathically—for example, murdering its siblings which have already hatched.

The weapons are silent, invisible, and many times deadlier than bombs and bullets. For example, there's a "knockout" force capable of dropping people in their tracks at a distance of 2,000 miles; there are "impulses" that can kill plants and birds (and possibly men); and there's "suggestology," the transmission of telepathic commands to large groups of people who obey them blindly and instantly. These are but a few of the fantastic new parapsychological armaments that are being developed—and tested—in ESP laboratories around the world, especially in Russia and Red China. Has WW III started and is the U.S. at this very moment suffering a

PSYCHIC PEARL HARBOR*

The article begins:

There's a savage war going on today. No, not the one in Vietnam; but an all-out struggle between the three greatest powers on earth . . . It's a silent war of unseen forces *beyond the five normal senses of mankind.* . . . The bombs explode in the brain. *Psychic weapons* form the frightful arsenal in this paranormal conflict. Every facet of ESP—telepathy, clairvoyance, psychokinesis, psihypnosis, even the darker psychic variants—will eventually be used when this psi-battle rises to its mind-smashing climax.†

Good grief! Is this where Dobbs's psitrons and Sir John Eccles' "will" have been leading? Some of the particulars that Binder gives in his article are even more alarming. Early on he quotes "one American scientist who must remain anonymous to protect his reputation" to the effect that "There are four known forces in the universe: gravitational, electromagnetic and two nuclear binding forces. If psi-force proves real, as it may, it will be the fifth power in the cosmos, *and the greatest of them all!*"‡

Mr. Binder's main source of information, however, is more exotic.

* Title of article.
† Italics original.
‡ Italics original.

How de we know this fantastic psi-war—or its preliminary skirmishes—has really started? The answer has come from UFOs. To the occupants of flying saucers, this kind of psychic battle is ancient history. The UFOs have used ESP to contact an undisclosed number of "channels" (people who are psychic sensitives) and have warned them of the coming psi-Armageddon. . . . These people will be America's last line of defense when the psi-invasion comes. . . .

According to saucer sources, "the Sino-Soviet psi-scientists have achieved a major breakthrough and have produced a 'cybernetic psi-weapon' of tremendous power. It's an electronic device combined with a computer that can *amplify and concentrate** human psi-energy to mind-blasting force. . . . That's what the UFOs revealed. . . . They said the Sino-Soviet Bloc has only one burning aim—to create 'mental havoc' in the United States." Possibly we are already seeing signs of it.

But by all odds the most electrifying report—Binder himself calls it a "strange and horrifying revelation"—came from the UFOs via a pseudonymous "channel," Norma Cathy, who put everything they told her on tape. Here is some of it:

Either as a test or to keep people in line, the Sino-Soviet leaders had a secret psi-projector (advanced psychotron) placed on an unnamed Siberian slope to bathe all of the Chinese in its insidious beams. The saucer people say it has "mechanized antenna" and sends out both telepathic and clairvoyant impulses that cause *delusions*. The chilling result . . . was that "a thought-disease was created in Asia and zombie-like obedience was forced upon the entranced Chinese."

That may be a frightful forecast of what Sino-Soviet psi-masters hope someday to attack America with. But it seems that psi-forces can be converted into even more diabolical variations, which the [saucer people] on Norma's tape describe in blood-chilling phrases like—"The mass exodus of rea-

* Italics original.

son . . . insanity taint . . . mental equilibrium destroyed
. . . greater blows to the mass mind than the nuclear bomb
. . . poisonous polluted thought" and "psi-energy ignited into
panic riots."

Whew!*

Apropos of the psychotron, Binder says: "It reminds us of prior
psi-geniuses such as Reichenback [sic] and his Odic Force, Wilhelm Reich and his Etheric Forces, Mesmer and his Animal Magnetism, Keely and his Motor Force,† Delawarr and his Universal
Energy. The ancient Chinese spoke of 'vital energy' and the Hin-
dus called it Prana."

The point is whether the antiquity of this notion is any sign
that it is correct. Another point is that some of the men Mr. Koestler is quoting are essentially concerned with problems of explanation that have arisen in quantum physics. Why have they made
the jump from quantum mechanics to parapsychology? Had they
other, extrascientific, motives too strong to resist? Or did they act
in the belief that the evidence for ESP is already so overwhelming
that a new theory is urgently needed to account for it?

Here we must be extremely cautious. There are certain results
reported, for instance, from Dr. Rhine's laboratory or in the earlier *Proceedings of the British Society for Psychical Research* that
are quite difficult to explain. Koestler gives an example of the latter—a set of six figure-drawings made by a "sender" in one room
and reproduced with astonishing accuracy by a "receiver" in another.

* Note that Binder's article appeared in 1971. A year later (March 12, 1972),
on the eve of a *détente* between this country and the two major Communist
nations, the *National Enquirer* ran an interview headlined: RUSSIANS ARE
SCARED THEIR PSYCHIC DISCOVERIES WILL BE ABUSED, SAY
RESEARCHERS. The researchers, of course, were Sheila Ostrander and Lynn
Schroeder.
† According to Martin Gardner, Baron Karl von Reichenbach was a nineteenth-
century physicist who discovered a force he called Od, but "other scientists
were unable to duplicate the baron's experiments." (By another report he detected flames coming from magnets.) John Keely appears to have been a confidence man who attracted the attention of Roger Babson's Gravity Research
Foundation with his perpetual-motion machine known around the crank circuit
as Keely's Motor. (It turned out to run on compressed air.)

This last, of course, is a much better experiment than card guessing, because the "sender" can choose from an unlimited number of things to draw, so the "receiver's" odds maker would presumably be at a loss for good guesses. At least, that would be the case if this were Experiment Number One and the sender and receiver were not acquainted. However, if the two knew each other, or had performed a series of trial runs prior to their near-100-percent success (or both), then the situation is changed. The receiver's odds maker might have *some* clues as to the sort of thing the sender was likely to draw. Even then, to achieve an almost perfect score would be an event of very low probability, if one excludes any possibility of unconscious collusion between the two parties. Being an event of such low probability, it would then (if it occurred) be very hard to duplicate—which was, I believe, the Society's experience, and one reason why orthodox science at the time took so little interest in its findings.*

For needless to say, in the sciences, repeatability of results is fundamental. To be believable, experiments must travel. Koestler maintains, however, that to apply this criterion to ESP studies is unfair. He points out that results in medicine are less repeatable than those of physics, the scatter increasing even more "in those branches of psychology which involve unconscious processes and the autonomic nervous system." That is quite true, but it is explainable on the basis of the much larger number of variables involved in experiments of the latter types. Many of the variables are in fact not known (for instance, those in experimental psychology), which does not mean they may not become so. In other words, Koestler is here invoking a pseudo-Indeterminacy principle to explain the fact that ESP phenomena, being "governed by unconscious processes which are not under voluntary control," are notoriously hard to reproduce—witness, among other things, the "decline effect" in card guessing.

Moreover, ESP transmission is evidently noisy (in the electronic

---

* It is also one reason for believing the odds maker may have played the part I have suggested. The humiliating corollary is that in our seemingly private and unique mental lives we may be much more alike than we have any notion of—an explanation of ESP that is naturally among the last to occur to us.

sense); messages may or may not get through, and 100-percent reception is rare. Much information is apt to be lost in transit, and
items arriving at the receiving end often do so in strangely disguised or garbled forms, so that interpreting them is rather like
reading Nostradamus. The impression one gets is that even if "psitrons" do exist and brains can thereby radiate messages back and
forth, conventional methods of communication still, on the whole,
work better. As a colonel, say, I would much rather that my com-
manding general contact me via field telephone or walkie-talkie
than give his orders by going into his "alpha" state and "projecting" them to me. What with the roar of battle and the static on
my own ESP line, nothing might get through at all. Likewise, any
great power that is tooling up, as Binder claims the "Sino-Soviet
Bloc" is doing, to wage an all-out psi war is certainly putting its
money on a dark horse. Suppose that when D-day comes they
switch on their monster psychotrons, hoping to touch off "panic
riots" or zap us into "zombie-like obedience"—and nothing happens? Why, as in so many everyday ESP experiments, mightn't the
transmission fail?*

On the other hand, it may be that the latest psychotron is so
much more powerful than ordinary unamplified brains that its
beams are absolutely surefire—in which case, as the UFO people
are saying, we may have had it. Further evidence on ESP phenomena in general is certainly needed, but with so many of us at
work on the problem, we will doubtless soon have it cracked.†

To my mind, it is not Mr. Koestler but Otto O. Binder who put
his finger on it, when he remarked that the present intense interest
in psi phenomena "reminds us of such prior psi-geniuses as Reichenback . . . Wilhelm Reich . . . Mesmer." And in Mesmer's
case at least, it is clear enough where that interest was leading,
since its immediate sequel was not an explosion of new knowledge
but simply an explosion.

---

* Other interesting questions come up here. If psychic energy is still a mystery
—if, apart from its existence, next to nothing is known about it—what sort of
system would one use to concentrate and broadcast it? If electronic, wouldn't
the broadcast psychic energy then have to be demodulated, just as sound waves
are, on the receiving end? How is that done?
† Either that or the other way around.

vii

Hello Out There... Hello... Hello

You will have noticed, in the last chapter, that Mr. Otto O. Binder's chief source of information about the impending psi war was not earthly; or, as he puts it: "The answer has come from the UFOs." Until quite recently I had paid no attention to UFOs at all. I was vaguely aware that there had been "flap" periods (in '52–'53, '57–'59, and '65–'67) during which people all over the country were reporting unusual experiences, mostly involving lights in the sky at night. I had no idea, however, of how vast the literature on this strange topic was becoming, or of the trouble to which the Air Force, the CIA, and various interested individuals, had gone in trying to decide whether UFOs do or don't exist. The whole thing struck me—as I'm sure it did many others—as a mania natural to the space age and probably limited to a small subgroup of sci-fi freaks and quack prophets.

When people such as Major Kehoe began appearing on network TV, and John Fuller's and Frank Edwards' books came out in paperback, it was clear that we were confronted by a phenomenon of much grander dimensions. The conclusion became inescapable when the *National Enquirer*, which is a sort of Everyman's cumulative nonsense index,* offered $50,000 to the first person to come up with hard evidence for the fact that we are being visited by spacecraft from Out There.

Public opinion certainly leans toward that idea. The popular

---

* For some time the *Enquirer* has featured UFO stories in almost every issue. Sample headlines: UFO SIGHTING MYSTIFIES ENGLAND; AMAZING UFO SIGHTINGS IN ARGENTINA—an *Enquirer* Special Investigation; 2,000 UFO SIGHTINGS IN PENNSYLVANIA.

UFO cult seems to be divided between the "angel" school which sees the coming invasion as benign and the "devil" school which feels sure it will be a calamity. The former believes that we are being watched over by Higher Beings.* These extraterrestrial guardians were so alarmed by World War II and the atomic bomb that they have been stepping up their surveillance of us ever since, conceivably in preparation for some form of corrective intervention. Hence the "ghost rockets"† which appeared over Russia and Scandinavia in 1946, and the UFOs which, starting in America in 1947, have been turning up since almost everywhere.

The "devil" school attributes these events to similar causes (the appearance of radio communication on earth; the two World Wars; the Bomb); its interpretation of them is merely reversed. A war between worlds is coming in which ours will surely get the worst of it. Both schools agree that we have probably been visited off and on for centuries by patrols from beyond the stars. Several writers have sought to explain passages in the Bible on the hypothesis that angels, pillars of fire, etc., were poetic descriptions of the landings of spacecraft. Frank Edwards, in his *Flying Saucers, Serious Business*, cites a supposedly ancient source, the Book of Dzyan, which (according to him) includes an account of space visitors to India.[6] The colonists, it seems, fell out among themselves and fought a brief nuclear war, after which the survivors climbed into their interplanetary vehicle and departed.

A few scientists think that we may have been reconnoitered in the distant past. "Dr. Thomas Gold, of Cornell, has suggested that life itself may have originated on earth as a result of such a visit, billions of years ago . . . The visitors came, explored and departed, but left behind them 'rubbish'—primordial garbage containing micro-organisms that grew, multiplied, evolved . . ."[7] This

* For instance, Binder's UFO people, who seem to side with us, since they are telling us about the Communist bloc's more sinister intentions. Because, however, their object is supposedly to head off Armageddon, they may also be keeping Russian and Chinese psychics advised as to what *our* military people are up to, which should hardly be welcome news at the Pentagon.
† Whose predecessors were the "Foo Fighters" seen by pilots on both sides during World War II—mysterious lights or lighted objects which flew among the Allied bomber squadrons over Germany.

hypothesis does not, of course, simplify the problem of how life originated. It merely shifts the site of origin to another planet and possibly to another galaxy.

Moreover, if we have been visited before, why is it that the pale-ontological record has so far shown no sharp discontinuities? Why among all the primitive flint scraping tools and bits of prehistoric pottery have we not found the remains of transistor radios, discarded space gear, or ray guns left behind by mistake? Possibly we will—the question being, if we do, who will ever believe us? Most UFO writers tell us that from about 1870 on, mysterious objects began appearing in the sky over various countries (Turkey; Mexico). In 1896–97 there was a wave of "airship" sightings in America.[8] On one such occasion (in 1897) a farmer named Hamilton of Leroy, Kansas, allegedly lost a calf which was hoisted up by a cable into a large, lighted cigar-shaped craft.[9] Parts of the calf were found a few days later in a neighbor's field. The neighbor reported that there were no tracks in the soft ground around the remains. Not to be outdone, Texans at Farmersville reported that they had seen an airship with creatures aboard, and one witness stated that "he could clearly hear them singing 'Nearer My God to Thee.' " (This would have to be classed as a sighting of the "angel" school.)

Frank Edwards, a "devil"-school advocate, connects events later in this century with Nikola Tesla's attempts, around 1900, to send powerful electrical signals into space from an installation he had set up in Colorado. Subsequently, in the 1920s (when radio was coming in), a Dr. Todd, with covert backing of the Navy, repeated the attempt to communicate electromagnetically with some other world and, by Edwards' account, received some very weird signals back. This prompt reply Edwards attributed to the presence of monitors presumably somewhere in our solar system (and therefore only a few seconds' or minutes' transmission time away). He considered bases on the moon or Mars a definite possibility.[10] His theory is that our visitors may come from planets around stars such as Tau Ceti, some ten or eleven light-years off. Having reconnoitered us before and found nothing much of interest, they may then have received Tesla's signals, by relay, on the home planet and decided to investigate further.

Supposing Tesla's broadcast had reached them by about 1910, one can see that if their expedition was got together promptly and their speed of travel approached 90 percent of c (the speed of light),* they could have been installed on Mars or the moon by 1924, and so be in a position to answer Dr. Todd's signals with little delay. Why have they been silent since? So as not to disclose their presence, one imagines. But then, why did they respond at all? This is something of a puzzle.

Possibly, having studied us more closely, they decided we were too dangerous to have anything to do with. For whatever reasons, the line has meanwhile gone dead. An international meeting of radio astronomers appears to have concluded that since Dr. Todd's day, nothing definite has come in.† Dr. Ronald Bracewell of Stanford's Radio Astronomy Institute suggests that we may be under surveillance by space probes and refers to "the strange radio 'echoes' that were picked up in 1927, 1928, and 1964 and are still unexplained."[11] Frank Edwards had an even spookier story along these lines. He reports that in the 1950s, television viewers all over Britain suddenly received the call letters of station KLEE-TV in Texas.[12] He considered a hoax unlikely, on the ground that British officials had calculated it would have cost $100,000 to carry out. Nor could the phenomenon have been due to the usual forms of freak transmission, because upon investigation it was found that KLEE had gone off the air three years before. The implication seemed to be that some alien space station was replaying an old tape and accidentally beaming it in the wrong direction.

Starting from such premises, several writers of the "devil" school

* At 0.9c, the mass gain predicted by Einstein's equation would be substantial but perhaps not yet critical. Expressed as a ratio of the moving mass to the mass of the same body at rest, $\frac{m}{m_0}$, the mass at 0.5c is 1.159—a gain of roughly 16 percent. At 0.9c it has increased by a factor of 7, and at 0.999c by a factor of over 22. Even to push a body through space at 70 percent of the speed of light would, according to this relationship, increase its virtual mass by 40 percent.
† They don't seem to feel anything came in then, either.

—notably Major Kehoe, Frank Edwards, and Coral Lorenzen— have attempted to detect a timetable in UFO events, their conclusion in common being that the contact phase may not be far off. How one feels about *that* possibility is, of course, entirely a matter of one's temperamental bias. Kindly, old-fashioned astronomers have inclined to favor establishing some sort of communication with distant worlds. More modern, hard-boiled types feel that would be lunacy,* and many UFO experts take a similar position. It is the "mystics," they say, who think a benign power is watching over us and may soon take a direct hand in human affairs. In fact, there are numerous UFO cults of this sort. Their ideas are regarded, by volunteer UFO organizations such as NICAP (National Investigations Committee on Aerial Phenomena, Washington, D.C.), APRO (Aerial Phenomena Research Organization, Tucson, Arizona), or AIAA (American Institute of Aeronautics and Astronautics, New York City), as utter nonsense.

UFO literature is roughly divisible into three categories: pop, serious, and skeptical. The first two can be called believer categories, and the line between them is sometimes vague. The tone of Major Kehoe's books is definitely pop, but their intent and most of their methods are serious. The volunteer civilian groups named above are serious, many of their members being engineers and the like. The Condon Committee, which was semiofficial and investigated UFOs with the help of a sizable public grant, was mostly skeptical. The best-known skeptics, besides Condon, are Donald Menzel, a Harvard astronomer, and Philip Klass, an electrical engineer and Senior Avionics Editor with *Aviation Week and Space Technology*.

In general, the skeptics' investigative techniques are better than the believers'. The Condon Committee's inquiry into magnetic effects supposedly induced in cars by the proximity of UFOs was a masterpiece of straightforward scientific demolition. They also did a most minute analysis of the photographs of a UFO allegedly

* For instance, Dr. Albert Hibbs, of Caltech's Jet Propulsion Laboratory, does. An NICAP publication reports that when asked what we should do if we received a message from outer space, he replied: "Hang up. Look what happened to the Indians."

taken by a Mr. Paul Trent of McMinnville, Oregon, in the early 1950s. The photos were finally cleared, in the Condon report, as "unexplained" (i.e., probably not faked), only to be put in doubt again by a later study made by Philip Klass, who showed that the pictures had probably been taken in the morning, not in the early evening as Trent had claimed.[13] Klass then checked into the case further. He found that in two newspaper interviews given by Mr. and Mrs. Trent at the time, there were odd discrepancies in their stories. He also discovered that they were "repeaters" (had seen UFOs before). "Most experienced UFO investigators," he says, "have learned to be extremely suspicious of 'repeaters.'"

Klass's report raises other questions. The Condon Committee's analysis of the film apparently ruled out the possibility that the Trents' saucer was really a small object thrown into the air and photographed. What, then, *did* they photograph? And why was it necessary to make the picture in the morning but *pretend* that it had been taken at nightfall? In other words, if they'd gone to the trouble of contriving a clever forgery, why did they make so elementary a mistake as to lie about the time of day when the picture was taken? The exasperating thing, as in many of these cases, is that we will probably never know what did happen.

On the whole, though, the skeptics are very thorough. Klass's analysis of the supposedly "classic" sighting in Socorro, New Mexico, is a fine example of the technique.[14] A police officer, Lonnie Zamora, had said that he had seen a UFO land near the town. Driving to the spot, he had caught sight of a four-legged craft on the ground with little men outside of it.* Evidently because they saw *him*, they had hustled back into their ship, which then zoomed away on a jet of flame. Klass showed that the supposed pad prints left by the craft were unsymmetrically spaced, requiring a very strange arrangement of landing legs. Moreover, the "feet" were oblong and oriented with their long axes in parallel—a design feature he considered suspiciously poor. Further checking showed

---

* Among other things, Klass showed that from the place from which Zamora said he had seen the Little Men, full-sized human beings were hard to make out.

that the sighting had occurred at a point situated between two main roads, making it readily accessible to the numbers of tourists who soon showed up. The land on which the little men had briefly debarked happened to be owned by the mayor.

The skeptics have developed various explanations to cover cases that defy this sort of close scrutiny. Menzel puts much stress on radar "ghosts"; on certain types of meteorites; on the "lens effect," or reflections from ice crystals which cause planets under some atmospheric conditions to look like bright lights nearby; and on miragelike phenomena occurring during air inversions. I have often tried to mistake planets for lights flying around in the sky, but with no success. However, it is common for independent observers to see the same phenomenon quite differently. Klass has documented a case of this kind which occurred on the night of March 3, 1968.[15] He gives the reports of a number of people in Indiana, Ohio, and Tennessee who saw a fiery flying object overhead. Some described it in detail, as cigar-shaped, with ports in the side, etc. One lady, a science teacher, was convinced "this is no natural phenomenon. It's UFOs." In fact, according to Klass, what all these people were seeing was "the re-entry of debris from the rocket booster which the Russians had used to launch the Zond 4 spacecraft." (So the lady science teacher was right, in a way.)

One naturally becomes cautious after reading enough of this sort of thing. Menzel's theory that many UFOs are actually meteorites or meteors[16] and Klass's idea that some UFOs may be plasmas[17] or possibly coronas which have detached themselves from high-tension wires and begun erratically zipping about* make it necessary to rule out most night sightings or any in which a flaming or glowing object keeps to a fixed course. The day of the sighting should preferably be clear, minimizing the likelihood of mirages, reflections from clouds, ice crystals, etc. Anything that *looks* like a cloud, or that glows without having definite outlines, should also be excluded. If a distinct but unidentifiable object is clearly seen in the sky in broad daylight, if it maneuvers, if it can

---

* He writes to me, as of October, 1971, that he would put plasma-UFO sightings at less than 5 percent of all those reported.

be observed by pilots or others thoroughly familiar with aircraft, and if the same object can be tracked on plane or ground radar as it is being visually observed, one has at least the start of a case. Ideally there should be several independent witnesses, observing the same object from different vantage points and between whom there is little reason to suspect collusion. Photographs are helpful but not conclusive.

It turns out to be difficult to find cases that meet *all* of these requirements or even most of them. One that nearly does is given in a volume of NICAP reports:

> May 14, 1954. Near Dallas, Texas, a flight of Marine Corps jets led by Major Charles Scarborough, was headed north in mid-afternoon. At a point 6 miles west of the city, Major Scarborough sighted 16 unidentified objects in groups of four, dead ahead but at higher altitude, 15 degrees above. He radioed Captain Roy Jorgensen, whose jet he had in sight by its contrail. Captain Jorgensen, at a higher altitude, saw the UFOs below his left wing. Just as the two pilots tried to box in the UFOs, Major Scarborough saw them fade from glowing white to orange and disappear, apparently speeding away due north. . . . Based on Captain Jorgensen's position, the UFOs were 3 miles ahead of Major Scarborough's plane and 15 degrees above him. Triangulation shows that the UFOs were at about 32,000 feet.

On September 21, 1962, during the NATO war games known as Operation Mainbrace,

> six Royal Air Force pilots flying a formation of jets over the North Sea observed a shiny sphere approaching from the direction of the fleet. The UFO eluded their pursuit and disappeared. When returning to the base, one of the pilots looked back and saw the UFO following him. He turned to chase it, and the UFO also turned and sped away.[18]

There are some dozens of reports of this kind in the literature. The question is, what do they mean? Pilots are known to be a high-spirited lot. If you assume that half of the daytime UFO sightings reported by them were really hoaxes, what about the other half? It is notoriously easy, even for men used to scanning the heavens, to be deceived by familiar objects, if the latter are far enough away or oddly enough lit. I read an account by one pilot of a sighting he made toward evening during cloudy weather. As he flew along, he saw a glowing, disk-shaped object emerge from a cloud bank. Having read about UFOs, he knew at once what this object probably was—but a few seconds later, as the light on it changed, he saw that it was a DC-3.

However, in the Major Scarborough case, cited above, misidentification of this sort would seem to have been next to impossible. The UFOs the major saw were not weather balloons at 70,000 feet, mirages due to air inversion, or slow-flying meteors—but they *may*, of course, have been plasmas flying in squadrons of four each. The fact that the pilot flying above Scarborough saw the objects as below his own plane establishes within limits the altitude of the UFOs, and so rules out the possibility of an illusion due to great distance. And while the UFOs glowed, it appears, from the NICAP report, that all concerned perceived them as *things*, executing definite maneuvers. What, in fact, had they seen? (Or was the sighting a hoax?)

UFO source-works have reported some radar-visual sightings, one of the more interesting having occurred at Lakenheath in England.[19] Ground radar picked up a flying object (at night) and an RAF fighter was scrambled to investigate it. The pilot got a visual fix, started to close with the object, and found it suddenly behind him, apparently tracking him. Having made several unsuccessful attempts to turn fast enough to put the object in front of him again, the pilot, with noticeable agitation, reported these events on air-to-ground radio and shortly afterward returned to base. (He was reportedly "low on petrol." A second interceptor developed engine trouble.) The Lakenheath incident is listed in the Condon Committee's report as "unexplained."*

A common feature of the more credible reports is that the ob-

* A case very like this one, involving multiple visual and radar sightings, pursuit of the object by aircraft, and finally of the aircraft by the object, is reported to have occurred at Ellsworth Air Force Base near Rapid City, South Dakota, in August of 1953. See *The UFO Evidence*, p. 4.

jects (if observed from the ground) are nearly or perfectly sound-less. In addition they often have a metallic look, are capable of high-speed turns, tend to glow and to change color as they accel-erate or decelerate, and frequently vanish by ascending straight up at phenomenal speeds, turning on edge as they do so. They can also hover, and sometimes exhibit falling-leaf movements. In Feb-ruary, 1953, a pilot, John Bean, gave a quite detailed account of an afternoon sighting of this kind.[20] He had stopped his car by the side of the road near Livermore, California, and was watching a DC-6 coming in for a landing when he caught sight of a flying ob-ject headed away southward. "It began a shallow left turn, and at that point I could see that it was perfectly round and had a metal-lic sheen somewhat similar to that of aluminum with a satin fin-ish. . . . It did not have a sharp glint which one often sees when light is reflected from a conventional aluminum aircraft. . . . Having gathered my wits about me . . . I followed its course, and suddenly it began to alter direction, at first seemingly heading due south again, and then suddenly making a steep righthand turn. It also began climbing at the most terrific rate of ascent I have ever witnessed." As "the disc" was heading up and away, Bean saw a jet flying in from the east roughly on the same course but, he es-timated, at a lower altitude. The jet left a contrail. The object did not. He heard no sound from either aircraft, attributing this fact to the wind, which was blowing from him toward them at "about 15 to 20 knots." He judged the whole sighting to have taken no more than nine or ten seconds, of which three "were counted time." "As soon as the sighting was over, I glanced at my watch and noticed the time to be 13:43. The date was the afternoon of January 27, 1953, and the atmospheric conditions were CAVU." (Clear atmosphere, visibility unlimited.)

So many reports from apparently sober professionals stress the absence of contrails or other signs of conventional propulsion that one learns to expect fraud when, for instance, sightings involve jets of flame which burn the surface of blacktop roads, or singe shrubbery. In the Socorro case, mentioned above, as in others, brush was alleged to have been burned in this way.

One comes after a while to distinguish reports that *seem* believable (partly because of their consistency with others like them) from those which contain more or less obvious inventions. But what are the believable reports reporting? This is a very difficult question. For instance, is the consistency one finds among the more believable UFO accounts a matter of independent observers reliably describing a class of essentially similar events? Or were the observers actually seeing one or more types of familiar event and *making* their reports consistent (i.e., with other high-quality reports of UFO sightings) as a result of an unconscious disposition to believe?

There can be no doubt that all of us have such dispositions to believe—the difficulty being that the more intelligent and highly trained a man is, the more plausibly he can falsify the (often ambiguous) evidence of his senses. There is also no question but that numbers of people, doubtless including pilots, have a disposition to believe in UFOs. The earth, in recent years, has come to seem rather confined, almost suffocating with its prospects of irreversible pollution and nuclear war. In this cheerless atmosphere, the prospect of contact with visitors from another world, while it certainly entails some sinister possibilities,* is at least exciting. It suggests that our world might become an "open" system once again, whose frontiers lie not in the Indies or far Cathay, but among the stars.

The thought that we might get into friendly touch with a people in some other solar system is consequently one that an imaginative man finds hard to resist. And since unidentifiable lights or objects maneuvering around in our skies do suggest that possibility (or to pessimists, the equally stimulating possibility of an attack by supermen), it is clear that we have a strong, if not always conscious, bias toward seeing them as messengers from Out There. That bias, combined with a knowledge of what other intelligent UFO observers have reported, may have gone far toward creating that consistency among the better type of UFO sightings which I have mentioned. Just as the hoaxers crib from the reports of others like them, or use the most obvious earth evidence in fabricating

* Not merely martial but medical (see *The Andromeda Strain*).

their accounts, so observers of the "higher" type may unconsciously make their reports conform to those of their intellectual peers. So it is conceivable that, starting with just a few reports, an epidemic of quite plausible "findings" might follow, resulting in a mass of testimony so impressive as to make the reality of the reported phenomena appear all but certain.

Swift, short-lived mass conversions of this kind have occurred in the sciences. Klass and, before him, Martin Gardner[21] described the case of Professor R. Blondlot, a physicist at the University of Nancy, who in 1903 announced the discovery of N-rays (N for Nancy). These, he said, were emitted by various metals and acted in some way to increase the acuity of the dark-adapted eye.* A number of papers by other investigators shortly confirmed the existence of these rays, whose properties turned out to be quite remarkable. (Among other things, they sharpened hearing and the sense of smell, were emitted by brain and muscle tissue, could be transmitted down a wire, etc.) An American physicist, R. W. Wood, abruptly put an end to the whole business by visiting Blondlot's laboratory, where he surreptitiously removed a prism from the spectroscope through which Blondlot was observing N-rays. The professor's observations were unaffected. Not long afterward the boom in N-rays collapsed, and poor Blondlot committed suicide.

It is interesting to note the circumstances under which this odd delusion sprang up. Radiations were very much the thing at the time.† Roentgen had discovered X rays not long before, and Bec-

---

* Such an increase in acuity may have occurred, but from psychological causes, as a kind of expectancy effect. It is known that keen interest can cause dilatation of the pupil.
† Even, of course, in quack medicine. I have in my library, for instance, a little book called *The Prismatic Ray* (Chicago: New Medicine Publishing Co., 1910). The author, Emily Lloyd, was apparently plugging a machine which, from the text and pictures, appears to have been a sort of spark coil. "It is true," the author admits, "that the first sight of the machine . . . strikes terror to the heart of the novice . . . The crackling noise, weird blue light in the vacuum tubes, peculiar odor of the Ozone, the shower of sparks as the applicator is brought near the surface of the body, combine to make a really awe-inspiring spectacle." Not only that, but the gadget could cure boils, remove warts without scarring, stop hair from falling or cause it to grow again, and perform any number of other medical services.

querel had demonstrated some sort of electromagnetic or particle emission from pitchblende. In the early 1900s, when the topic was still hot, a physicist who discovered a new form of radiant energy might well earn a Nobel.

What makes one suspect that UFOs could be an instance of group self-deception, similar in principle to the N-ray flap of seventy years ago, is that other, more objective evidence for their existence is still wholly lacking. Of the hundreds of photos of UFOs that have allegedly been made, few or none are acceptable (i.e., many may be pictures of rare natural phenomena or of familiar objects taken under conditions that radically falsify their appearance both to the eye and to the camera). Klass quotes the late Dr. James E. MacDonald, a believer, as saying he was "uncomfortable about the fact that most UFO photos have turned out to be hoaxes." Klass adds that by 1969 the pictures on which MacDonald had put his dwindling hopes were those taken by the Trents, at McMinnville.[22] (Dr. MacDonald was subsequently a suicide, though not, it is believed, for reasons connected with his UFO investigations.)

With all the extraterrestrial surveillance we are supposed to have been under, it is odd that there is still no evidence that UFOs come from another world, no wreckage to indicate that they even exist. If only 1 percent of the strange activity recently reported in our skies represents genuine UFOs, how does it happen that not one has ever been shot down? According to Frank Edwards, one has been.[23] He reports that in 1963, in the South Atlantic, one of our missile ships, on orders from its home base, fired on a UFO and destroyed it. However, he says, "the subsequent search for debris was futile." As in so many other cases, he does not name his sources. Nor does he identify the ship or give any details which would make it clear that the destroyed object was really a UFO. It is this sort of reporting which makes a good deal of the UFO literature so irritating and difficult to believe.

Another of Edwards' cases was one in which a UFO was reported to have crashed on Spitzbergen Island, off the coast of Norway.[24] Several years later (by Edwards' account), the *Stuttgarter Tageblatt* quoted a Norwegian official as saying that the craft was definitely not of Soviet or other earthly origin and was made of materials still unidentified. In NICAP's opinion, this incident was most probably a journalistic hoax.[25]

There is, however, *one* bit of physical evidence which has received the most detailed attention, not only from a "believer" organization (APRO) but from the Condon Committee. It consisted of some pieces of light metal, reported to have been obtained in 1957 when a UFO dived toward the sea near Ubatuba in Brazil, pulled out of its dive at the last minute, and blew up, spattering the ocean's surface with flaming debris. Three chunks of the latter, having fallen into shallow water, were gathered up by an anonymous witness, who sent them to a society columnist in Rio de Janeiro, along with a letter describing the incident.* The late Dr. Olavo Fontes, an APRO representative in Brazil, arranged to have chemical, spectrographic, and X-ray diffraction studies made of the material. These showed it to be magnesium "absolutely pure in the spectrographic sense." What remained of the samples was sent by Fontes to the Lorenzens of Tucson (APRO), who in turn released an even smaller sample to the Condon Committee. David Saunders—then a committee member—says that the metal fragment was "about the size of the last joint of your little finger and weighed less than five grams."[26] It was subjected to neutron-activation analysis, a technique by which the unknown material is made radioactive by neutron saturation, its gamma-ray spectrum then showing the elements of which it consists.

The composition of the fragment was indeed odd, not only in the absence of some elements usually found in terrestrial magnesium, but in the presence of certain others, notably strontium. After thorough checking, the Condon Committee concluded that the fragment, though unusual, *might* have been part of a batch of magnesium prepared as early as March 25, 1940, by the Dow Chemical Company, which contained "nominally" the same concentration of strontium. Saunders, who subsequently left the committee, feels that the earthly origin of the sample is doubtful on these grounds:

1. It contained no aluminum and "only a trace of copper."

* The letter was signed, but the signature was reported to be illegible.

2. If terrestrial, it should also have contained calcium.

3. Removal of the calcium (in the interest of fraud) would "almost certainly" have involved a quartz vessel, which would have left traces of silicon in the sample. (Silicon was not reported.)

4. Purification of the sample by the "best techniques available" in 1968 would have depended upon vacuum sublimation of the metal, resulting in contamination of the specimen with mercury from the mercury-vapor pump. No mercury was present.

If the Ubatuba fragment was a hoax, Saunders says that it must rank as one of the most sophisticated in history. There is another possibility, however. The original witness in the case has never to my knowledge been identified. So far as one can tell, nobody *went* to Ubatuba immediately after the incident had been covered in the press, nor was any other sort of debris from the explosion apparently ever collected. Except for the fact that the object reportedly zoomed upward at the last moment, we have nothing to indicate that all this fuss may not have been over a piece of meteoritic magnesium. The fallibility of observers being what it is, it is quite possible that just before a meteorite or bolide* exploded over the beach, part of it broke off, falling away at an angle which suggested to the witnesses that they were watching a manned vehicle trying to pull out of a dive. That is, if they had *wanted* to see the phenomenon in that light, a little stretching of the sensory evidence and a little sharing of views, or a confabulatory session immediately afterward, might easily have done the trick.

Two other notable episodes occurred in Brazil during the same period. In one (December, 1954), a UFO seemingly in trouble sprayed "silver rain" over the housetops of a town.[27] It was first reported to consist of pure tin, but analyses made by the Brazilian Air Force, and later by a chemist in the United States, showed it to be solder—a finding that was thought to discredit the whole sighting. Why, one wonders, should it be more plausible for a UFO to be leaking pure tin (a metal of limited usefulness) than solder, which plays such a huge part in our own electronics industry?

* Except that bolides or meteorites are not usually made of pure magnesium. Most commonly, if metallic, they are iron-nickel mixtures.

In the other episode, a UFO came clanking down over a village that stands on the banks of the Peropava River in Brazil.[28] The craft, apparently out of control, nicked a palm tree, caromed off into the water, and sank, issuing a cloud of bubbles as it did so. The incident attracted considerable attention. Newsmen, skin divers, and salvage gear were rushed to the place, but unfortunately, nothing was ever found.

NICAP's monthly newsletter for March, 1971, carries a story that originated much closer to home. It involves a sighting that occurred at Scargo Lake, on Cape Cod, "just after sunrise" in February, 1971. The lake is roughly pear-shaped, with the neck of the pear pointing a few degrees east of north. Route 6A passes close to its western shore, and on the road, roughly 500 feet west of the lake at its widest point, stands a little settlement. In this settlement, on the morning of the sighting, two boys, one on Whig Street and the other about half a mile away, on Elm, were starting for the school bus. Each saw a bright object moving slowly through the sky. (One reported that he watched it for some three minutes.) Both said that it settled over the lower end of the lake and disappeared.

It then appears that one of the boys (John Brogan, 12, of Elm Street),* together with Martha Koempel, 13, and Robert Bottcher, 12, went to the lake, and at the approximate spot where the object had settled, they found a large hole in the ice. They noticed vapor rising from the water and reported some turbulence (though that could have been due to a breeze). Walter H. Webb, of the Charles Hayden Planetarium in Boston, went to Scargo three days later. "Using a topographic map of the area, I plotted my compass bearings and found that the lines of direction to the UFO from each boy's viewing spot converged exactly over the hole in the lake. . . . We have the unanimous claim by uninvolved residents and skaters that there was no hole in the ice on the day before. . . . No one could recall ever seeing such a large hole (approximately 100 by 30 feet) or one of that shape, on Scargo Lake. After viewing the hole myself . . . I believe [it] was formed by a

* The boy on Whig Street was Paul McCarthy (aged 13).

151

rather sudden melting process. There was no evidence of radial cracking or scattered ice fragments. To this investigator, and to the skin diver who inspected the hole, it would appear unlikely that an underwater spring could melt away a three-inch layer of ice at the subfreezing temperatures that existed on the night before the sighting."

Webb then gives reasons for not attributing the sightings and the hole to a fireball. Bright planets were checked out and the conclusion was that none could have been responsible for the sighting. Webb then ruled out other possibilities on various grounds. Two separate attempts by a skin diver to search the lake bottom failed because of the murkiness of the water. If anything is still down there, it will have to be located by its sonar profile or through a full-scale diving operation, and it seems unlikely at this date that anyone can be persuaded to make the effort. We have been baffled too often before. Moreover, as a friend of mine suggested, it may be that the UFO did not crash: it may just have landed; thawed a hole in the ice; submerged; collected samples of marine life, mud, etc.; and then stealthily departed. (No one that I know of reported seeing it go, however.)

I have sketched out this case in some detail to illustrate the methods of the better investigators of the believer school, and also to underscore the great difficulties which this sort of inquiry presents. A hoax seems improbable, since one can think of no way that two boys, aged 12 and 13, might, before dawn of the sighting day, have melted a 100-by-30-foot hole through 3 inches of ice. My own view is that *any* of the explanations we are apt to get of this incident are fairly certain to be nonsense—unless, of course, a thing measuring about 100 by 30 feet can be pulled out of Scargo Lake.

The point is, what are we to make of the UFO question as a whole? The sightings and the controversies over them continue, but still without issue. The theoretical obstacles in the way of an ETI (extraterrestrial intelligence) theory of UFOs are almost as great as the difficulties we have had in turning up "hard" evidence for UFOs themselves. A West Coast physicist, Dr. Nicholas Der, says the main one is communications.[29] Even if a spacecraft had come from a solar system as nearby as four and a fraction light-years away, contact between it and mission control would be as good as cut. This would put space travel on the same freewheeling basis as the trading or whaling voyages of past centuries, when a ship might not be heard from for years. Space travel, Der seems to think, cannot work that way; and indeed, communications aside, the problems presented by this sort of travel are awesome, to say the least. To provision a spaceship and give it sufficient fuel to see it through a one-way journey of four to six years, let alone twelve to fourteen, is an undertaking at the moment quite beyond us.

However, one hears rumors. New discoveries are said to be at hand. In a multidimensional universe there may be shortcuts. (Remember Dobbs's "second time dimension.") Don't the UFOs we have seen execute unbelievably swift maneuvers? Why not swifter ones? Doesn't the (verbal) evidence we have to date suggest that UFOs have somehow overcome gravity? A number of reports by motorists who have been buzzed by UFOs mention strange antigravity effects—cars or trucks being lifted into the air and deposited some yards away, off the road. One said that his headlight beams were deflected by a UFO—arguing a *very* strong gravitational effect. As to how the crews of these craft can withstand the tremendous inertial and g-forces involved in their abrupt changes of course, Gerald Heard had an interesting explanation for that. The spacemen, he declared, are insects—as I recall, beautifully colored ants. (He said they came from Mars—a point we may soon be able to settle.)

A large majority of scientists will have nothing to do with these puzzles, for reasons perhaps best summarized in a memo by Dr. Robert Low, Project Co-ordinator for the Condon Committee.[30] Writing to two colleagues, "Jim and Ted," Low said in part: "In order to undertake such a project, one has to approach it objectively. That is, one has to admit the possibility that such things as UFOs exist. It is not respectable to give serious consideration to such a possibility. Believers, in other words, remain outcasts . . . The simple act of admitting these possibilities . . . puts us beyond the pale."

A few scientifically trained people *are* interested in UFOs and evidently are willing to risk the sort of censure Dr. Low is talking about. One of these is Dr. James Harder, a believer who nevertheless puts his case with some caution.[31] "Over the past twenty years a vast amount of evidence has been accumulating *that bears on* the existence of UFOs. Most of this is little known to the general public or to most scientists. But on the basis of the data and ordinary rules of evidence, *as would be applied in civil or criminal courts*, the physical reality of UFOs has been proved beyond a reasonable doubt. With some effort we can accept this on an intellectual level but find a difficulty in accepting it on an emotional level, *in such a way that the facts give a feeling of reality*." (Italics added.) Dr. Harder has put his finger right on it, except that I would reverse the sense of his last statement. It is not at the emotional level that the trouble lies: quite the reverse. All would be in order there, if only we could shut up our minds.

My own difficulty is that I can't shut up mine. The great assortment of theories about UFOs presents, on the whole, no problem. But the visual, or radar and visual, sightings reported by trained, apparently reliable people are, in a few cases, hard to dispose of, even on the psychological grounds I have suggested.

To look at the question statistically, *some* sightings of this sort probably were a result of misidentifications made either innocently or out of a disposition to believe in UFOs in the first place. But did *all* of them originate in this way? (I am discounting practical jokes on the ground that, while probably tempted, most pilots avoid them for career reasons.) If even some (say 1 percent) of the visual or radar-visual reports were accurate, the question remains, what were they reporting? I do not share the easy attitude of theorists on either side of this question.

There can be no doubt that purely psychological factors have played an enormous part in making UFOs a worldwide phenomenon. If one were to study the major events or social trends of the period between 1945 and 1970, one might draw a graph representing the successive peaks that our collective anxiety reached during those years. One such peak very likely developed as the postwar alignments of power took shape, resulting in a decade or so of the

Cold War, Dulles' "brinksmanship" and the opening phases of the race into space. A second peak may have developed in the United States as we entangled ourselves in Vietnam. By no startling coincidence, the major UFO flaps appear to correspond to these peaks (e.g., '52, '57, '65–'67).* Skeptics such as Donald Menzel or Philip Klass would doubtless take this to mean that the phenomenon *is* largely psychological—a case of our being so unsettled that our tendency to misperceive natural events was greater even than usual.

But what about that tiny percentage of cases which the Condon report classifies as "unexplained"? From a list of 27 of these, I screened out all but 6. Applying the same criteria† to the NICAP reports in *The UFO Evidence*, I ended up with a similarly small number that might rate as unexplainable. If one grants that out of the thousands of UFO sightings which have been made in the past twenty-five years, a few tens must stand as unaccounted for, what is the sensible position to take? Does this small percentage mean anything?

A statistician would be likely to say it means that the probability that UFOs are real is zero—the small unexplained remainder being due to observer error or to some rare natural phenomenon which, when finally discovered and certified officially, will clear up our marginal uncertainty. I think of myself as a rational man; I would like to accept that analysis. I have made it, in fact, partly to convince myself that I *must* accept it. Yet I find a curious resistance in myself to doing so.

Major Scarborough's experience; the methodical report of pilot John Bean, the RAF airman who was scrambled only to find the object he was supposed to be pursuing pursuing *him*—these and some few other reports like them haunt me. Am I the victim of my own topic, then? Do I too have a secret disposition to believe? It is quite possible.

The fact remains, however, that the strongest argument against

* I have since learned that a study of this kind, correlating UFO sightings with apparent epidemics of anxiety, has appeared in *Science*.
† I.e., those mentioned earlier: professional observers, daytime sightings preferred; also radar confirmation of visual fixes, object not merely in straight-line flight, etc.

UFOs as visitors from outer space is the astronomical one, pre-sented in Walter Sullivan's *We Are Not Alone*.[32] If we assume that life on other planets requires conditions similar to those on earth, then the number of stars in the so-called main sequence likely to have "habitable zones" for planets becomes rather small. The large, bright stars may endure too short a time to permit bio-logical evolution; the small ones at the opposite end of the se-quence may not give off enough radiation. A great many stars are binaries and therefore not apt to have planets in sufficiently stable orbits. Our own earth is, as Sullivan puts it, in a kind of quaran-tine. It is situated not in an inner arm of our galaxy—where star-planet systems may be within one light-year of each other—but on an outer part of the spiral and slightly above it. Our closest neigh-bor, Alpha Centauri (4.3 light-years away), is a triple star system, hence unlikely to have planets in a habitable zone. Next out is Barnard's star, which appears to have a planet one and a half times the size of Jupiter, with an orbital period of twenty-four years. Here at least is one possibility.

The astronomer Su-shu Huang considers that two stars, Epsilon Eridani and Tau Ceti, both about eleven light-years off, are the best bets to have life-supporting planets. Even if they do, of course, there is no telling whether biological evolution there began at the same time as it did on earth; or if so, has proceeded at the same rate.* Moreover, as Sullivan points out, we do not know what the life expectancy of civilizations may be, once they reach the high-technology stage; it could, to judge from our own, be rather short. Relative to the whole course of biological evolution, eras equiva-lent to those on earth which we call historic may amount only to a split second. In that case, the chance that our civilization coin-cides in time with *any* other, even thousands of light-years off, is small; the chance that it is nearly simultaneous with civilizations which happen to have evolved on the handful of planets within ten or twelve light-years of us is even smaller.

* If the galaxy is about 10^{10} years old and the earth half that, or 5 billion years (5×10^9), it seems that on a slightly warmer planet, suitably supplied with water, oxygen, etc., evolution similar to our own might have begun and perhaps ended, hundreds of millions of years ahead of us, the converse being true of cooler planets. Even simultaneous starters may not finish together.

Granted the outside possibility that such civilizations do co-exist with ours, the chances that they could send spaceships here over the relatively short distances that separate us (6 to 11 light-years) seem also very small. Travel at speeds approaching the velocity of light involves extremely serious collision and radiation hazards, not to mention staggering problems in propulsion engineering, on-board maintenance, and navigation.

Pending further discoveries concerning planet X* in our own solar system, we are forced to the conclusion that it is highly unlikely that we are being visited by spacecraft from other planets. A very few UFO sightings may correspond to some other, as yet unclassified, phenomenon. But the strongest possibility seems to be that UFOs are simply a variant of the New Nonsense—a result of the same willful personal belief that has made a culture hero out of Immanuel Velikovsky and caused millions of us to look to the stars not as modern astronomers do but in the way our Chaldean ancestors did. There have been some changes, of course. As a final example, consider the following:

The first act of this aerial melodrama opened at Selby, in the West Riding of Yorkshire. There were four witnesses. (1) A solicitor of Selby saw two hovering lights in the sky, at 9:15 of Friday evening, February 21. (2) An insurance manager, standing in Church Fenton Station with a party of Selby businessmen, observed—not three quarters of an hour later—"an airship with strong searchlights, playing on the railway lines." It was high at first, he said, but descended almost to the roofs of Church Fenton. There it lingered for some twenty minutes, while he and the businessmen held their breaths; then it was off at a great speed, showing for the first time, a wicked green and red light along each side. (3) A countryman of Riccall in the East Riding saw an airship at 8 P.M. and being sharper of hearing than the rest, distinguished the whirr of its engines. (4) A commercial traveller was driving near Ellerton between ten and eleven that night, when he and his horse were startled by a very bright light "from an airship or something" which passed across the road in front of him . . .

* Whose existence has recently been inferred from data on comet flight paths.

To the veteran reader of UFO literature, it is all there—the hovering at low altitude, swift ascent, varicolored lights, whirring sounds. But these reports were not supposed to be about spaceships. According to George Dangerfield,[33] they were made in February, 1913, in England, and taken as firm evidence that the country was being scouted by German dirigibles. That, at least, was what people were looking for. What were they seeing?

viii
Speaking of Flying Objects...

Of all the popular thinkers whom this busy era has produced, few have been more despised than Immanuel Velikovsky—unfairly perhaps, but for reasons not hard to understand. Like his rival-in-martyrdom Wilhelm Reich, he had been a psychoanalyst; and for the inventive theoretician, there is probably no better beginning.

After all, the primary datum in Freud's *Totem and Taboo*—the drama of the prehistoric sons' killing and eating the father—was invented, a fact that seems in no way to have discouraged a generation of psychotherapists and lay believers from accepting the momentous conclusions which Freud drew from it.* Ernest Jones speaks of the difficulty in "tracing . . . the genesis of Freud's original discoveries" and thinks that "the greatest of them" was very likely his discovery of "the universality of the Oedipus complex." It was, in any event, the closest Freud came to a one-factor explanation of human behavior—the point being that Reich and Velikovsky developed similarly monolithic theories. Reich centered his on the universal essence, orgone, whereas Velikovsky undertook to explain many of the riddles of geology and evolution with his catastrophe hypothesis. How did he arrive at it? How did Freud arrive at his notion of primal patricide? While writing *Totem and Taboo* he said he considered it his masterpiece, and in a letter written during that period, he remarked: "The *Totem* work

* Jones says in *The Life and Works of Sigmund Freud*, "There is a notable sentence toward the end [of *Totem and Taboo*] where Freud spoke of 'the beginnings of religion, morality, social life and art meeting in the Oedipus complex.'"

is a beastly business. I am reading thick books without being really interested in them since I already know the results; my instinct tells me that . . ." It was possibly the same instinct which told Dr. Velikovsky that the catastrophes which he found described in ancient records from all over the world were due to a single agency —a comet, which passed dangerously close to the earth apparently circa 1500 B.C. and again about 750–650 B.C., later becoming the planet Venus. Had he spent his earlier years as a professional astronomer, would he have come up with this extraordinary hypothesis?

As a result of it, however, Velikovsky arrived at certain conclusions which were contrary to the conventional science of 1950 but have subsequently proved out, the most famous being his conclusion that the surface temperature of Venus must be much higher than was then supposed. He also said that the earth's magnetosphere extended farther into space than it seemed reasonable at the time to expect,* and foretold that remanent magnetism would be discovered in rocks on the moon, the orientation of these small magnets not necessarily coinciding with any former or existing magnetic axis in the moon itself. What, if anything, are we to make of these hits, particularly in view of the odd way he made them and the number of fantastic things he says in addition? Did a part of our crude-oil deposits *really* fall down from the sky? Can we seriously suppose that one of the plagues of Biblical times consisted of vermin from Venus?

To judge from his material and the way he mostly uses it, Velikovsky is a sort of twentieth-century Talmudic Schoolman. In fact, one of the themes that crop up in his work is a strong pan-Semitism. He dedicates *Ages in Chaos* to his father, whom he describes as having "devoted his life, his fortune, his peace of mind, all that he had, to the realization of what was once an idea, the renaissance of the Jewish people in its ancient land. He contributed to the revival of the language of the Bible . . . by publishing . . . collective works on Hebrew philology. . . . He was the

---

* At the earth's surface the magnetic field is variable and extremely weak—on the order of 0.5–1.0 gauss.

first to redeem the land in Negeb. . . . I do not know whom I have to thank for intellectual preparedness for this reconstruction of ancient history if not my late father, Simon." Velikovsky himself practiced psychoanalysis in Palestine in the 1920s and '30s.

In fairness one should add that this chauvinistic note turns up only occasionally in his work—for instance, in the passage in *Worlds in Collision* in which he contrasts the bloody religious practices of the Central American Indians with the relative humanity of the Jews during the trials of the Exodus.

This theme in Velikovsky's work is important, however, in that it suggests that his real affiliations are not with modern science or supposedly supranationalistic scholarship. At bottom, he seems more akin to Christian divines of the past several centuries who had the same belief that people of their faith were the chosen, and who studied the Scriptures for hidden messages, often also of a self-serving kind. Velikovsky, of course, ventures much farther than any Puritan theologian would have been likely or able to do. Nevertheless, there is a basic resemblance. His logic is not quite the logic of modern science, and in that, I suspect, lies his great popular appeal, as well as his extraordinary power to infuriate the learned. The latter sense in him the Wave of the Future, and have reacted with the ferocity of men who believe that their cause, although just, is about to be lost. The reaction was ill advised, however sound some of the motives for it may have been.

The parts of Velikovsky's work in which the reasoning seems clearest and the assembled evidence most impressive are those based upon ancient texts or inscriptions (and in some cases, surviving oral traditions), all of which tell of periods of catastrophe—notably, he says, around 1500 B.C. and again circa 750–650 B.C. The records he cites include pre-Christian papyri; the Talmud and Old Testament; the "Shoo-king" (this seems to be the Shu Ching, a collection of documents dating as far back as Shang times in China); the work of classical authors (Plato, Strabo, Diodorus Siculus, *et al.*); the Zend-Avesta of Zoroastrian Persia; the Icelandic *Edda*; the sixteenth-century Mexican Annals of Cuauhtitlán; legends of the Polynesian islanders, the Incas, the Greenland Eskimos, the Choctaw and various African tribes; the *Vedas*, and so on and so on.

Merely to have gotten all this stuff together and extracted from it certain surprisingly similar, if not universal, themes would have been enough for most scholars, and possibly should have been for Dr. Velikovsky.* From features that he found common to these various accounts he reached the following conclusions:

—That several times most ancient peoples were visited by calamities which profoundly disturbed the earth, causing floods, conflagrations, earthquakes, "pillars of fire," rains of stones, arrest of the sun in the sky, and protracted veiling of the sun by dust or haze.

—That in one or more of these upheavals, the earth's orbit, axis of rotation, or direction of rotation changed. Thus the old records he cites speak of the order of the heavenly bodies being suddenly altered, the sky "falling" or getting "lower," the points of the compass having to be determined anew (ancient China), and the sun rising where it used to set (Egypt; Central America).

—That whereas for a period most ancient peoples had a calendar of twelve 30-day months, after one of the calamities just mentioned the length of the year in days changed, with the result that circa 750–650 B.C. or later, calendars across the globe were reformed to harmonize (as an account from Ptolemaic times in Egypt says) with the "present arrangement of the world."

In support of the many tales and traditions which say that the earth once turned upside down, he tells of a star map found in the tomb of Senmut, an Egyptian who lived during the reign of Queen Hatshepsut (1501–1479 B.C.). The map shows "the celestial sphere with the signs of the zodiac and other constellations in a 'reversed orientation.'" The Harris papyrus "speaks of a cosmic upheaval of fire and water when 'the south becomes north and the Earth turns over.'"

The Ipuwer (Leiden) papyrus contains similar, if somewhat

---

* Indeed, he is to be praised for the breadth of his work in a field in which specialization has become so intense that a student of Coptic texts may be only vaguely aware of the Saite period and never have heard of the Shoo-king.

more ambiguous, descriptions. The difficulty here is that the Leiden papyrus is usually taken as reporting a social catastrophe or revolution that occurred in Egypt some two centuries earlier, at the beginning of a period of invasion and foreign occupation known as the Hyksos. If, as Velikovsky seems to think, Ipuwer was really talking about a great upheaval of nature, then the inversion of the poles may have taken place not after Senmut's time but before it—in which case how do we explain the star map in his tomb? Was the map simply a commemoration of the celestial sphere as it had once been?

According to Velikovsky, the Egyptian word "Harakhte" is "the name for the setting sun. As there is but one sun in the sky, it is supposed that Harakhte means the sun at its setting. But why should the sun at its setting be regarded as a deity different from the morning sun? . . . The inscriptions do not leave any room for misunderstanding: 'Harakhte, he riseth in the west.' The texts found in the pyramids say that the luminary 'ceased to live in the occident and shines; a new one, in the orient.' . . ."

One reason why the sun at its setting might have been regarded as a deity is given by Sir Joseph N. Lockyer. From his detailed study of the temple of Karnak he concluded that it was so oriented that at sunset on the evening of the summer solstice, a beam of light penetrated the long hall to the inmost shrine. He remarked that Karnak was complementary to Stonehenge in that the latter was oriented so as to sight the sun at its rising on the same day. Stonehenge is thought to have been built in the nineteenth century* B.C., so that if perturbation in the earth's orbit, direction of rotation, or inclination to the plane of the ecliptic had occurred in the meantime, its present orientation should have been badly out of whack—perhaps so badly that we could not have said what its original astronomical purpose was. How could Thebes, as Velikovsky suggests, have changed latitude and Stonehenge not?

In the passage just quoted he says, "the texts found in the pyramids" indicate a west-to-east switch in the sun's rising—but here

* Actually built and rebuilt, over the period 1900–1500 B.C.

again we are in chronological trouble. For if, as he proposes else-where, *the* great disaster befell us somewhere around 1500 B.C., the pyramid texts would be unlikely to mention it, since most pyramids were built long before, during the fourth to twelfth dynasties, and none were built in the Empire period, which began at the end of the Hyksos.

As for the number of days in the year increasing, so as to cause the worldwide calendar reforms mentioned, there should here too be certain definite cutoff dates. Velikovsky's notion, if I understand him, is that the 360-day year was an interim phenomenon (fifteen to eight centuries B.C.). During the earlier Middle Kingdom, he assures us, the year was *less* than 360 days because "the earth then revolved on an orbit somewhat closer to the present orbit of Venus." In that case, no people before roughly 1800 B.C. should have had a year of 365¼ days. The astronomer Giorgio Abetti reports,* though perhaps not very reliably, that the Chinese in the reign of the emperor Yao (circa 2300 B.C.) did have a year of that length.

A more important line of evidence relates to lunar calendars, used by most ancient peoples—including the Sumerians, who go back approximately to the middle of the fourth millennium B.C. (circa 3600). The lunar month is 29.530588 days, which makes the lunar year 354.3670 days long. Velikovsky doesn't tell us how much less than 360 days the precatastrophic year was; but if it was, say, a week shorter (353 days), then no ancient peoples would have had an *intercalary* lunar calendar; that is, instead of adding days, at intervals, to correct to the true solar year, they would have had to subtract some; but the Sumerians added them. Therefore their solar year was at least longer than 354.3670 days and may even have been its present length.

Velikovsky might argue that the lunar as well as the solar year was altered by comet Venus after its first visit in 1500 B.C. or somewhat earlier. So in the period when the solar year was 360

* *The History of Astronomy*, p. 26. The much more scholarly work of Joseph Needham, mentioned below, casts doubt on this date, but suggests that the present solar year was in effect in China in Shang times, or the period when Velikovsky says that the year was 5¼ days short.

days long, or during the centuries when it was even shorter, the lunar year might have been shorter too. There is some evidence against that conclusion. Needham reports in *Science and Civilisation in China* that the "oracle bones from the thirteenth century B.C. of the Shang period indicate a lunar month of 29.53 days."

In the closing pages of *Worlds*, Velikovsky refuses to say exactly what, in his opinion, *did* take place. Maybe the earth slowed down or stopped, and then started spinning in the other direction; its axis of rotation may have tilted or turned 180°, and then come back or not come back to where it started. But it is clear, earlier, that he means us to take seriously the Egyptian and other stories that speak of the sun standing still, the orientation of the celestial sphere changing, etc. For these things to have happened—for Harakhte to have become the East-Rising One and Senmut's map to have slipped 180° out of phase with the heavens—the earth must have reversed its direction of rotation and inverted its axis of rotation both.*

If this double change had occurred fairly quickly, as Velikovsky implies it did, would the earth have been able to withstand it without major disruptions of its crust? Why is the geological record, otherwise so explicit, silent about these very recent events? It tells us of many similar ones in the more distant past—of glaciation during the Paleozoic, of repeated periods of vulcanism and mountain building, of continents rising or sinking, of the "Laramide revolution" at the end of the Cretaceous that produced the Rocky Mountains, and of the seas that once covered middle America, leaving behind coral beds as much as 1,000 feet deep and beautifully sculptured fossils of crinoids. If all these apparently slower changes have left traces of themselves, why shouldn't the catastrophes of 1500 and 750–650 B.C. have done likewise? Or have we, as Velikovsky hints in his opening chapters, just not read the record correctly? Is geology as a whole on the wrong track?

The agency that he thinks may have stopped and then reversed

---

* If the poles were inverted but the earth's direction of rotation remained the same, the heavens would be inverted, as in Senmut's map, but the sun would still rise in the east.

the earth's rotation was a passing comet. This body he supposes exerted some sort of magnetic torque on earth's liquid ferrous core. As the body approached, it had a braking effect on the earth's rotation. Presumably then at the body's closest approach, the rotation might have become zero and begun to accelerate in the opposite direction until, when the comet had passed out of effective range, the earth was rotating at approximately its old speed but now (viewed from above the North Pole) clockwise.* How long shall we allow for the whole process? If days or weeks, the conclusion is that part of the globe must have been exposed for a very long time to the sun, while another part (the New World, if we are to believe the Central American legends) was in prolonged darkness. Would life have survived that amount of cooking or cooling? What would the meteorological effects of such unequal heating have been? Obviously we are into physical problems of great intricacy, not the least of which is the mechanism of the rotational slowing itself.

If we assume that slowing and finally reversal of rotation took place in a matter of hours, then unequal heating ceases to be a major problem but the survival of the earth proper becomes one. The main reason is that a *constant* deceleration of the earth's rotation, under the conditions Velikovsky outlines, would be most unlikely. The slowing forces, acting at a distance, would presumably be subject to the law of inverse squares, which would mean that the deceleration would accelerate to a sharp maximum as the comet reached its point of nearest approach. In the last few moments, what had been a barely perceptible slowing some while before would become a violent wrench, followed by an equally violent reverse movement as rotation in the opposite direction began. In this crucial interval not only would the pyramids themselves possibly have been laid flat, but the earth's crust might have started breaking up.

For according to the present view, the earth consists of a liquid or semiliquid core and several overlying layers of rock, with a thin layer, no more than about twenty miles below the surface, where

* Actually the reverse, for now it is rotating counterclockwise.

volcanic activity originates. A slowing force, acting on the core, would tend to set it in motion relative to the next layer, the same being true the rest of the way out. That is, the outermost layer would be the last to respond, and would tend to shift in relation to the next-underlying "volcanic layer." A deceleration, starting in the core and rising to a sharp maximum, could therefore cause the outermost mantle at the last moment to grind over the layer beneath it like an ungreased wheel, generating immense heat and creating huge faults or instant anticlines. The net result might be a succession of volcanic explosions dwarfing any that had occurred in the remotest past—upheavals that would transform the continents and fill the air with debris which would take decades or centuries to come down again. What damage vulcanism and sheer mechanical fracture had failed to do would be done by the oceans massed up into great tidal waves and hurled upon the suffering land.*

To try, in all seriousness, to work out the means—say, electromagnetic induction—by which a passing body might set up counterforces in the earth's core sufficient to reverse its direction of rotation, and then to calculate the stresses that would be generated within the earth at various rates of rates of change in rotation, and the effect of these on oceans, mountains, buildings, etc., is a job no physicist in his senses would want to tackle, because it is, for all practical purposes, impossible. There are too many unknowns; and even if these were reasonably estimated, there would be no way to test the result. About the most one could shoot for is a

---

* Note too that the earth is at present oblate—that is, bulged out at the equator, probably as a result of centrifugal force. In the last critical moments of rotational slowing, a considerable percentage of that force would die out, resulting perhaps in an enormous counterthrust along the axis of the poles—i.e., the earth might tend to assume more nearly spherical form, with what changes in the existing crust one can imagine. These stresses would be only momentary, but to them one would have to add the stress of rotation commencing, at a very high rate of acceleration, in the opposite direction.

The magnitude of the floods that would accompany these events may be judged from the fact that earthquakes detectable globally only by means of instruments are nonetheless sometimes sufficient to raise tsunamis, or "tidal waves," a hundred feet high or more and traveling at over 400 miles an hour. (See The Larousse Encyclopedia of the Earth, p. 165.)

few critical values—rates of deceleration that would topple 90 percent of all man-made structures or raise tidal waves sufficient to flood 90 percent of all habitable lands.

So Velikovsky seems to be on safe ground here except for one point: namely, that the law of inverse squares—which holds for gravitation, induction, electrostatic attraction, etc.—makes some such crescendo effect as I have described appear quite probable. Consequently, any passing body that caused the earth to stop rotating in one direction and start rotating in another should have left a highly legible record of these events. Where is it? The stones in pyramids do not appear to have shifted. Stonehenge is still there. Excavation, of which we have done a good deal, ought to have disclosed bands, of very recent origin, in which the pre-existing strata were broken up and jumbled together in ways typical of no other era.* The doctor is silent on this point.

As it turns out, he has some other cards to play, but by far his best one is the mammoths. We are so used, he says, to the gradualism of classroom geology and evolution that we cannot consider anything resembling the catastrophe theories of Baron Cuvier, even when the evidence suggests we should. But how, then, did so many mammoths come to be frozen whole in the ice of Siberia, some with fresh food in their mouths and stomachs? If the cold only very gradually invaded that region, how could these animals have been trapped by it or have been eating temperate-zone vegetation at the time of their sudden demise?

Approaching the matter without preconceived notions, one would say that to last so long in such a state of preservation, the Siberian mammoths must somehow have been quick-frozen. Even if we make the unlikely assumption that the animals were bacteria-free and therefore decayproof, their bodies would have *weathered* away before a conventional ice sheet could have caught up with them. Did they fall into chilly aseptic bogs which in effect embalmed them before freezing? Possibly, although the problem of their preserved insides remains. To be embalmed effectively, bodies must be opened and are usually eviscerated.

* Or few others. If I understand him, Velikovsky is edging toward a catastrophe hypothesis to account for *all* previous ages of geologic upheaval.

Velikovsky has raised an embarrassing question here. Some of
his others, relating to supposed geological puzzles, struck me as in
no way crucial, either to his argument or to the security of established views. Given all the convulsions which the earth's surface
has apparently undergone over the 600 million or so years since
pre-Cambrian times right down into the Pleistocene, is it really
surprising that "occasionally . . . during mining operations, a human skull is found in the middle of a mountain, under a thick
cover of basalt or granite, like the Calaveras skull of California?"*
Admittedly, the genesis of mountains raises questions not yet satisfactorily answered. But since the evidence from geology is that in
the past continents have risen or sunk many times, and that the
weight of enlarged seas or accumulated ice can cause the earth's
crust to sag down here and thrust up somewhere else, and since
volcanic activity may have brought about many direct or indirect
changes in the earth's outer mantle,† it follows, I think, that we
may in time get all this sorted out by the same combination of
methods that has allowed us to learn the little we already know.

Up to this point it is clear how Velikovsky reached his conclusions. If so many peoples scattered all over the earth have left parallel accounts of great physical calamities and have in addition
done such strikingly similar things as switching from a 360-day
year to one of 365¼ days, then he reasons that these calamities
may actually have occurred and the year may actually have increased in day length. Granted that his reasoning contains apparent mistakes, we can still, in a general way, follow him.

It is when he comes to the core of his theory, the Leap of Ge-

* *Worlds*, p. 37. This question is easier to see in perspective when one considers the recorded effects of earthquakes. The one in Japan in 1923 "uplifted
the coast 3 to 6 feet. Beds of oysters were found afterwards above sea-level,
and the bottom of Sagami Bay had been raised by 300 to 800 feet in some
places, and in others had subsided by more than 700 feet." (Larousse, *op. cit.*,
p. 165.) Similar catastrophes on a larger scale could produce fossil fish on
mountaintops and other mysteries of which the doctor makes so much.
† The evidence from geology is that at the end of almost every clearly defined
era, from Cambrian times on, volcanic activity, mountain building, and changes
in the height of continents and the extent of seas have occurred. During the
later Carboniferous (350–270 million years ago), and in the early Permian,
just after it, there seem to have been Ice Ages. The Laramide revolution came
in the Cretaceous; and so on.

nius part, that we begin to lose our bearings. The essentials of this part are:

—That the present planet Venus originated from an upheaval on Jupiter's surface, which cast forth a comet.

—That at least once this comet passed disastrously close to the earth, causing meteorite falls, clouds of colored dust, and rains of petroleum (the Biblical "naphtha"), of "manna" (an edible organic compound or group of them), and of "vermin" (insects).

—That the comet Venus induced changes in the earth's rate and/or direction of rotation and released huge lightninglike discharges of static electricity between its own head and tail, or between itself and earth (the Biblical "pillars of fire").

—That later it disturbed Mars' orbit, causing the latter body to approach near enough to us to set off a second round of disasters.

—That finally Venus settled into an orbit of its own, and the solar system into its present, deceptively stable state.

One result of all this commotion (which included the parting of the Red Sea), was evidently to prepare the Jewish people by successive trials for its future spiritual leadership of mankind. Does Dr. Velikovsky intend us to see the hand of the Almighty at work here? He does not say so straight out, but the suggestion is clear (see above, pages 160–61).

What are we to make of his hypothesis that Venus was once a comet and only in very recent historical times became a planet? Even after she joined the great stars, Velikovsky says, she retained some of her cometlike characteristics. The people of pre-Columbian Mexico called her "the star that smoked"; according to the Chaldeans she had a beard or, alternatively, was "the bright torch of heaven." "The people of faraway Samoa, primitive tribes that depend on an oral tradition . . . repeat to this day: 'The planet Venus became wild and horns grew out of her head.'"

However, the popular historian Will Durant, in *The Story of Civilization*, cites George Sarton to the effect that "as far back as 2000 B.C." the Babylonians made "accurate records of the heliacal rising of Venus." Durant also mentions the great ziggurat at Borsippa, built in seven steps, representing the five visible planets, the moon, and the sun. Borsippa predated Assyria, since its library was copied and incorporated into that of Assurbanipal (669–626 B.C.). Lockyer says: ". . . It is well known that from the very earliest times pyramidal structures, called ziggurats, some 150 feet high, were erected in each important city [in Babylonia and in Sumeria]. These were really observatories; they were pyramids built in steps, as is clearly shown from pictures found on contemporary tablets; and one with seven steps, and of great antiquity, it is known, was restored by Nebuchadnezzar II about 600 B.C. at Babylon." Lockyer thinks that the very old step pyramids in Egypt may have been patterned on Babylonian models;* all of which suggests that the Babylonians had begun observing the planet Venus at least five hundred years before Velikovsky tells us they could have done so. And if the symbolism of the seven steps, like the ziggurat itself, dates from the Sumerians, who go back to 3600 B.C. or earlier, then Venus may have been in her present orbit for roughly the past 5,600 years.

Though Velikovsky does not tell us where he got the idea that Venus originated as a comet, ejected from Jupiter during some calamity on that planet, one can think of several facts that might have led him to it. There is, for example, what is known as Jupiter's family of comets, defined as including forty percent of the hundred or more comets having well-established orbits.† While there is nothing to indicate that these *originated* on Jupiter, more than half have orbits that bring them within 15 million miles of it; and one comet, Lexell's, which had a period of 5.5 years in 1770, "subsequently made a close approach to Jupiter and has never since been seen." Perhaps this suggested to the doctor a similar event in reverse: a launching instead of a crash.

---

* And Flinders Petrie tells us that the pyramid at Medum—"the first true pyramid"—was stepped seven times. If this was not sheer coincidence but an imitation of the ziggurat, it implies that Venus was one of the planets quite early in the Pyramid Age, or roughly 3000 B.C.
† Robert H. Baker, *Astronomy*, pp. 225–26. There is also the fact that Jupiter has a number of satellites (some quite large) and a very turbulent atmosphere. In the nineteenth century it was thought to be hot; now the view is that it is cold. Its mass is 388 times the earth's, and it receives about 4 percent as much solar radiation per square mile.

The present evidence is that comets do not contain planetary amounts of matter. The astronomer Raymond A. Lyttleton, for instance, says that "even the largest of them if compressed solid would probably make a ball of rock only a mile or two in diameter." A current hypothesis suggests that some fifty astronomical units out, beyond the farthest known planet, we may have a comet belt, which serves as a reservoir from which "new" comets appear as their orbits are perturbed—for instance, by a passing star. Some astronomers think that members of the solar system, excepting Jupiter and Saturn, "froze out" of the sun's "rotating disk of gas" as collections of smaller bodies which later accreted into their present forms, including not only planets, but the asteroids, comets, and some satellites.*

So again, one is left with a view of matters quite different from Velikovsky's. Comets may represent a truncated form of the accreting process which generated the solar system as a whole. And while comets could have come together to produce a planet, there is no evidence at present that any planet came apart to produce a comet. Secondly, the evidence as to the mass of comets makes it unlikely, though perhaps not impossible, that one of them could have had the effects on the earth's rotation which the doctor has proposed. For example, in 1770 Lexell's comet came within one and a half million miles of us. If its mass had been only one ten-thousandth of the earth's, astronomers calculate that it would have changed the length of the year by over a second; but there was no change at all.

The conclusion is that we have no grounds for supposing that Jupiter, at least in the present stage of the solar system's evolution, ever gave birth to a comet; and even if it had done so, the chances that the comet itself would have had a mass equal to that of Venus (81.4 percent of the earth's) seem very small. For one

* No scientist would say a comet *couldn't* be as big as Venus in mass. He would just say none so far has come close to it. Nor would he say (as Velikovsky implies) that the solar system couldn't be seriously perturbed by an errant mass. It's just that the evidence so far is that the solar system hasn't been perturbed for the past few thousand years. So the crux of Velikovsky's argument is his contention that contrary evidence exists: that Venus was not in the sky in her present place until quite recently.

thing, no observed comet has come anywhere near that size; for another, if Jupiter had ejected such a quantity of matter, its own orbit might very well have been noticeably perturbed.* Between that and the wanderings of comet Venus among the other planets, it is quite conceivable that the whole solar system would have been disarranged, so that star maps made before the Velikovskian revolution would have shown the planets standing in relations to each other and to the fixed stars quite different from those we see today.

Since the evidence for a disarrangement of the heavens in pre-Christian times appears none too strong, another approach might be to concede that the convulsions Velikovsky reports may actually have occurred, but from conventional causes. A shower of exceptionally large meteorites or even falls of single big ones could have resulted in many of the events reported by the ancients. Here, for instance, is an account of the great Tunguska meteorite:

> At 7:00 on June 20, 1908, in fair weather, a large bolide or fireball was observed flying from south to north through the cloudless sky over the Yenissei River basin in Central Siberia. After the fall of the mass, a column of fire rose over the taiga; it was observed in Kirensk . . . at a distance of 400 km. The appearance of the "column of fire" was followed by three or four powerful claps and a crashing sound which were recorded over radii of more than 1000 kilometers, and by powerful air waves. The blast caused a radial windfall of trees . . . to a distance of several dozen kilometers from the point of the fall. . . . Eyewitnesses related that individual trees were felled in the vicinity of Vanovara. . . . In Kirensk . . . fences were torn up; in Kezhma, grain loaders were thrown off their feet; in Kansk, 600 kilometers away, rafters were cast

---

* Jupiter's mass being close to 400 times that of the earth, that might not be a factor, since Venus' mass would be roughly $\frac{(.8)}{400} = .002$ that of Jupiter. However, its escape velocity would have been *very* large, so the event on Jupiter that ejected Venus-to-be must have been an upheaval of some violence—more violent than any we have observed to date, and possibly violent enough to change Jupiter's flight path.

into the river, while south of Kansk, at a distance of 700 kilometers, horses could not stand up. . . . The air waves were so powerful they set in motion microbarographs in North America, as well as in Western Europe; they circled the world and were recorded a second time at Potsdam in Germany.

Throughout the world, seismographs at stations as far from each other as Irkutsk and Tashkent, Tbilisi and Jena, Washington and Java, recorded the powerful earthquake wave caused by the explosion of the meteorite as it struck the earth's crust. . . . The large masses of fine particles of matter sprayed in the atmosphere during the flight of the meteorite and by the explosion when it struck the earth's crust at cosmic speed, created a thick dust layer in the upper strata of the atmosphere, formed "silvery clouds" (luminous clouds) at an altitude of 83–85 kilometers, and dust screens in the ceiling and lower layers of the atmosphere. This produced the remarkable and incomparably beautiful phenomenon known as white nights. They were observed over the territory stretching from the region of the fall to Spain, and from Scandinavia to the Black Sea.*

Interestingly enough, the Tunguska object left no large crater and no meteoritic fragments of any size.

If only one largish bolide or smallish comet could produce such startling effects, imagine what disasters, and what a hubbub among the superstitious, a fall of many meteorites, or of one exceptionally big one, might touch off. Such falls are known to have occurred, and studies are beginning to show that the earth, like the moon, has been struck in the past by some extraordinarily large chunks of matter. To date, the biggest "fossil" meteorite crater seems to be the Vredefort Dome in South Africa, which is 75 miles in diameter with a granite core 25 miles across. The volume of crushed rock in the vicinity has been estimated at 200 cubic *miles*, and there is no evidence that volcanic activity was in any way involved. A multiple fall of smaller meteorites occurred in southwest Africa, where "at least 65 masses totaling over 20 tons

* L. A. Kulik, "The Tunguska Meteorite," from *Source Book in Astronomy.*

are known to have been found in an area of several hundred square miles."*

Had it fallen in historic times, the object that created the Vredefort Dome might have been seen by many people as it entered the atmosphere, and its impact might well have caused temblors and related events—far more serious ones than the Tunguska meteorite did. Thus in addition to the fact that comets or falling bolides often create an awesome spectacle, there may be firmer grounds for the almost global tradition that regards such phenomena as bad omens. Moreover, since the Tunguska object created great amounts of dust, a much bigger one, or a swarm of smaller meteorites, could possibly have produced a haze of particles sufficient to shroud the sun for some time—an event capable of spoiling harvests, causing rainfalls tinted with iron oxide ("rains of blood"), and plunging the earth into a portentous gloom. My point is that many features of the old tales of cosmic disaster do not require that we invent a special agency such as the comet Venus to explain them.

Having invented that agency, however, Velikovsky is prepared to invest it with quite extraordinary powers. In *Worlds* he tells us "the rain of fire-water contributed to the earth's supply of petroleum; rock oil in the ground appears to be partly at least 'star oil' brought down at the close of world ages, notably the age that came to its end in the middle of the second millennium before the present era."

How did petroleum come to be present in the comet Venus? Here is the explanation: "The tails of comets are composed mainly of carbon and hydrogen gases. Lacking oxygen they do not burn in flight, but the inflammable gases, passing through an atmosphere containing oxygen, will be set on fire. If carbon or hydrogen gases *or a vapor of a composition of these two elements*† enter

---

* See Menzel, *et al.*, Bibliography.
† Comets, according to Menzel *et al.*, have "dust tails" or "ion tails." Unless adsorbed on solid matter, free hydrogen is probably not present in them, since its freezing point is too close to Absolute Zero for it to be part of the icy head. Spectral analysis shows comets to contain heavier elements (silicon, calcium, nickel, etc.), along with simple molecules made up of carbon, hydrogen, oxygen, and nitrogen.

the atmosphere in large masses, a part of them will burn, binding all the oxygen available at the moment; the rest will escape combustion, *but in swift transition* will become liquid." (Italics added.) This liquid is, of course, crude oil, some of which then sinks into rock formations, to be discovered centuries later by Texaco and others.

But what does the phrase "in swift transition" mean? The reference is obviously to some set of chemical reactions by which, under the conditions described, the simple molecules or free radicals of the comet became the hydrocarbons found in petroleum. What are these reactions?

The mystery surrounding the synthesis of manna is even deeper, since it is supposed to have consisted of carbohydrates, which contain oxygen and are furthermore quite combustible. If manna came in on comet Venus at high velocity it would (as Velikovsky suggests in the case of carbon and hydrogen) have burned up. Lightning discharges in an oxygen-free atmosphere could not produce it, by definition. Where did the manna come from, then?

Velikovsky tells us it was formed while the "veil of gloom" lay over the world following the catastrophe. It was evidently both liquid (nectar) and solid (ambrosia) and could be baked into bread, used for cattle feed, stored for future use, or even applied as an unguent or cologne. Was it synthesized by some sort of catalytic molecule-building process in the upper atmosphere after comet Venus had passed? If so, we are not told what the process was, merely that it was at work.

On the matter of "vermin," Velikovsky notes that old reports of cosmic catastrophes often include references to plagues of hornets, frogs, serpents, and the like. He adds that "the internal heat developed by the earth and the scorching gases of the comet were in themselves sufficient to make the vermin of the earth propagate at a very feverish rate. . . . The question arises here whether or not the comet Venus infested the earth with vermin which it may have carried in its trailing atmosphere in the form of larvae together with stones and gases. It is significant that all around the world peoples have associated the planet Venus with flies."

SPEAKING OF FLYING OBJECTS . . .

(Earlier he mentions that "after the close of the Middle Kingdom, the Egyptian standard bore the emblem of a fly." The logic of this move, if it is relevant, is hard to follow. Why would the post-catastrophe Egyptians adopt a reminder of that dreadful era as one of their national symbols? And in any case, if Venus became universally associated with flies, why should we assume these were not ordinary earth flies, of which Egypt has unusually large numbers even today?)

Velikovsky sums up his vermin hypothesis as follows: "Modern biologists toy with the idea that micro-organisms arrive on earth from interstellar spaces. . . . Whether there is truth in this supposition of larval contamination of the earth is anyone's guess. The ability of many small insects and their larvae to endure great cold and heat and to live in an atmosphere devoid of oxygen renders not entirely improbable the hypothesis that Venus (and also Jupiter from which Venus sprang), may be populated by vermin."

He omits to note that, Venus having passed at least as close to the sun as the earth does (since it nearly collided with us), any larvae traveling on the rocks in its tail must have been exposed to stiff doses of ultraviolet and cosmic radiation, and that for reasonably long periods.* Moreover, he postulates great head-to-tail electrical discharges in the comet itself, which cannot have favored the survival on it of life in any form—larval, encysted, or hidden as chance inclusions in rock. Most scientists or professional scholars would say, I imagine, that once you had gotten as far as proposing that Venus was recently a comet wandering around in the solar system, any hypothesis you tacked onto that one was perfectly okay. I still find that these additions of Velikovsky's bother me almost more than the Venus-as-comet theory itself.

One line of evidence crucial to Velikovsky's theory is that relating to the arrangement of the heavens prior to the two eras of catastrophe he is talking about. In *Pensée* he has a paper describ-

* The errant period of Venus, according to him, lasted at least from the fifteenth to the seventh century B.C., and (since he gives no data on its flight path) may well have included quite close approaches to the sun.

ing the work lately done by an astronomer, Professor Gerald Hawkins, which purported to show that Stonehenge was (and still can be) used to sight the sun on the morning of the summer solstice (June 21). Moreover, Hawkins said, a ring of 56 holes, known as the Aubrey or X holes, had been used of old to predict lunar eclipses—adding that he and other modern astronomers had learned of a 56-year cycle in lunar eclipses from those holes.

But then, Velikovsky reports, Hawkins' work was demolished by an archaeologist and recognized expert on Stonehenge, Professor R. J. C. Atkinson, who maintained, in effect, that Hawkins' measurements were made from maps not accurate enough for the purpose, and that in addition he forced his evidence, such as it was, in order to achieve a fit with his theory. Moreover, the lunar-eclipse cycle is not 56 but 65 years long. According to Atkinson, Stonehenge was not built in any one period, but pulled down and rearranged some five times over an interval of 400 years. Later rings (the Y and Z holes) were made but, says Atkinson ". . . For some reason, *perhaps an unforeseen catastrophe* or an unlucky omen, the project was abandoned unfinished. . . . The date of this final reconstruction is not known for certain; but it seems likely that . . . Stonehenge as we see it today was already complete by 1400 B.C." (Italics added).

Velikovsky interprets Atkinson's account as meaning that the Stonehenge people had had to rebuild because of repeated changes in the heavens, giving up at last around the time, according to Velikovsky, when *the* big disaster—the brush with the comet Venus—took place. He is quite insistent on the need for more astronomical evidence on this point. In the library of Assurbanipal, he tells us, there are clay tablets that show the length of the day, month, and year, and the positions of the moon and the planets, to be all "wrong" by modern standards. He suggests that these and other ancient reports be studied in parallel; the data might even be computerized so as to turn up hidden regularities among them.* In this way we might discover whether Venus really was

* Here are some calculations I made myself. It is known that the "obliquity of the ecliptic," or tilt of the earth's axis relative to its plane of rotation, is de-

missing from the heavens prior to about 1500 B.C., and the heavens themselves reversed, as in Senmut's star map. If only because of the fuss there has been over his work, that study should certainly be made. One would still like to know how, if the earth was as convulsed as it must have been in those days, Stonehenge managed to stand up at all.

Since publishing *Worlds* in 1950, Velikovsky has evidently devoted himself to certain problems in astrophysics that are crucial to his theory. In the May, 1972, issue of *Pensée* he has, for example, a paper about the moon. The glazes on moon rocks and the thermal gradient found below its surface should be such, he said, as could have been caused by quite recent heating of that body (i.e., by comet Venus). "The 'extremely fresh' appearance of the interior of all crystalline lunar rocks; the vitrification of a large proportion of the lunar soil; the volatilization and transfer of lead; the glazing of the rocks that must be of recent date; the thermoluminescence studies indicating thermal disturbances in historical times;* and the steep thermal gradient [below the surface] that bewilders researchers; all point to the fact that the thermal history of the moon is not what it was thought to be only a few years ago."

On the question of remanent magnetism in moon rocks, which Velikovsky attributes to heating by comet Venus in the presence of that body's magnetic field, Robert Treash, in the same issue of *Pensée*, says: "The remanent (or 'fossil') magnetism of the lunar

creasing at the rate of about 1' every 128 years. The obliquity now is approximately 23°27'. Thom, a student of European megalithic observatories (probably contemporaneous with Stonehenge), calculated from their orientation what the obliquity back then must have been, and came up with an average value of 23°54.3'. This gives us an average date for the period when the megaliths may have been in use, which turns out to be about 1520 B.C. This is in fair agreement with the dates given by Atkinson for the later periods of Stonehenge. The question is, if Velikovsky's theory is correct, would one have been able to run through these calculations and come up with a result that made sense?
* Apparently a thermoluminescence study made on Apollo 12 cores indicated, in the words of the official report, "anomalies resulting from disturbances ≳10,000 years ago." Unless misprinted, the symbol means "approximately equal to or greater than"—which is a fit of sorts, but a rough one, with Velikovsky's prediction.

surface was confirmed on the rocks brought back from the sites of all subsequent Apollo missions." (Subsequent, apparently, to Apollo 12.) It was concluded that that magnetism could not have resulted from an approach of the moon to earth, since the approach would have had to be close enough to bring the moon within the "Roche limit," at which it would supposedly have begun to break up. According to Treash: "Another team of scientists found that the magnetization 'shows a well-defined Curie temperature at 775°': the lunar surface must have been heated above this temperature in the presence of a magnetic field and must have cooled off thereafter. (To melt the rock, a temperature of over 1200°C is needed.)" Treash evidently thinks there is something to the Venus hypothesis. Still other scientists appear to be coming around to Velikovsky's oil-from-the-sky hypothesis. The most spectacular example, given in *Pensée*, is a paper by A. T. Wilson, published in *Nature*,* which "claimed an extraterrestrial origin for *all* earth's oil."

Well, now. What is happening? Are scientists (as *Pensée* says) trying out some of Velikovsky's ideas without acknowledging that that is what they are doing? May we be in for a surprise, when the astronomical data from Assurbanipal's library and other ancient sources are decoded and compared? Will mountain building, as Velikovsky implies in *Worlds*, turn out to have been the result of a long succession of extraterrestrial visitations? Were frozen mammoths and fossils the result of catastrophes which suddenly shifted the geographic poles, or produced instant folding or fissuring of the earth's surface? Are the well-known discontinuities in the evolutionary record due to the same cause? Maybe so, but one would like more details; and then there's the business about manna and vermin. Is it mere prejudice that makes one distrust the work of a man who seems so sober and scholarly at one minute and so irresponsible the next?

When Velikovsky says things such as the following, I become uneasy: "If this unorthodox view [of Venus, etc.] is substantiated, it will bear greatly not only on many fields of science but also on

* *Nature* (1962, 196:11–13).

the phenomenon of repression of racial memories, with all the implications as to man's irrational behavior." What is a racial memory—a set of traces literally inherited (and so comparable to an instinct), or a tradition? If the latter, "repression" of a racial memory would simply mean that it ceased to be handed down,* while if we assume the former, we have the problem of showing that inherited memory traces exist to begin with—a question that psychiatrists like Jung have never bothered to settle. There is, I believe, little evidence that they do exist. We may inherit "learning dispositions" but not specific recollections. So when Velikovsky amplifies this remark in *Pensée* by saying, "The cause of the opposition to me was in great part psychological: my critics could not accept my bringing their unconscious to consciousness," I can only conclude that he is talking rubbish.

There is still another aspect of his work that troubles me. We live in an age that appears to crave simplifications. For all the labor which went into it, and which he has expended in its later defense and elaboration, Velikovsky's theory is itself a radical simplification. He takes the legends of various civilizations quite literally—to the point of using them as an argument for drastically revising accepted historical time schedules—and proceeds from there to an apparently arbitrary set of assumptions concerning the origin and wanderings of the planet Venus.

In turn, that suggested to the doctor a truly monolithic hypothesis—one which, he hints, accounts not only for folktales of the flood, war in heaven, etc., but for most or all geologic revolutions in the earth's past. Thanks to his cometary *deus ex machina*, fossils and frozen mammoths are now explained; the Sumerian account of the deluge too, presumably; and the story of Oannes who came from the sea, bringing all the arts of man with him.

Because he was such a simplifier, solving all sorts of intricate problems at a stroke and never lingering over the odd-shaped fact (petroleum, during Venus' passage, was formed "in a swift transition"; the "texts found in the pyramids" tell of events that hap-

---

* But then, by his account, racial memories *are* handed down, as stories of world calamities.

pened centuries later), Velikovsky was a great hit with the general public. *That* was the kind of history-cum-geology-cum-astronomy they'd always wanted, and which no schoolmaster or nit-picking professor would ever give them: straightaway stuff, ticking off the riddles of the past, one two three! No need to stop and rack your brains. Just listen to the old doc, he's got it all together—and what a downer for those scientists. No wonder they were mad, the way he showed them up.

The success of *Worlds* was Everyman's revenge on a world of intellect he never made and now would as soon be done with. For the literary sort—critics such as Clifton Fadiman—it perhaps represented a triumph of humane understanding over the barbarian mechanic: a mere scholar *shlepping* around in libraries, Velikovsky had beaten the measurers and calculators at their own game. For readers who had never much liked poetry or myths he had something too: he showed that legends were fact—not tedious inventions, but reportage; he brought the old tales, as it were, back to life. For the impatient he provided drama: none of your slow wrinkling and wearing away of the globe, but a series of super-spectacles—lightning, holocausts, the Chosen People scurrying through the parted waters. Even his book titles were boffo, perfect for a marquee:

DOUBLE FEATURE   TODAY ONLY

EARTH IN UPHEAVAL—AGES IN CHAOS

The more one gets involved with this strange man's work and his even stranger reputation, the more one wonders about him. He did make some predictions that were borne out—rather unexpectedly, too. Nor can one dismiss his theories merely because they are radical simplifications. Any theory is a simplification, which aims to show the order underlying diverse and puzzling events. Most theories, however, are wrong, and much minute effort is needed to establish whether they are or aren't. The issue, in Velikovsky's case, is responsibility. Is it responsible to say, "I have a theory that explains everything (lots of things)" until I have worked out the details? People like Einstein and Newton do it analytically, which is to say by mathematics; but even in words, much more care is possible than Velikovsky appears to take.*

Unlike Lockyer, a professional astronomer, who developed his ideas about Egyptian temple orientations in a most painstaking way, Velikovsky draws up no tentative tables of dates showing which documents fit into his time scheme and which don't. He seldom says such-and-such *may* have happened (Venus *may* have been a comet); he says it did happen (Venus *was* a comet). He does not deal in approximations, but is vague and dogmatic by turns. When the facts seem to be with him, he is quite the precise scholar, only to turn oratorical and evasive when in the final pages of *Worlds* the time for a grand summation comes. As primal patricide was to Freud, comet Venus is to him, the hook on which all else hangs but which, like the doctrine of the Virgin Birth, is itself beyond question. Is science, after three centuries, trying to take on the characteristics of a revealed religion? Is that what the violent division of opinion over Velikovsky is really about? Do we want to start "doing" science the way things are done by the new priesthood of the couch? And was it a certain concealed ambition in the doctor which led him to play to that impulse, addressing himself to a mass audience first and letting the aristocrats of intellect fulminate and make fools of themselves trying to stop him?

He is hard to fathom. He seems such a saintly dogged old party, a model of reasonableness at times. And one must grant him a certain wild originality. As a thinker he is certainly not afraid to take chances. Whether or not he has genius, he has the daring that is said to go with it. One feels that he is a misplaced and somehow corrupted theologian whom the times have encouraged

---

* Here again his psychoanalytic background may have had an effect on him. The dogmatism of analysts, the extreme reluctance of the profession to test its own basic presuppositions, is irresponsible in the sense meant here. Freud's career indeed began with a prophetic episode—a paper he wrote advocating the use of cocaine. When statistics on addiction to the drug (then relatively new to Europeans) began to come in, this enthusiasm of Freud's turned out to have been premature. According to Jones, his biographer, Freud did not make a public retraction and let it go at that. He appears to have suppressed his earlier paper, thus compounding his original hastiness with—what shall we say?

to become a Terrible Simplifier in the realm of ideas. At that, some of his conclusions (for instance, concerning the surface temperature of Venus) may turn out to have been more accurate than some of Freud's (for instance, concerning the universality of the Oedipus complex). What people unfamiliar with science do not usually understand is the principle enunciated by Poincaré— namely, that any number of theories can be devised to account for the same phenomenon. It is the *range* of things a theory can account for that determines its acceptability; and it goes without saying that its basic postulates must be at least plausible and its supporting data sound. Velikovsky, and even parts of Freud, do not meet these standards.

The great appeal of the quack, in revolutionary ages, is to the emotionally volatile majority who have come to hold a grudge against the whole world of culture, seeing in it nothing but a form of conspicuous consumption. The presumption is that those who become cultured do so not out of respect for an ideal or from a love of ideas, but simply to show off—to make their ignorant fellows feel worthless and excluded. Reason, on which the scientific part of our culture rests, has no great appeal at the best of times. Its results are too hard come by and even then do not yield the kind of certainty most of us demand. Therefore we dislike it, welcoming anyone who can make understanding seem easier and especially anyone who, in doing so, debunks the more cheerless forms of it—the laborious life of reason itself. Velikovsky is to us what the outsider savants were to the French public of 1785: an intuitive and a protorevolutionary whose struggle with the Establishment we feel in some sense to be our own.

In Germany during the rise of the Nazi party in the 1920s, a former engineer named Hans Hörbiger became a similar *cause célèbre* as a result of his strange cosmological theory known as the World Ice Doctrine.* Staring at the sky one night through a portable telescope, Hörbiger suddenly came to an astounding realization: a good deal of the universe, including the Milky Way, is made up of ice. His hypothesis included catastrophic features. A

* See Willy Ley, *Watchers of the Skies.*

184

dead star, composed of ice and heated by the "Star Mother," was (as Willy Ley puts it) "slowly changed into a steam bomb." Nor did Hörbiger omit the war-in-heaven theme. In the preface to the book he wrote with a high school teacher named Fauth, he described their work as "a new cosmogony of the universe and the solar system, based on the realization of a constant battle of a cosmic Neptunism against an equally universal Plutonism."

Like Velikovsky, Hörbiger was slighted by astronomers, but his publisher in Leipzig found his works highly salable. The *Welteislehre*, shortened to WEL, soon became a movement, with a monthly magazine, a lecture circuit, and a national membership which per capita probably equaled or exceeded that of mesmerism in pre-Revolutionary France. His popular appeal was in principle the same as the Nazis', since both traded on the anti-intellectual bias of the masses. However, when the revolution itself came, Hörbiger the (probably sincere) quack, who had cashed in on its imminence, found himself pushed aside, just as Mesmer was in France after 1789. Both had ceased to be relevant for reasons neither apparently understood. (Hörbiger's disciples tried to ally the WEL movement with the Nazis, as their official scientific arm, but Hitler would have none of it.)

Velikovsky apparently does not see himself in this light. For today (1973), after years of excellent book sales and of fame as a hero of the intellectual *sans-culottes*, he seems to be making determined efforts to win the acceptance of orthodox science. Having gotten in, so to speak, through the back door, he wants now to make a final triumphant entry through the front. Academia will never let him get away with it. No matter *how* many of his predictions prove correct, it will see him dead first.* It will maintain,

---

* Back in the disturbed McCarthyite era when *Worlds in Collision* first appeared, some scientists responded with a ferocity that smacked of panic. Macmillan, the original publisher of the book, turned it over to another house, apparently for fear that its line of textbooks would be boycotted if it continued to support and make money out of a work that academicians found so outrageous. It is important to recall that this masterpiece of the New Nonsense came along just at a time when academics, as such, found themselves under attack as literal, or crypto-, Communists—when the whole Republic of Letters felt itself threatened by a public animosity of quite unexpected scope.

with some justice, that even his historical first premise is absurd; if one is to take all the old legends at face value, then to judge from Chinese mythology alone, the heavens must have been in an uproar for centuries. The ancient Chinese represented every conjunction of heavenly bodies as a battle, and according to Needham, there was a time, during the reign of the emperor Yao, when ten suns were seen in the sky at once! What are we to make of reports like that? Perhaps in some later volume Dr. Velikovsky will tell us.

PART THREE

ix

Lawrence and
the New Psychological Poor

If Velikovsky, both in the character of his work and in its reception, represents the disordered common sense of today, D. H. Lawrence, a far abler and more talented man, prophesied that downturn in events as long as sixty years ago, in his violent rejection of the Renaissance ideal of rationality. The curious thing is that Lawrence, for all his vehemence, and notwithstanding that unreason was fundamental to his own theories of art and the Good Life, was never entirely consistent on this point. Mostly he regarded mind—"*knowing*"—as a crime against the flesh, the beginning of a division within the self whose final result was to destroy it. In *Introduction to These Paintings* he tells us that the Renaissance in England was the time when Chaucerian wholesomeness died away and the corruption of everything by thought began:

"The real 'mortal coil' in Hamlet is all sexual; the young man's horror of his mother's incest, sex carrying with it a wild and nameless terror which, it seems to me, it had never carried before . . . He is horrified at the merest suggestion of physical connexion, as if it were an unspeakable taint." This, no doubt, is all in the course of the growth of the "spiritual-mental" consciousness at the expense of the instinctive-intuitive consciousness.*

---

* However, to judge from such contemporary documents as Pepys's and Boswell's diaries, sexual life in the seventeenth and eighteenth centuries in England was pretty vigorous, even by modern standards, so the pale cast of thought that Lawrence says it acquired in Shakespeare's time cannot have been too lasting, unless one sees the Victorian Age as a delayed outbreak of the same disorder.

In short, as their tradition matures and men attain to "spiritual-mental consciousness," there is no improvement in their inner harmony. On the contrary, relations among the Freudian trinity—Ego, Superego, and Id—stay fundamentally the same. Conscience becomes no less blind and the instinct no less inhuman or despotic. All that happens is that conscience (thanks to that gadfly, mind) becomes morbidly inflamed, and so more blind and tyrannical than ever, the result not being to make people more moral but only to make such natural acts as lovemaking seem suddenly monstrous and disgusting. Vacillation, a profound loss of gut certainty, above all a poisonous awareness of self, an appetitive narcissism, become Western Man's distinguishing characteristics thereafter. We are all Hamlet today—an idea that disciples of Lawrence such as Henry Miller have turned into one of the clichés of the avant-garde. But elsewhere, Lawrence appears to gainsay his own doctrine. In his "Study of Thomas Hardy" (*Phoenix*, p. 454) he tells us:

> During the medieval times God had been Christ on the Cross, the Body Crucified, the flesh destroyed, the Virgin Chastity combating desire. Such had been the God of Aspiration. . . . *But now, with the Renaissance, the God of Aspiration became in accord with the God of Knowledge, and there was a great outburst of joy,* and the theme was not Christ Crucified but Christ born of woman, the Infant Savior and the Virgin; or of the Annunciation, the Spirit embracing the flesh in a pure embrace. [Italics added.]

But the "God of Aspiration . . . in accord with the God of Knowledge" comes down to the ideal I mentioned earlier—the Renaissance concept of Universal Man, in whom the full development of the waking self through culture or the "humanities" produced a being not only worthy at last to be called human but one *less* at war with himself than in past ages he had been. This, indeed, had been the hope that underlay the moral strivings of the Middle Ages—"the Virgin Chastity combating desire," not so much because desire in itself is bad as because, like the other instincts, it acts when poorly controlled to debase us, plunging us into inner struggles we invariably lose, reducing us to automata. Likewise fear or anger, to which the Christian solution was forgiveness. Only forgive and thou shalt see. Only possess thy (given, automatic) self and thou shalt be no longer possessed.

So in the Renaissance, as *l'uomo universale* began to be a hope and in some small degree a reality, there was, says Lawrence, "a great outburst of joy," and properly so. For by then the long, if often betrayed and perverted, effort at man's inner improvement which had been the declared object of Christianity was showing signs that it might work, which in turn meant that mankind might, in a very real sense, be delivered—that a humane, imaginative lucidity might one day lie within reach of all. What had lately proved possible for a handful of the privileged could conceivably—in some future world, in which everyone was educated and culture had been made widely available—become a way of life for millions. The psychological stunting to which a majority of men had had to submit since the beginning of history* might at last come to an end and an era of freedom in the truest sense set in—a Golden Age in which Everyman, to the limit of his native abilities (and regardless of class) might enlarge the powers of his waking self to the point at which he was fully human.

A similar idea underlay Jeffersonian democracy. Essentially it presumed that the process begun in the remote Christian past had gone far enough so that now Everyman *was* human—which is to say, no longer the beastly lout he had been in the Middle Ages, but a rationally self-possessed being, capable of deciding who should govern him, what form his institutions should take, and how and on what scale his children should be educated.† Justice at law, greater consideration for the weak or the afflicted, con-

* Either because no culture existed or because, when it did, they had neither access to it nor the leisure they would have needed in order to develop with its help.
† Hence it is no paradox that eighteenth-century aristocrats such as Jefferson were precursors of modern egalitarianism, although in its present form it might have shaken their faith in the rational ideal which appeared to underlie their political convictions.

cessions in general to those who lacked the power to exact them—in a word, liberalism, in the sense in which Ortega y Gasset understood the word fifty years ago—were natural descendants of the union of the "God of Aspiration" with the "God of Knowledge."

But clearly as, for the moment, he seemed to see it, Lawrence was too much the child of his times to allow the vision to stick. To him, "spiritual-mental consciousness"—knowing or, worse still, the *craving* to know—was the archenemy; and strangely enough, the part of the Western world in which he appears to have found that craving most intense was America. This theme crops up repeatedly in his *Studies of Classic American Literature*.

Poe's Ligeia is a woman hollowed out and turned into a thing—in the end, literally killed—by her lover's obscene determination to know her, not in the old, straightforward Biblical sense, but in the sense of possessing her totally in his consciousness. This knowing, Lawrence says, is a way of murdering the beloved. "To *know* a living thing is to kill it. You have to kill a thing to know it satisfactorily. For this reason, the desirous consciousness, the *spirit*, is a vampire. . . . Beware oh woman of the man who wants to *find out who you are*." (Italics original.)

Though millions of people now evidently have the same idea, believing that to see with the eye of the mind somehow kills, Lawrence's way of putting it is surely a bit extreme. How exactly did being *known* kill Ligeia? His implied use of science as an illustration of the thought-equals-murder theorem is equally absurd. A common complaint against biologists is that they chop up the subjects of their interest, giving us "dead" knowledge. The truth is that while postmortem studies are often necessary and of great value (how else, for instance, is one to discover such things as the fine structure of the brain, information possibly of some ultimate value to our self-understanding?), biologists have lately put much effort and ingenuity into finding ways of studying the behavior or the internal processes of living things as nearly as possible under "physiological" conditions—*in vivo* and undisturbed. The ethologists in particular have developed a considerable delicacy of approach, observing animals in the wild and at long range so as minimally to disturb their natural behavior. The problem is in fact an "operational" one common to all the sciences: how to study the motions of nature in a way that will least interfere with them. To know is not necessarily to kill the known, but may be to impinge upon and therefore distort it, a great deal of the tact of science being aimed to avoid just that.

Lawrence, however, is no more consistent on this point than on any other. In one breath he tells us that "surely all material things have a *form* of sentience . . . some subtle and complicated tension of vibration which makes them sensitive to external influence and causes them to have an effect on other external objects, irrespective of contact." Eight pages earlier in the same essay (on Poe), he advises us: "Keep *knowledge* for the world of matter, force, and function. It has got nothing to do with being." But if objects *have* being—a "form of sentience" connecting all to each— then either knowledge has something to do with being (of a low sort) or nothing to do at all.*

Six pages later, Lawrence is quoting psychoanalysis to the effect that "almost every trouble in the psyche is traced to an incest-desire." He thinks that interpretation too narrow; but he at least takes psychoanalysis seriously enough to dispute it, whereas by his own definition it is not a proper branch of knowledge to begin with and so should be beneath mention. In reality, he may be using it only because of the weight he knows it will have with his audience, since it is clear that he himself has little use for science in any form.

In an essay on Lawrence, Aldous Huxley said: "His dislike of scientists was passionate, and expressed itself in the most fantastically unreasonable terms. 'All scientists are liars' he would say, when I brought up some experimentally established fact which he happened to dislike. 'Liars, liars!' " This dislike did not prevent him from talking quasi-scientifically himself when the mood was on him. In his essay on Poe he tells us:

---

* Which is perhaps really what he intends—to leave it nothing, to destroy it by denying its usefulness in any direction.

Love can be terribly obscene. It is love that causes the neu-
roticism of the day. It is love that is the prime cause of tuberculosis. The nerves that vibrate most intensely in spiritual
unisons are the sympathetic ganglia of the breast, of the
throat and hind brain. Drive this vibration over-intensely and
you weaken the sympathetic tissues of the chest—the lungs—
or of the throat or the lower brain, and the tubercles are given
a ripe field.

No physiologist would be able to make much sense of this passage. In what way, for instance, are the lungs the "sympathetic tissues of the chest"? The heart (often implicated in love) is just as
much so, in that it receives both sympathetic and parasympathetic
fibers of the autonomic nervous system; and the prime innervation
of the sexual organs is *para*sympathetic.*

But since knowledge "has got nothing to do with being," one
should probably not even bring such questions up. Lawrence in
any case is speaking not from nature knowledge but from intuition, a faculty that generates not pedestrian statements of fact
but myths embodying truth. Who cares about strict scientific accuracy if a bit of inspired nonsense—almost, it would seem, admittedly, deliberately that—will take him straight to the heart of
things?

Admitted and deliberate it had to be in Lawrence's case, since
clearly he was anything but stupid. Huxley said of him:

> It was not an incapacity to understand that made him re-
> ject those generalizations and abstractions by means of which
> the philosophers and the men of science try to open a path
> for the human spirit through the chaos of phenomena. Not
> incapacity, I repeat; for Lawrence had, over and above his
> peculiar gift, an extremely acute intelligence. He was a clever
> man as well as a genius. . . . He could have understood the
> aim and methods of science perfectly well if he had wanted

---

* Ejaculation, however—the temporary terminus of lovemaking—is controlled
by sympathetic fibers (of the hypogastric plexus).

In speaking of nervous tissue as vibrating (which it does chiefly in an
electrical sense), Lawrence anticipates the current emphasis on "vibes."

to. Indeed he did understand them perfectly well; and it was for that very reason he rejected them. For the methods of science and philosophy were incompatible with the exercise of his gift—the immediate perception and artistic rendering of divine otherness.

The "otherness" Huxley means is that within. For Lawrence, he says,

> the significance of the sexual experience was this: that in it, the immediate non-mental knowledge of divine otherness is brought, so to speak, to a focus—a focus of darkness. . . . We may say that sex is something not ourselves that makes for . . . life, for divineness, for union with the mystery. Paradoxically this something not ourselves is yet a something lodged within us; this quintessence of otherness is yet the quintessence of our proper being. "And God the Father, the Inscrutable, the Unknowable, we know in the flesh, in woman. . . . In her we go back to the Father; but like the witnesses of the transfiguration, blind and unconscious." Yes, blind and unconscious; otherwise it is a revelation not of divine otherness but of very human evil.

But the "otherness" within us is not, of course, just sexual. It is all of the Id, including the instinct for survival, which moves us through fear or its complement, anger, and the instinct for self-maintenance, which will let us think of nothing but eating or drinking as we become acutely hungry or thirsty. Why do we not experience God the Father, the Inscrutable, in these as well? Why is a good dinner not as much of a divine union as a night in bed with the beloved?

The answer, I should think, is obvious. Except for an eccentric few, gourmet meals are not as keen a pleasure; they do not, to the same degree as sexual passion, convulse us with delight. Nor do the passions arising out of our survival instinct. A minority of men—many of them Germans, but also including our own Ernest Hemingway and professional groups such as test pilots, high-wire artists, policemen and sky divers—find the contest with fear, or fear itself, pleasurable, some defeating it by coolness and skill, others by converting it into a hot or cold ferocity. These same groups often develop a mystique of danger and death and sacrifice for the Fatherland, of a brutal "biker"-style *machismo*, of plain stoicism; but the exaltation is never quite what it is in sex— basically, one suspects, because the sensory returns are not as great. In fact, as has often been noted, it is those in some way deficient or damaged in their erotic lives who are apt to be drawn to the careers mentioned—who turn hotly or coldly ferocious, who court death rather than mates, who back into orgasm by way of inflicted or endured pain, or who console themselves by stuffing at the dinner table.

To talk of sex as *the* mystery is *kitsch*. All being is mysterious, and if it takes the Big "O" to make us aware of the fact, that is not because sex is somehow magical or transcendent (we "transcend" ourselves in fear or fury too) but simply because we are so deficient in imagination that it takes a crisis of bodily and psychic pleasure to bring us, as it were, to ourselves—to make us poets for fifteen minutes. Sex, in short, for men of declining civilizations, may be a natural substitute for faculties they no longer quite have. It is this epochal process* of which Lawrence was the prophet and passing spokesman—for the deification of sex may be a transitional phenomenon. In old civilizations, long past the stage ours is now in, no such mystic glamour attaches to it. Over the centuries, in China or Islam, it has been merely one among several opiates of the masses. (And indeed, even as we try to glamorize it, sex is becoming as banal among us—a form of therapy or calisthenics or, in the extreme, a secular diabolism: joy-through-degradation. *L'amour fait passer le temps; le temps fait passer l'amour*, say those romantics, the French.)

Early in our history, with the troubadours and Eleanor of Aquitaine, and again today, with the mass production of romance, and finally plain sex, in our movies, in fiction, in popular songs, even in advertising, love-sex became a lodestar and a monomania—then

---

* "Epoch" meaning a beginning or turning point.

because the "I" was just stirring into life, ceasing itself to be a mere function; now perhaps for the opposite reason: because it has begun to lapse into the "otherness" out of which it arose, becoming a slave faculty once more, obedient to the demands of the flesh and the tribe, a function among other functions.

In the twelfth century all the world lay before us, nor had that been the case for long. A bare two hundred years earlier, the Carolingian power had collapsed and Frankish civilization very nearly did likewise. That men not only outlasted that brutal era but emerged from it immensely grown in imagination and sensibility must have seemed to them a sign. God loved His children and had put it within their power to become men. The "I" was to prevail after all.

So, in the same century as the Gothic, there appeared the lovely court culture of Provence; and instead of the mindless rutting which it had been, love, with the help of poets such as Christian of Troyes, became that passion "complicated beyond modern conception" of which Henry Adams wrote long afterward.* As an ideal, it began woman's slow release from chattelhood and subjection to male *force majeure*, by making her, in one sphere at least, all-powerful—Queen of the Boudoir as Mary was the Queen of Heaven. Along with notions of courtesy and the chivalric gentleman, it expressed a hope we had started to have, not of love alone, but of our own humanity. It told, in poetic images, of what our desire and our ferocity might become, sufficiently illumined by awareness of the Other—of how the life of the Id might be transformed by that of the mind.

It was precisely that ideal which Lawrence saw had gone dead among us, and the remains of which he set out, with a singular vindictiveness, to destroy. For in the 1910s and '20s when he was writing, if not in his late-Victorian boyhood, romantic love had become a fraud. Like the cult of youth and pep and "It" of the '20s, it stood for the one thing which, as skeptical materialists, we still felt we could believe in: the happiness of the body. Repre-

* In *Mont-Saint-Michel and Chartres.*

senting no real effort of aspiration, it led naturally to a repulsive sentimental sort of prurience, a *voyeuriste* obsession with what Lawrence called "the dirty little secret." More and more, our lending-library romances and ever-so-clean Boy Meets Girl movies became the thinnest cover for out-and-out obscenity; and that mawkishness, Lawrence maintained, was an obscenity in itself, encouraging us all to become masturbators, trapping us in a world of fantasies we only rarely dared to act out, so that even our sexual behavior with others was often a form of masturbation *à deux*, guilty and feverish and essentially private.

In his view, this was the supreme evil, and mind—*knowing*—was its cause. The cure, he thought, was equally straightforward; to save sex in the bed, sex-in-the-head must go. Love must be made what it had been in the days before the troubadours, "blind and unconscious." And modern man (who mostly never heard of Lawrence) has gone on to do just that, in ways and on a scale Lawrence himself might have found quite amazing.

For in fact Lawrence never fully thought out his ideas. He made no distinction between fantasy and imagination—between mind as an instrument of the libido and mind as a force for transforming it. For him, all awareness was a profanation of the one bit of divinity left to us, the sexual act proper. And in that he anticipated our own ultimate materialism. Back in the '20s, while our popular culture was still pseudo-idealistic, we were already practicing a hard-boiled Doublethink, paying lip service to love while looking for mates who were "compatible" or "good in bed" (and who could always be dumped, at a price, in divorce court when the kicks wore off).

What neither he nor we recognized is that radical egoism, which begins as a reasoned animality, ends as a tic. And just as the fantasies arising out of the Id are incessant and impersonal, so are our love lives coming to be—a development leading in the extreme to the orgy or "polymorphous-perverse" sex romp, in which all present are simply bodies, each available to any other, a largess of *things* like the largess in our supermarkets. For the swinger set, if not for many married people, physical novelty has become a "must," so by mutual agreement, other, more human, considerations have had to be waived. Man the animal must forever be moving on; and man the poet who sang of the unique and essential, who would *know* the Other, and whose knowing Lawrence saw as a crime against the flesh, is ceasing to exist among us.* Far from being a cause of our condition, he is one casualty of it, a sacrifice to the flesh triumphant. Not through poetry but by falsification of it, all that Lawrence so bitterly objected to became possible, along with much else he could hardly have foreseen.

Like Lawrence, the angry, dejected, nonsense-prone children of the '60s were not stupid. The element of "camp"—mocking themselves, mocking existence—showed that in a part of themselves, they knew what they were doing.† In a sense, they understood the situation better than he had, if only because for them it was the more inescapable. Their reliance on sex was, as he might have said, a *pis aller*, of the same sort as their reliance on drugs. Both invited in "otherness" as though the house were almost empty and needed a tenant. No matter how sinister he might turn out to be, he was at least company, breaking the inner monotony, making life real again. Saint Leary had shown the way. For the few who believed the Megamachine could be stopped, there were thousands who merely fled it, creating overnight huge ghettos of their own kind, the New Psychological Poor. But even there, the problem of "communication," of establishing "meaningful relationships," remained,[34] and with it the chemical or sexual addictions which to the hippies seemed the only possible solution.

Lawrence's hopes of sexual love were only slightly more inflated than theirs;‡ and in his attitude toward the "straights" he foretold the Generation Gap and the commune. He was at odds with everyone. The existing order infuriated him. His novels are not

* Literally; our few poets survive on charity and seldom now take love as a major theme.
† As it did in Dada and Surrealism fifty years ago, and does still in Andy Warhol movies; in Nikki de St. Phalle's "action" paintings (and her lover's self-destroying art objects); in John Cage's "composition" consisting of several minutes of silence at the piano; in "paintings" consisting of blank canvases; etc.
‡ But basically in agreement on one point: that "repressions" were bad, leading to most of the war and nastiness in the world.

really about ordinary existence, and his own life was a continual flight from one provincial outpost to another, in none of which could he ever be at peace.

Like Lawrence, the hippies admit a little science when it is convenient. Hi-fi sets and old Volkswagens are parts of technology one can forgive; scientific diets promising long life are also okay, as of course is emergency medical help. But the sort of thinking that originally made these things possible or now causes them to be available to the general public is out. That way lies dehumanization, the vampire knowledge. To *feel* is the thing. Sixty years ago, Lawrence said it:

"My great religion," he was already saying in 1912, "is a belief in the blood, the flesh, as being wiser than the intellect." He forecast us all, and like the seers of modern politics, had the passionate certainty of a man who knew he was onto something—knew it because he was a part of it, a fellow victim, but one triumphing in his own way over his own condition. It was not a stretch of the truth to call him, as some did in the '30s, a fascist, for at bottom the same forces drove him as drove the German revolution. Indeed, as he showed in a remarkable letter written from Germany, probably in 1924, Lawrence saw exactly what was happening in that country.

Immediately you are over the Rhine, the spirit of the place has changed. There is no more attempt at the bluff of geniality. . . . The moment you are in Germany, you know. It feels empty and somehow menacing. So must the Roman soldiers have watched those black massive round hills: with a certain fear, and with a knowledge that they were at their own limit. A fear of the invisible natives . . . of the invisible life lurking among the woods . . . Germany, this bit of Germany, is very different from what it was two and a half years ago when I was here. Then it was still open to Europe. . . . Now that is over. The inevitable, mysterious barrier has fallen again. . . . The positivity of our civilization has broken. . . . So . . . all Germany reads *Beasts, Men and Gods* with a kind of fascination . . .

. . . At night you feel strange things stirring in the darkness, strange feelings stirring out of this still-unconquered
Black Forest. . . . Out of the very air comes a sense of danger, a queer *bristling* feeling of uncanny danger. Something
has happened. Something has happened which has not yet
eventuated. The old spell of the old world has broken . . .
The old adherence has ruptured. And a still older flow has set
in . . . away from the polarity of civilized Christian Europe.
This, it seems to me, has already happened. And it is a happening of far more profound import than any actual *event*.
It is the father of the next phase of events.*

In Heidelberg he found everything, on the surface, as usual.

Students, the same youths with rucksacks in gangs come
down from the hills. The same and not the same. These queer
gangs of *Young Socialists*, youths and girls, with their non-
materialistic professions, their half-mystic assertions, they
strike one as strange. Something primitive, like loose roving
gangs of broken, scattered tribes, so they affect one. And the
swarms of people somehow produce an impression of silence,
of secrecy, of stealth. It is as if everything and everybody re-
coiled away from the old unison, as barbarians lurking in a
wood out of sight. . . . And it all looks as if the years were
wheeling swiftly backwards . . . whirling to the ghost of the
old Middle Ages . . . then to the Roman days, then to the
days of the silent forest and the dangerous lurking barbarians.

Compare this with Ortega y Gasset's observation, made circa
1930, that the modern European "at times leaves the impression of
a primitive man suddenly risen in the midst of a very old civilization." Compare the atmosphere that Lawrence describes in the
Germany of 1924 with the one that developed in this country
during the days of Joseph McCarthy and the Beats, or later, during the Vietnam-war years. Our own young people, in their withdrawal and queer religiosity, their "non-materialistic professions,

* As if to prove him right, the *New Statesman* ran his letter ten years afterward, in 1934, the year of Hitler's Night of the Long Knives.

their half-mystic assertions"—in the restlessness that carried them off from "good homes" to become street people or made them take to the road in droves in their microbuses—struck us as no less strange. They too were like "loose roving gangs of broken scattered tribes";* while still others from the lower social depths began making life in our big cities more dangerous than it had been since the era of the great fighting gangs in New York a century earlier—the Dead Rabbits, or the violent Irish proletariat who devastated the lower city in the so-called Draft Riots of 1863. Such progress as we thought we had made since then seemed suddenly to have gone into reverse. Suspicion of one's neighbors and one's children, of casual passersby (especially young ones in groups); uneasiness as to the future; withdrawal under the "bluff of geniality" into stealthy hatreds and a slow-growing extremism became characteristics of American life during the 1960s, many of them personified in Mr. Nixon himself, the fake-Christian, venomous, nonexistent man.

As Lawrence had, forty-odd years earlier, one felt a "sense of uncanny danger" and it was indeed "as if the years were wheeling swiftly backwards . . . whirling to the ghost of the old Middle Ages . . . then to the days of the silent forest and the dangerous lurking barbarians." Because that was what was happening—although why, neither Lawrence nor anyone else at the time could say.† And as it was in Germany in 1924, it may well be, for us, "the father of the next phase of events."

But there is another side to the matter—namely, the contribution that intellect itself has made to the low esteem in which so many now hold it. It was easy enough to see why Lawrence, the son of a Welsh coal miner, may never have recovered from cer-

---

* Who spoke an increasingly broken and scattered English, and in the "family" of Charles Manson gave us a hint of where the Love Generation might really be headed.

† And having no explanation, many tried to deny that it was happening at all. So sociologists of the period argued over whether youth formed *a* subculture, or several subcultures, or any. Didn't youth *always* rebel? Etc. etc. See, for instance, *Science* 134: 1061–62, 1961.

tain of the psychological handicaps under which he began life. He chose from an intuition of necessity to join the forces of "dark otherness" he could not lick—to deify them, even, but it was never a comfortable worship. His intelligence guaranteed that it could not be. And in his disparagement of mind—in such extreme notions as that knowing amounts to murder—there is more than a hint of revenge.

Whereas H. G. Wells never forgave society the fact of class and what it had cost him, Lawrence may have recognized the graver psychological injustice underlying the material one. Besides money and position, it was the advantages of a gentle upbringing that he had lacked and whose lack had crippled him. Not to have been formed soon enough in mind was as much fate for the poor man as to have been undernourished in body*—and for an intelligent poor man, as Lawrence was, a fate perhaps worse than physical stunting, since it meant that, struggle as he might, the "I" in him would never securely realize itself and so give him peace. Whatever else he may have been, Lawrence was not wise, remaining always the turbulent seer, half of his visions the brilliant truth and half, nonsense.

In just that, Lawrence was modern to the core. It was he, not Hamlet, who was the prototype of us all. Even his dates are significant. His views on the wisdom of the blood he held, Huxley tells us, in 1912, on the eve of World War I, the watershed of our own era—the beginnings of radical egoism and of the progressive retreat and diminution of the "I" that have occurred since. In him, as in us, there is a jealousy not so much of what mind is as of what it might have been. Like him, we revenge ourselves upon an enemy already wounded and failing—on what remains of a promise that never came true. The real complaint of children against their parents today is not that they have been abused in any crude sense (mostly they haven't) but that they have somehow been cheated of themselves. Instead of the fullness they

* And both were suffered by most men of the Renaissance to a degree we can hardly appreciate today, which makes the Renaissance itself all the more remarkable—in a sense, pure promise.

might have expected of life, they find that much that should have had meaning for them has none; much that should have been the keenest of pleasures is mysteriously painful and difficult,* or simply nothing—not "relevant," a blank.

In school, our culture flows through their heads and leaves scarcely a trace. They are "now" people, far more parochial than Lawrence himself, but sophisticated in a thin way, and arrogant as he was—ready to "put down" anything they don't understand. And like Lawrence they are unhappy, as if aware of the real truth. "I see only enough of how I am crippled," wrote Michael Rossman (in the *Wedding Within the War*), "to guess at how much I will not let myself see."

But these, like Lawrence, are the most dramatically penalized, the Bravest and the Best, who feel their impoverishment most acutely because they are often among the most natively intelligent. The gap between the possible and the actual is more evident to them than it is to the run of men, and also a greater threat to their peace of mind, or in the extreme, to their sanity.

For an amorphous good mind, if only because of its greater innate activity, is more prone to disorders arising from conditioning or from the pressures of the Id than is a mediocre or dull one. It fights back—not necessarily with more effect, just more; so the confusion and ultimate destruction of self are apt to be the greater. From this arises the apparent paradox that today in particular our great wits to madness nearly are allied. It is no doubt a risk they run at the best of times, but one seems to read less about it in the London of Gay and Goldsmith; nor was it evidently a major problem among the poets and artists and madrigalists of the Renaissance.

The "creative" type, in short, has always inclined to be "neurotic," but never more so, one feels, than in the twentieth century, the period when everything should have been going its way: when

* Which according to Masters and Johnson is true even of sex. They find our young people struggling with the same old problems that troubled Mom and Dad. They are, say these experts, "still caught culturally"—which may be true in a far deeper sense than they meant. (*The New York Times*, Sunday, June 27, 1971, Sect. 1, p. 21.)

the Victorian rational consensus should have matured into an era of genuine civilization; when public education should have worked and Everyman joined the ranks of the delivered.

It has not turned out that way. And in the meantime, the extreme vulnerability of the "I" in writers from Poe's day to this—the alcoholism of Scott Fitzgerald and Faulkner and countless others,* the violence of some (Mailer; Hemingway), the madness and suicide of Virginia Woolf, the suicides of Hemingway and Jack London and Hart Crane, the forever-threatened sanity of Theodore Roethke†—has been used by the mediocre as a stick to beat intellect with. All artists or thinkers are cracked: *ergo*, who in his right mind would want to be one (a contradiction right there); who could take anything they said seriously? And it is true that in the very small population of our *literati* a very large percentage seem to be borderline mental cases—though to conclude that that is the *necessary* condition of mind, the price one pays for developing it, may still be a disastrous mistake. For in fact it may be the necessary condition of mind not developed highly enough—in "creative" people, the result of having grown up in a world in which the Renaissance ideal of universality has never really taken.

Because it has not, the majority of us today never become what we might. Nor do we understand exactly in what that deficiency consists—what our upbringing and education have left out of us. More and more, we feel *something* is wrong, but whatever it is, we do not usually connect it with our ideas of the waking self. On the contrary, as Lawrence did, we seek help elsewhere, in the Unconscious or the solar plexus. Our concept of intellect remains trivial. We tend to see it as mere cleverness. To have "brains" is to have mastered an assortment of none-too-trustworthy mental tricks. Out of a physicist's repertoire come such things as the Bomb; out of an intellectual's, mostly just words. Nor does it appear to strike us as odd that a faculty so superficial should also be

---

* John Berryman, Malcolm Lowry (also a suicide), Dylan Thomas, etc.
† One might also mention such possibly psychosomatic diseases as duodenal ulcers (which killed Joyce) and tuberculosis, which killed Lawrence and Orwell and Robert Louis Stevenson—and long before, Keats.

so treacherous—that to have brains and use them should invite insanity.

For a time, the sons corroborated the fathers' trivial concept of mind by developing into adults still more specialized or partial than the fathers had been. The more mediocre of them are still doing so, which means that the caliber of those soon to be running the Establishment is likely to decline.* The specialist mentality, as it became general, gave us (real) grounds for distrusting and devaluating mind still further. There are, for example, few scientists now who have the idealistic sense of mission that seems to have motivated men such as Tyndall and Thomas Huxley a century ago.

And even if they still existed among us, would many workingmen leave their TV sets to go and listen to them? Those who do spread the word nowadays are either popularizers, in it for the money, or institutional scientists interested in maintaining good public relations. In short, our scientists have for the most part become as partial as the rest of us. To be partial in one's sympathies —to have interests overriding mere interest—follows naturally perhaps from being partial in the sense of incomplete.

It is this type of mind—really the adaptive one transferred to the field of learning—that we sense to be heartless and amoral: one incapable of the generosity of a Tyndall, but perfectly capable of releasing nuclear fission or germ warfare upon the world without a qualm. The sufferings of a man like Oppenheimer, caught between loyalty to the humane ideals still residual in his calling and loyalty to country, were perhaps never very real to us, if only because so many of his colleagues were clearly impervious to them. Business is business, the latter seemed to say, and in the 1960s showed it by a flagrant careerism—in the cheapness, for instance, of James Watson's little memoir describing his and Francis

* That is to say, the specialist type, which was as much the creator of the modern world as its creation, may itself be passing in favor of the Amorph— the New Psychological Poor.

Already, by the mid-1960s, The Wall Street Journal noted a sharp fall in the number of Ivy League students planning to go into business. By 1970 enough Bachelors of Arts or Science were leaving Yale and Harvard to become day laborers (carpenters, notably) that Time considered it a trend and ran a story about it.

Crick's race against Linus Pauling for the Nobel.* No ideal of any kind is involved here; we are watching rival manufacturers racing to be first on the market with a new product.

So our children are given no reason to see in science the embodiment of any unique transcendent character, moral or psychological; and writers such as Mumford and Marcuse are given the text they need. All science, everywhere, is what it is becoming with us today: supertechnics—a business as self-interested as any other and more closely tied to the state than some. Bacon's distinction between experiments of "light" and of "fruit" was nonsense, and two recent presidents, Lyndon Johnson and Nixon, have put pressure on the research community to work along lines that are more obviously useful. For all one can tell, the public and possibly not a few scientists concur in this change of policy. It is very much a part of the *Geist*. Real objectivity, disinterested interest in one's subject, concern with truth for its own sake, we now know to be mere pretenses by which mind seeks to give itself special status.

At that, the position of scientists may be somewhat better, psychologically, than the average man's. As Aldous Huxley remarked in his *Collected Essays*: "There are general abilities and there are special talents. A man who is born with a great share of some special talent is probably less deeply affected by nurture than one whose ability is generalized. His gift is his fate and he follows a predestined course . . ."

It is particularly his fate if he happens to be heir to a highly developed tradition. (What would a mathematician such as Euler or Galois have become, growing up in Polynesia?) If, however, he inherits it at a time when much is being dropped from the repertoire of traditional ideals, he may turn out to be not a "natural philosopher" but a "science freak," one of that class of new intellectual barbarians whose prevalence has been the excuse for endless tirades against science as such—as somehow the great bar-

* Not that this sort of rivalry is new in science. It began with Newton and Robert Hooke—but on the other hand did not exist, as it might have, between many—between Clerk Maxwell and Gibbs, for example, who were men of a character we scarcely believe in any longer.

barizer. For the public fantasy that sees in such developments as the Bomb the handiwork of a comic-book Mad Scientist is, although absurd, not without a kind of truth. The people out front have certain well-founded suspicions as to what their intellectual betters today actually amount to—the trouble being that, like Freud, they mistake the present limitations of intellect for inherent and permanent ones, and so feel perfectly justified in their own rejection of it as anything but an adaptive gimmick. And unlike some Victorians, they see science and culture in general not as transcending class, but as a badge of it.*

Among people known as intellectuals, this same deficit—this partiality in both senses—has become even more apparent because, in contrast to scientific specialists, intellectuals pretend to large-scale understanding. They are the would-be Renaissance men of our day and frequently not up to the role. Many incline to scientism—a bits-and-pieces familiarity with nature knowledge, a glibness in psychoanalytic or politicoeconomic talk—under which it is difficult to detect any really coherent point of view. As Gertrude Stein once said of us all, they lack "vital singularity"—are defenders of an eclectic Received Opinion, with nothing of their own to say. In proportion as the public senses that to be the case, it ceases to take them seriously. In the vulgar view, they are just windbags. And when our intellectuals have involved themselves, à la Walt Rostow and the Bundy brothers, in the actual making of policy, the ordinary citizen has often discovered that neither their presumed capability nor their supposedly high principles (in this case liberal ones) have much real foundation. They are folks just like the rest of us—a bit more educated and much better connected, but in no way less partial or prone to the sort of gross errors and gross inhumanity to which rationalization so readily leads.

The parallel in private life to this sad public failure of the promises of intellect is the uses to which mind is commonly put in the introverted and "neurotic"—i.e., in those in whom mind,

---

* And hence send their children to college not to get educated but to get ahead.

falling short of what it might be, is forced permanently on the defensive. In the man of this type "intellectualizing" becomes the purest exercise in futility.*

For besides being driven to continual rationalization to explain his own behavior, he resorts to the supreme form of it; he uses words and symbolic situations—imaginary triumphs, injustices suffered with honor, etc.—as a way to inflate a self-image which to begin with hardly exists. That is, he invents or contrives a self to replace the one he might have had—the harmonious union of mind with its darker companions. And because this other self *is* an invention, he must defend it with a most elaborate, indefatigable skill, avoiding any test which might cause it to crumble. For in that event, as he knows, he would be left with nothing. Even his vanity is in a sense a fraud—a desperate recourse in the face of his own nonexistence.

Hence the perennial cry of the neurotic or tormented intellectual of this century: "Who am I?" Hence the violent, the egregious insecurity of writers otherwise as different from one another as Hemingway, Virginia Woolf, Theodore Roethke, and Norman Mailer. Hence the touchiness of neurotics and intellectuals generally. In many, the whole ground of their imaginative life, the compass of their waking being, is a tiny island, risen from the volcanic depths and forever threatening to sink back into them. Whether by means of alcohol or self-destruction outright, or by some succession of compulsive provocations against others, by the verbal demolition of friends and competitors,† by literal assault, each feels he may go under, into the interior darkness, and not a few have done so.

So to the spectacle of the intellectual as a man of mere words is added the spectacle of him as a near-madman, a psychiatric

---

* And in turn the best possible stick for "disciplines" such as Mind Control or Encounter or Scream to beat it with. "Stop thinking!" they tell us, "it's getting you nowhere!"—and in this they are like the religions of "the annihilation of consciousness" which come at the end of old civilizations, cures for the incurable.

† Much practiced by Hemingway, Gertrude Stein, and other literary people—especially, it would seem, of the '20s.

casualty making art out of his disorder.* And with that the public case against intellect appears to be complete. Of the purity and breadth of reason, as in science and philosophy; of the superhuman quality of the "creative" in poetry and painting and music and mathematics; of mind as the realization of an ideal of wholeness and humanity, little remains. The edifice we have been longing, in our distraction, to bring down has obliged us by collapsing unassisted.

The last stage is what one might call the biologization of life—the use of science to prove that the Naked Ape has almost nothing to distinguish him from his hairy brothers. Any number of writers have grown rich pounding away at this theme. Its importance is that it says *there are no exceptions*; *everything* is adaptation—that is, animal behavior. There is no escape from the treadmill of subservience to the (given, brute) self and to the tribe. Intellect is simply a mark of pecking-order status, another device for self-promotion or for advertising the rank one already has.

So a century ago, when Tyndall and Huxley brought "the hard science of the day" to the workingman, it only *seemed* that they did so out of spontaneous generosity, or from a genuine belief in certain ideals. And it only *seemed* that their audiences came to hear them for similar reasons—because speaker and audience both felt science to be "an intellectual good"; because culture after all transcended class; because something of the Renaissance, lingering on in that age of child labor and the dark satanic Midland mills,

---

* Having started with such genuine madmen as Rimbaud and Céline, this genre has gone on to become mannerist *Grand Guignol* in America: Susan Sontag's *Death Kit*, Alice Cooper, a sisters–of–Sylvia Plath movement in poetry.

Armed Love by Eleanor Lerman.

Eleanor Lerman's first book of poetry is an astonishing accomplishment. Hallucinatory, yet intimately in touch with their sources, her poems focus on homosexuality and insanity, cruelty and degradation, bitterness and terror, in a Manhattan *demimonde* where people react to each other in violent need because they no longer have any choice or even want a choice, accepting, embracing a survival beyond desire, beyond reason . . .

(From the Wesleyan University Press Fall Catalog for 1973.) To a reader of my age, it sounds almost like *The Tale of Peter Rabbit*.

could still bring oppressor and oppressed together in the interest of an idea both saw to be great, and not in its material promise alone.

Because in honoring it, each forgave the other, as Dostoevski said the peasant in his rags once forgave the rich man—for in looking at him he felt, "I am a man too." Now the rich man reciprocated, saying, "So are we both"—each suspending his partiality, each forgiving the other and in that, if only for an hour, the whole sorry business of our life together as animals, our adaptiveness. For that impartiality, that forgiveness of ultimate nature is truly what culture comes down to—is why we freed our slaves; why Victorian scientists felt moved to bring their learning to classes ordinarily denied all but bare literacy, and Victorian reformers struggled to lighten the burden of those same classes; why liberal democracy, as Ortega y Gasset said, decided to "share existence with the enemy, more than that, with an enemy which is weak. 't was incredible that the human species should have arrived at ' noble an attitude, so paradoxical . . . so anti-natural."*

Universal Man conceals a Christian few Christians ever were— as Tyndall demonstrated when he gave away the several thousand pounds his American lecture tour had earned him to a society for the advancement of the pure understanding in which he and his audiences so ardently believed.

But of course we know now it was probably nothing like that. Tyndall was just on an "ego trip" and his audiences were bumpkins who had nothing better to do. Lawrence, our prophet, would have seen through the whole business in an instant ("Liars, liars!"), even though he himself had once described it: ". . . The God of Aspiration became in accord with the God of Knowledge, and there was a great outburst of joy . . ."—muted enough, perhaps, by mid-Victorian times; nowhere to be heard today.

* *The Revolt of the Masses*, p. 88.

X

Homo Fabricator

Compared with D. H. Lawrence, who had brilliance and passionate conviction, there is a kind of prophet who, without either, makes capital of the predicament of which Lawrence was the victim and the oracle. Many of these are Establishment people who have found in some facet of our situation—Future Shock, Other-Directedness, the Managerial Revolution—material for a best seller. Others are nominal or maverick doctors, who have discovered that Scream or a honey-and-vinegar diet or jogging or thirty-two chews or a quarter of an hour a day of *samadhi* will cure practically anything—not just your nervous stomach, hypertension, or piles but the World Sadness in which these disorders originate.*

What all of these seers have in common is a clear understanding of what the modern public wants: namely, marvels plus simplicity—magic. It has been said that magic is primitive science, but actually it is not. Science promises understanding not necessarily concerned with use. Magic promises shortcuts, and is very directly concerned with use (how to hex an enemy, bring on rain, make gold out of lead, etc.). Magic is what the man in the street thinks science is—what today he demands that it become: Science for the People. He conceives of research as a series of crash programs that will solve the problem of cancer, say, the way the Manhattan Project solved the problem of the Bomb. Even then science is not

---

* Ever since the psychiatric movies of the post-World War II period (the one I especially recall starred Hedy Lamarr as an electrifying lady analyst), everyone knows that diseases are mostly psychosomatic.

really to his taste. The faster its miracles come, the sooner his interest in them seems to fade. His own restlessness outruns them; he yearns back to magic. And when there are enough of him, when he amounts to a market in the millions, the New Nonsense is born. Indeed, out of his ranks come most of those who create it: mass man with a degree or simply the gift of hokum; the canaille intellectual who knows his own by instinct.

According to one historian of nonsense, Daniel Cohen: "The reason for astrology's decline from the seventeenth through the nineteenth century is easy enough to account for. Scientific knowledge had overtaken astrological concepts." By the close of the Victorian Age, the apparent gains of Reason had been so great that a contributor to the 1898 edition of *Larousse* could say of astrology: "It has hardly any adherents other than swindlers who play on public credulity, and even these are fast disappearing." He spoke too soon.

"Astrology came back strong after the First World War," Cohen continues, "when newspapers began printing syndicated astrological columns. At first they were considered a mere game . . . But the readers did not take them so lightly; they proved to be marvelous circulation builders . . . The Second World War was a period of further growth for astrology, until at the present time, this ancient practice probably has more influence in the West than at any time in the past 300 years."

Among other uses to which this "ancient practice" has lately been put, Cohen mentions weather and stock-market forecasting (which involves taking a company's birth date and casting its horoscope) and even political astrology. An article in *Life* (February 22, 1960) reported that "A handful of psychologists have for years been quietly experimenting with astrological techniques. Psychoanalysts of several persuasions report that a horoscope, properly cast and intelligently interpreted, is a valuable diagnostic tool. Said one Manhattan analyst: 'I think a horoscope is more useful than a Rorschach test. A Rorschach shows only the patient's condition at the time the test is taken. A horoscope reveals his basic psychological setup' "—not to mention the therapist's.

Understanding Your Child Through Astrology was written by
the principal of an elementary school in Pennsylvania, and proposes a system of character appraisal based upon the young ones'
birth dates. The book has a certain idiotic charm, but it is still
rather startling to read that a school principal is basing his analysis
of difficult pupils on their horoscopes or transferring a girl from
one classroom to another so that she and her teacher won't be of
clashing zodiacal signs.

Apropos of the connection between nonsense and revolution,
it is interesting, if perhaps coincidental, that 1848, the year in
which spiritualism was born in America, was a great year for revolutions overseas. In the same way, astrology, all but dead by the turn
of the century, began its recrudescence here in the 1920s, when the
Bolsheviks and Italian Fascists were consolidating their regimes and
the Nazis laying the groundwork of theirs.

Since World War II, primacy in the mass production of nonsense appears to have shifted to the United States.* The Scan-
dinavians were ahead of us in that they had the first postwar UFO
"flap"; but even before that (in 1944), Raymond A. Palmer, the
editor of *Fantastic Adventures* and *Amazing Stories,* had prepared
us to see all kinds of weird things with his series *The Great Shaver
Mystery.* Shaver, a professional welder, anticipated scientology in
being able to go back in memory to previous incarnations—as far
back as the time of the Lost Atlantis. The data he turned up in
this way seemed to lead to a Hollow Earth theory.

According to Shaver, a whole population, unknown to us, lives
underground, sometimes sending forth *deros* (detrimental robots)
to explore our world or simply to terrify us. One school of Flying
Saucer theorists, apparently including Ivan Sanderson, now believes that UFOs may come out of the sea and be, in effect, *deros.*
Needless to say, *The Great Shaver Mystery,* like most other
Palmer features, sold very well.†

It was at the start of the volatile '50s that Immanuel Velikovsky

* I believe we were the first country in which, for a modest fee, one could have
one's horoscope cast by a computer.
† Palmer in fact was a genius in his field. Long before the current vogue for
Kirlian photography he was selling "aura goggles" equipped, Martin Gardner
tells us, with "pinacyanole bromide" filters.

published *Worlds in Collision*. The response which this work evoked was as alarming in its way as the McCarthyism of the same period. The fact that apparently responsible critics (including John J. O'Neill, the New York *Herald Tribune*'s science editor; Gordon Atwater, chairman and curator of the Hayden Planetarium; Horace Kallen of the New School for Social Research; and Clifton Fadiman, a sometime reviewer of books for *The New Yorker*) were impressed by Velikovsky's theory seems to have stunned the scientific community, as well it might have. The book's partially favorable press and subsequent immense sales argued that all the billions we had spent on education since 1900 (when astrology seemed to be on the way out) had had no great effect. In a supposedly rational age, in which the mass of men were believed to be better informed and more aware of the principles of clear thinking than they had ever been, scientists suddenly found themselves obliged to remind us of the most elementary rules of evidence, which they did with little enough effect, as it turned out. Velikovsky sold and sold. When one publisher dropped him out of embarrassment, another was only too glad to snatch him up. Wilhelm Reich was soon to be selling, too —any number* of "orgone boxes."

Both Reich and Velikovsky were treated by the scientific establishment with great harshness, a part of which might better have been directed against the educated laity who supported them. To this day, champions of Reich, such as Orson Bean† or the cartoonist William Steig, remind us that his books were literally burned and the man himself hounded to an early death. In an ostensibly free society it was odd and ominous that such a special case should have been made of Reich. At bottom, one feels, his persecutors were frightened—not by the man himself (he was probably insane) but by the fact that he could establish such a following, and not among certified ignoramuses only.

To men raised in the older tradition of scientific reason, it was

---

* Actually, according to David Elkind (*The New York Times Magazine*, Sunday, April 18, 1971), a rather small number—perhaps 50 to 100—but all the talk about them and the later legal proceedings made it seem much larger.
† The TV comedian, who was evidently much helped by Reichian therapy and subsequently wrote a successful book about it—*Me and the Orgone*.

as though reason itself were coming unstuck, to such a degree that the public needed to be defended against its own credulity by police-state methods. The same argument was used by the political reaction in Germany in the '30s. The public had lost its wits— was going Communist and needed discipline. But of course, that too was nonsense. If notwithstanding the most astronomical outlays for education, the average citizen *cannot* be taught much—if the signs are that intellectually he is losing ground—it is absurd to suppose that any sort of radical censorship or mistreatment of false prophets is going to be very effective. On the contrary, Reich's following is probably the bigger today (1973) for the fact that his books *were* burned.

Velikovsky too, after a period of obscurity, appears to have made a comeback, beginning, of all places, at Harvard.

IMMANUEL VELIKOVSKY DELIVERS LECTURE HERE AFTER TWENTY YEARS AS A SCIENTIFIC OUTCAST, The *Crimson* reported on its front page, February 19, 1972. The news story says that Velikovsky, "a stony-faced man," began his address to a capacity crowd at Lowell Lecture Hall with the words "I have been waiting for this moment for 22 years."

The *Crimson* described some of the sage's tribulations over this period, and summarized his *Worlds in Collision*:

. . . Around 1500 B.C. a comet which later became the planet Venus passed very near the earth, causing the earth to turn on its axis and temporarily stop rotating. The book stated that this catastrophic event caused many of the "miracles" described by the Old Testament . . . None of Velikovsky's major theories have yet been conclusively disproved, and a number of them have been confirmed by recent scientific discoveries. . . . Space probes have discovered that the temperature of Venus is 600 degrees Fahrenheit, a figure close to Velikovsky's prediction. *When Velikovsky suggested the existence of a magnetic field surrounding the earth, he was ridiculed, but in recent years a magnetic field has been discovered.* [Italics added.]

216

If this last is correctly stated,* then how, prior to Dr. Velikovsky, did we explain the workings of the old-fashioned magnetic compass (or are such nuts-and-bolts items no longer supposed to be part of a Harvard man's general knowledge)?

In any case, it is clear that persecution has turned out to be good business for the doctor. Had he simply been ignored as a crank, organizations such as The Student Academic Freedom Forum would not now be trying to win him a second hearing. And had *Worlds in Collision* not been so controverted when it appeared, it probably would not have sold a tenth as well then or since. It was the scientific establishment, in short, which may have given Velikovsky that little extra push he needed—the break that made him a star.

Voltaire once said: "If you are desirous of obtaining a great name, of becoming the founder of a sect or establishment, be completely mad; but be sure that your madness corresponds with the turn and temper of the age. Have in your madness reason enough to guide your extravagances; do not forget to be excessively opinionated and obstinate. It is certainly possible you may get hanged; but if you escape you will have altars erected to you." If you are hanged in effigy, so much the better, since that will increase your royalties while leaving you still around to enjoy them.

An important point is that the present demand for nonsense appears to have been stumbled upon rather than deliberately created.† If we take astrology as an indicator, the nonsense market was stable or declining around 1900 and began growing again after World War I—slowly at first, then more rapidly after World War II, and finally at an explosive rate in the 1960s. According to *Time* (June 19, 1972), books on witchcraft, satanism, spirit phenomena, etc., had had steady but not spectacular sales until about 1965,

* It is not; what Velikovsky said was that the magnetosphere of the earth extended much farther into space than had been supposed. Subsequent data have supported his conclusion.
† Just as the market for rock was stumbled upon by recording-company executives and bookers, back in the 1950s, when they discovered that rhythm-and-blues, a debased jazz, sold better than jazz itself. The next step was obvious: to make R & B even worse.

when they began to skyrocket. The same article quotes Sybil Leek ("America's most famous witch") as saying she has made close to a million dollars from her writings. It is unlikely that she would have done as well thirty years ago, let alone a hundred.

The effect of this phenomenal growth in the public appetite for the marvelous has been to turn a flagging old business into an economic frontier overnight. In racing language, the nag has turned out to be a sleeper. In this sector of the economy, it is as though we had suddenly reverted to Adam Smith's ideal early stage of capitalism, in which no one producer controls more than a small percentage of the market, and anyone who is able to scrape up several hundred or thousand dollars can try his luck in the arena of pure competition. A short-term lease on a rundown storefront, a few bags of sunflower seeds, soy meal, herb teas, and unbleached flour, bought on thirty-day terms, are enough to start you in the macrobiotic-food business.* With a bigger nut and some technical aides, partly paid in stock, you can found a rival to the *Mother Earth News* or the *Wretched Mess Calendar*. Once your publication is rolling, you can, like *Wretched Mess*, branch out into the mail-order field, selling assorted notions by way of unbooked advertising space in your own pages.

Already, however, the entrepreneurs of the New Nonsense are beginning to sort themselves out into two groups: small operators who run stable, "ma-and-pa"–type ventures, and big ones who work in the rapid-growth corporate format. One of the most impressive of the latter is José Silva, the founder of Mind Control Inc. Beginning a little over a decade ago with a small-scale operation in Laredo, Texas, he has since built an organization that operates in all fifty of the United States and several foreign countries as well. Whereas the Maharishi is still a one-man

---

* A great advantage of such stores being that they can sell substandard merchandise at higher-than-standard prices. A macrobiotic-food market across from my apartment in Cambridge, Massachusetts, was recently (1971) offering "organic" apples—small, blighted, sour things such as can be gathered free in abandoned orchards throughout New England—for 20 percent more than one would have paid for unblighted apples at the A&P down the street. (The A&P has since moved away, incidentally.)

show, Silva has become a chain. Like Mesmer, he covers the realm; and unlike L. Ron Hubbard, he has stayed clear of the law. Tests show that his EEG-management technique really can alleviate migraine. And as long as you make no false claims about physical cures, what medical society is going to prosecute you?

Will nonsense, then, go the way of heavy industry and become dominated by a few monster corporations? Will Silva Mind Control soon be the GM in its field, absorbing Transcendental Meditation and Scream Therapy or such related ventures as Esalen, Alexander-Granberry Associates, and the Athena Center for Creative Living? I doubt it, for the following reasons: Since we are talking about a type of business ordinarily involving no tangible product, its capital requirements are small and the number of competitors who can spring up at any given moment correspondingly enormous. Moreover, the incentive to build one's pitch into a sort of vertical nonsense trust may be lacking, simply because one can make such large amounts of money without going to all that trouble. Some months ago, I recall seeing, in a nationally circulated newsmagazine, a photograph of a swami doing a headstand on the wing of his private DC-6. The accompanying story explained that the demand for his spiritual services was so great that he needed the plane to meet his tight lecture schedule. The DC-6, therefore, became deductible as a business expense, and to that extent, self-supporting. Add the wisdom of the East to that of a good tax accountant, and who needs more?

Corporate liability is another reason for not expanding. The chain operator, seeing the vast horizons opening before him, may be tempted to offer the public more nonsense than it is ready for, and so end up in court. That seems to have been what befell Glenn Turner, who based his miniconglomerate originally upon the assertedly remarkable skin-toning properties of mink oil, and/or a related course in self-help called Dare To Be Great. In the end, Turner made most of his money selling distributorships for an allegedly nonexistent line of cosmetics. At pep sessions, a friend reports, distributor trainees were given a hint of what to expect by the great man himself, who told them: "Four out of five of you are going to be financial failures in life." Those who, in fact, were could tackle that problem by taking Turner's Dare To Be Great course.* After legal rumblings in several states, Turner was indicted in 1972 under the Florida securities laws.

The moral is obvious: avoid tangible goods. Looking back, one can surmise that Reich might have escaped much of the abuse heaped upon him by the medical profession if only he had not started manufacturing orgone boxes. Similarly, it is advisable to avoid making physical claims of a kind which can be easily checked out. It is perfectly okay to say that your graduates can project their thoughts to Mars, provided that NASA does not yet have enough photographic evidence to prove that their reports of what they saw there were erroneous. But by no means make the mistake of saying you can cure cancer by administering blue light or orgone or "glyoxylide" (Dr. William F. Koch's famous remedy, which, on analysis, seemed to be distilled water). That cancer patients may do only slightly better following surgery or radioactive-cobalt treatments is not a point in your favor. On the contrary, the fact that the cancer problem is so far from being solved means that medical men will be all the quicker to jump on you as unfair competition—unfair, that is, to the suffering public. (Of course, if they had solved the problem, you wouldn't be competition at all.)

On the other hand, you can do very well as a one-horse operator in the paramedical field if you avoid flagrant claims, and particularly if you have a certificate of some sort to start with. Koch, one of the more spectacular quacks described by Martin Gardner, was an M.D. and also a Ph.D. in chemistry. Gardner reports that in "two sensational trials, in 1943 and 1946," the government failed to convict Dr. Koch, a failure possibly not unconnected with his impressive credentials. The patients who come to a quack must want to believe in the nonsense he is offering or they wouldn't be there. At the same time, their latent suspicion that they may be fooling themselves requires that he take special pains

---

* Some Turner distributors did not fail and therefore did not need the course. These were the ones who sold other distributorships, rather than trying to push the product line.

to reassure them. Hence a medical degree is worth more to him than it is to an ordinary doctor—worth whatever it may cost him—and should be kept, framed and in full view, in his office. Otherwise, however, the same cautions apply, so some oddball version of psychiatry is infinitely preferable to therapies involving machines or chemicals.

One of my favorites in the parapsychiatric field is Dr. Francis I. Regardie of Los Angeles, who in the 1950s introduced a technique he called vomit therapy. Gardner quotes an article by the doctor himself, who said his procedure was "to ask the patient to regurgitate by using a tongue depressor and a kidney pan. Usually the patient is puzzled and resists with some vigor. If a brief simplified explanation is given, or if the therapist states unequivocally that this is not the time for intellectual discussion . . . the patient as a rule will comply. My procedure is to let him gag up to a dozen times, depending on the type of response. In itself the *style* of gagging is an admirable index to the magnitude of the inhibitory apparatus. Some gag with finesse, with delicacy, without noise. These are categorically the most difficult patients to deal with. Their character armor is almost impenetrable, and their personalities rigid to the point of putrefaction. They require to be encouraged to regurgitate with noise, without concealment of their discomfort and disgust, and with some fullness. Others will cough and spit and yet remain unproductive. Still others sneer and find the whole procedure a source of cynical amusement. Yet another group will retch with hideous completeness." This would appear to be a quite literal application of the Freudian concept of catharsis—and one that must have made the maintenance of pleasant premises something of a problem.

Some parapsychiatrists content themselves with developing odd monomaniacal theories from which they make money, mainly through their writings. One of these was Dr. Edmund Bergler, whose best-remembered work is *The Writer and Psychoanalysis*. His basic idea was that every writer is a would-be, if not a practicing, plagiarist. Even though a writer may not *think* he wants to swipe the work of others, he still does, unconsciously. Ego—

Waking Conscious Me—is wrong as usual; putty in the hands of unseen forces. Bergler attacks his subject with awful gusto, writing in a hyped-up version of that style which has long since become standard in the psychoanalytic literature—a sort of genteel cardboard prose with touches of "liveliness" or "humanity" crayoned in, showing that, for all his learning, the doctor is really just like you and me.

His chapter titles mark the progress of his thought: "I—The Impulse to Write; II—Sublimation; IV—The Psychic Mechanism of the Writer; V—Writer, Alcoholic, Homosexual [Now, we're getting down to it]; IX—Hack and Huckster; X—Plagiarism; XI—The Myth of Objectivity." What is left?*

In Chapter X he lists twenty-four types of literary theft, some of them extremely odd (for instance, No. 17: "Plagiarism as a substitute for a 'cover' memory" or No. 20: "Plagiarism of the aging." I also liked No. 18—"Plagiarism of people in love"). The final item is of particular interest: "24—The plagiarist hunter. The man is always compulsively searching for plagiarisms of others. . . . He may be one of those paranoic [sic] plagiographs who write books about somebody else's plagiarism, real or imaginary."

In Bergler, as in much other psychoanalytic writing, Ego is clearly the fall guy. Whereas I think of myself as a single central embattled entity, struggling to manage my instincts and their attendant emotions just as I struggle to cope with external circumstances, I am really just a sort of resultant of forces. The various Little Men in my head† do it all, battling things out among themselves, while I simply provide the premises in which these events occur. Even my conscience is beyond my control. There is no question of my being able to reprogram it in any sensible way.‡ It is a *being*, and a very nasty and inflexible one at that.

---

* An appendix called "Supplement: Literary Critics Who Can Spell but Not Read."
† Not too different, really, from Thomas Edison's, or the Menorgs and Disorgs of Lawsonomy.
‡ Which, for those who have come to the battle of adolescence too underequipped to win it, is quite true. But note that Bergler, like most of his profession, seems to assume that that is always and inevitably the case.

Dr. Bergler would then appear to be a forerunner of such prophets as Lewis Mumford and Professor Marcuse (and a corroborator of Skinner)—intellectuals who, in their different ways, have all cast doubt on the powers, the good faith, or even the existence of objective reason. And if the "I" is as feeble as Bergler implies, objectivity is indeed a dream. But if that's the case—if the feebleness of the "I" is what drives every author to crib from others—how did the first book get written? And if scientific objectivity is likewise impossible, it would seem to follow that then *no* theory is to be trusted—including Mumford's and Marcuse's, about the true nature of science, or Skinner's, about the true nature of man.

Obviously these people expect us to make an exception of *their* theories; and obviously numbers of us do. Whereas if we were to be logical about it, we would conclude either that they are wrong and go on to other ideas, or else that all thinking, including theirs and the logical positivists', is Q.E.D. futile. In other words, these theories may, by some accident, have hit on the great truth that no theory is worth bothering about, so to all intents, thinking in the Western world is over. And *that* may be the message we were waiting for. Never mind the inherent contradiction of using reason to prove that reason itself is false; having grown weary of thinking—from being less and less good at it, perhaps—we want someone officially to tell us to give it up, in favor of the "dark otherness" within. And so the New Nonsense, in all its various forms, has obliged us—not always with the verve and grandeur of a Lawrence; sometimes in a prose so opaque and misshapen it's a wonder anyone can stand to read it. The fact that a whole generation of New Left students waded through Professor Marcuse is a tribute to the powers of sheer preconviction. Once the faithful have decided what the Word is, they will find it, it seems, no matter where.*

What happens, incidentally, if we apply Dr. Bergler's analytical methods to himself? Had he some secret grudge against writers, perhaps? Would one find in his files a drawerful of unpublished

---

* Just as the pre-Revolutionary French did, in what Darnton calls the "unlikely guise" of mesmerism.

novels? Do his frequent quotations from Freud betray some distrust of his own powers—an impulse, as he puts it, to plagiarize "from necessity to lean on a model"? What about the unconscious influence *of his own name* (Bergler; burglar)? Ostensibly, he wrote his book to help other writers, but then at moments he drops his guard and we seem to see what he is really getting at:

> The idea that the writer is objective and the highest representative of his time or of the culture in which he lives is, politely speaking, ridiculous. Of course, writers often proclaim that slogan as an inner rationalization, but why should we believe that rationalization *any more than that of any other neurotic?* . . . No, the writer is not the objective observer of his time. He is just a neurotic operating his defense mechanism without knowing it. Sometimes the defense mechanism coincides with the general trend; then he is successful . . . [Italics added.]

Arthur Janov, the inventor of Scream Therapy and author of the best-selling *Primal Scream,** is in effect continuing the good work begun by Bergler. A British psychiatrist, Anthony Storr (*The New York Times Book Review*, Sunday, November 5, 1972), says that in Janov's latest book "the existential psychiatrists . . . are dismissed out of hand, because in the Primal view, man's search for meaning in life is itself neurotic. Having thus implicitly disposed of the whole of religion and philosophy, Janov proceeds to dismiss all art as neurotic too."

So, thanks to Bergler and Janov, we discover the "hidden ends" of literature, art, and philosophy to be no more legitimate than those of science. With a little more work, one feels, we will have the whole structure down—religion, science, humanities, intellect, belief in any sort of personal initiative, or the genuineness of any aspiration. It is, one might say, the most imposing achievement of the New Nonsense to have brought about what reason alone never could: the ruin of an entire culture. Compared with this one, the

---

* Logically enough, Dr. Dan Casriel endorses Janov's theory and has published a book about it—*A Scream Away from Happiness* (Grosset and Dunlap, 1972).

program of demolition begun in France by Voltaire and continued by the later *philosophes* and the quacks of the 1780s was almost trifling.

Today (1973) there seems really not much left to do, although the tic of psychoanalytic "explanation" dies hard. An example of it, which I came across recently, seems relevant here. According to Dr. Joan FitzHerbert, "member of the British Psycho-Analytical Society and for 15 years head of a child guidance clinic in Kent":

> The double rhythm of much rock music—the slow rocking coupled with a steady fast beat—is similar to the rhythm that bombards the unborn baby in its mother's womb. . . . The slow rocking sound is that of its mother's heartbeat and the more rapid sound that of its own heart. When young people writhe and turn in this kind of music—sometimes for long periods without stopping, often in a dreamy, trancelike state —they are subconsciously responding to the memory of peace and security in the womb. They are in effect saying, "We wish we had never been born."

Poor loves, who can blame them?

Dr. FitzHerbert's remarks, incidentally, appeared not in some learned periodical or in a semipopular work on psychiatric self-help, as they might have done twenty-five years ago; they were quoted in the February 6, 1972, issue of the *National Enquirer*. The same issue featured a spectacular row (with photos) between Jackie and Ari Onassis at Heathrow Airport, and a front-page headline reading:

GROUP OF RESPONSIBLE SCIENTISTS AND EDUCATORS CLAIM . . .
EXISTENCE OF UFO's CAN NO LONGER BE DOUBTED

Having started among the philosophers of sixty or seventy years ago, and continuing still in dignified special forms, the New Nonsense is now spreading to the vulgus and becoming totally eclectic in the process. The Ostrander-Schroeder book, for instance, deals not only with Russian ESP work but with almost any branch of weird science one can think of, including treatment of schizophrenics by putting them in trapezoidal rooms, and the use of pyr-

amidal hats to cure headaches. This trend toward total compre-
hensiveness seems to be a recent development, as though nonsense,
like a true Toynbeean "late" religion, were becoming syncretistic.
Every form of it tends increasingly to contain all the others.

Drs. Regardie and Bergler did not work that way. Each had his
shtick and stuck to it.* Of all the old-time analysts, Jung was possibly the most modern in this respect. He appears to have believed
not merely in "synchronicity" and various spirit phenomena† but
finally in UFOs. He is also reported to have spent twenty years
studying alchemy.

One feels, in short, that a great synthesis may be at hand. A
new edifice is rising out of what, a few years ago, looked to be
mere rubble—a vast heap representing all the abandoned dwellings
and broken utensils of the mind that mankind has been accumulating probably since the last Ice Age. The idea seemed to be that
one never knew when some of this stuff might come in handy; and
since to arrive at *any* new thought is a matter of the greatest difficulty for most of us, we naturally cling to our old ones, the way we
store useless treasures in our attics: the difference being that the
things in the attic eventually get thrown out. Basic Nonsense, it
seems, never does.

The problem that concerns us here is the self—by which I mean
the I that thinks it thinks for itself: the part that seems most real
because it alone looks out upon all the rest. Is that self in trouble
because a generation or so of theoreticians have been saying it
doesn't exist; or has it never existed, and are we just catching on
to the fact? In any case, it is certain that our literal self-assurance
has been badly shaken, as can be seen in our public relations approach to the problem of who we are. A man is not apt to have a
nature or a character anymore; he has an "image." Maybe he's
identical with his façade, and maybe he isn't. Best not to pry. If I

---

* This is not quite true of Dr. Regardie, some of whose other interests are described in Francis King's *Rites of Modern Occult Magic.*
† One day while he and Freud were having an animated discussion, both heard
explosions in a nearby bookcase—projections, as Dr. Jung explained, of their
combined psychic energy. The streams of "psitrons" they were emitting were
apparently so concentrated that an audible collision with the furniture resulted.

speak of my "image" as a writer, Dr. Bergler can't catch me out, since I'm only talking about the aims, interests, and ideals I *seem* to have. My actual motives may be even fishier than those he imputes to me.

Appropriately enough, this use of the word "image" became current around the time of Richard Nixon's first try at the Presidency, in 1960. Few men in our public life have been more consistently, openly contrived than he. One must give him credit; he did it all right there onstage—switching hats, changing his delivery and diction, turning from the Good Bad Guy who fearlessly pursued Commies in the late 1940s to the Bad Good Guy, loathed by liberals and adored by Middle America, in 1968. In that same year, he permitted a picture story to be run in one of our nationally circulated magazines showing him in the new makeup that his team was using to brighten up his "image" for the coming campaign.

I tried to think of a past Presidential candidate who might have done the same, but none occurred to me. Even FDR, given as he was to effects, and careful always to be seen under circumstances that minimized his particular affliction, would not, I think, have resorted to cosmetics, or at any rate publicized the fact that he had. But of course, from the outset, he was a popular President. To have been seen too often or too dramatically as a cripple might have cost him votes, but a bit of Five O'Clock Shadow or that Used-Car Dealer persona, once so damaging to the present incumbent, probably wouldn't have hurt him much.

In principle there is nothing new about the "image" either in our politics or in life generally. What is new is the extent of our reliance on it—the perfectly bald way we set out to manipulate our own exteriors so as to produce a self which everyone knows is a fake, but which each of us feels to be essential to his career and his peace of mind, nevertheless. Mr. Nixon will surely go down in history as one of the great masters of the method. His original incentive may have been a somewhat unfortunate appearance. Besides lumpy features, he had a certain glowering, thuglike air which he made the mistake of corroborating by his behavior toward political opponents, most recently in the 1972 election campaign. After the tactics he used against Helen Gahagan Douglas and Representative Voorhis, his conduct at the Hiss trial, and his reply to a heckler during the 1960 campaign ("Never mind. We'll take care of you!"), one would have thought that, imagewise, he was done for. Not a bit of it. From his early appearance on TV (when his dog, Checkers, somehow cleared him of any imputation of financial fast dealing) to his restrained, humorous statesmanlike speech during the victory celebration on election night in 1972, Mr. Nixon always managed to turn the tables on his detractors— not by being a new man, but by tirelessly acting the part of one. In allowing himself to be shown in full makeup as the New Nixon, he even let us in on the fact—a stroke of candor inconceivable in a President such as Andrew Jackson.

The day of that sort of rough-hewn candidate is probably gone, because now we would feel he was being played by John Wayne or might better be. With our doubts about identity in general, the plain man in this century has come to seem simply one of a number of stock characters. He is no more genuine than the flamboyant type or the chameleons, just less interesting. Lincoln definitely lacked star quality. It is doubtful if he could have run successfully against Nixon, and Bobby Kennedy would have beaten him by a landslide. It is true that Lincoln's contemporaries, especially in the Northeast, made fun of him and considered him something of a hobbledehoy. Even for that era, perhaps, he was too down-home, had too clearly defined a character. Compared, say, with the Kennedys, he generated little excitement. His plain prose style, barely acceptable in Victorian times, would have been a dud today. In short, in the era of man-gone-hollow, he would have seemed as fake as any and not nearly as charismatic as some.

It is not necessary to labor the point that image building has become a major industry, which manufactures corporate and product images* as well as personal ones. The public relations concept has

---

* Note, too, that some ads in the past decade or two have begun to be frankly nonsensical. Bert and Harry put Piel's beer on the map not by plugging the product in the old pseudo-factual way, but by comedy routines. Much other advertising has since become pure camp.

penetrated even to the dinner table and the boudoir. The object of Dale Carnegie courses, of Sherwin Cody and his "spin-offs," the Mnemonics men, of the How-to sex books (Everything You Always Wanted to Know . . .) is to permit Everyman to shine: not by unveiling his inner light—since it is agreed that he has none—but by teaching him certain techniques which will add luster to his "image" the way a coat of paint adds luster to a house. The idea may seem outrageously bald until one understands the even balder one that lies behind it. *Inner man is a fiction*; the Real You doesn't exist, except in your outer relations, the impressions you create—in your success or failure as a lover, conversationalist, molder of opinion. Only a few, such as Skinner, have come right out and said it: we are machines. The notion is a logical descendant of the bare-bones practicality forced upon us back during our frontier days and cultivated since as if in a spirit of Protestant virtue. A man is what he can do, or seem, or get away with. All the rest is vaporing.

So long as we were still more or less religious, this sort of realism had to remain covert. It throve on the frontier or among the Robber Barons but was frowned upon in Boston. Now it is the moralists who are on the defensive, trying for an ethical consensus they suspect is without real foundation. In fact, some such compact to behave with an unrealistic decency is all that stands between us and the Skinnerian nightmare, and the signs are that it is holding up none too well. And with that, our uncertainty on matters of principle has become so profound that the "image" is almost all we have left. We prefer to be fooled, by others as well as ourselves.

So the Good Man has gradually been displaced by the Good Guy. Clear moral lines can no longer be drawn about anything. When we say, nowadays, that somebody is sincere, we seem to be talking not about his real character but about his effect on us. So long as he pleases us, what does it matter what he *is*? The sincere man is one who does not switch images on us, or if he does, switches to one we like even better. Nixon was more sincere in 1968 than in 1960 and the embodiment of sincerity in 1972. The one thing we used to hear said in favor of Hitler and Mussolini (up until World War II) was that they were sincere. And years ago, at the Alger Hiss trial, Whittaker Chambers wrung our hearts with his sincerity. He had switched images, of course, but to a better one.

From the nonsense personality or "image" to the scenario that treats the conduct of international affairs as something like moviemaking seems a quite natural progression. The basic assumption is that foreigners are as completely defined by their roles as we are, and can be pulled around by the same little strings of "interest." On that assumption, games theory was used in the 1960s in an attempt to "psych out" what the enemy might be up to next. The idea is that one doesn't, for example, have to be a Vietnamese Buddhist monk, or even to know any, in order to be able to forecast the reaction of the Buddhist clergy to some move by our government. All one needs is to "get the picture" as outlined by a young man from Rand or Auerbach, who probably doesn't know any Buddhist monks either, but has gotten the "scoop" from reading State Department documents (many of them written by people who never left Washington) or by talking with CIA officials (some of whom have never been in Vietnam either, but who have reliable "contacts"—American officials on the spot who pay natives for intelligence which the latter supply as nearly as possible to meet expectations). Somewhere at the end of this long chain of informers and the informed lie a few facts, and one is assured that they are the essential ones. Armed with these, one is ready to serve as a qualified player in the Game of Nations.

Is something wrong with this approach? One thing is certain: whether or not we played Rand Corporation games with them, the facts we collected in Cuba at the time of the Bay of Pigs, or in Vietnam roughly from 1954 to the present (1973), have served us poorly enough; nor was that, in Vietnam, for want of the means to act on what we thought we knew. The trouble here may lie deeper—in our radically impoverished conception of man, which has led us to imagine that he can be stage-managed into doing pretty much what we want. It has not worked out that way, either in the foreign lands mentioned or even in the case of our own children.

One does not hear much, nowadays, about strategic games playing, and perhaps the vogue for it is passing. There was a marvelous effrontery about the Bundy brothers' little scenarios in the Pentagon Papers. To deal so offhandedly, almost playfully, with matters affecting the lives of millions is surely aristocratic in the grand old sense. When one realizes moreover that many of those who lost their lives did so sheerly as a result of miscalculations made by some political scientist or State Department hack in an office thousands of miles away, the spectacle becomes truly impressive. That nonsense can now unloose the whirlwind on such a scale, and from such small beginnings, does, as we incorrectly say, boggle the mind.

So what do we find the New Nonsense has done for us up to now? It has proved that hard conscious thought is not likely to get us anywhere—is just "intellectualizing." The real you is hidden and automatic; you just learn to let it out. But there is still the world to cope with; to do so, you contrive a fake external self, an "image,"* and go on to base such things as foreign-policy decisions on games playing and "scenarios." All of these are what the New Nonsense aims for: shortcuts, surface ways of doing things which make life magically easier—except that they haven't.

The "image" we bought in the New Nixon simply blew up with Watergate. The "scenarios" we constructed to win in Vietnam failed. And in the Calley case, no one knew what to think. For, given a rational self that really has no powers, how can there be such a thing as moral responsibility? If Calley is no more responsible than any of us, why should the poor fellow be made a scapegoat? (One sympathizer even described him as "Christ on the Cross.")

But it was President Nixon who gave the whole affair the blessing, as it were, of his own confusion. Having originally described the My Lai slaughter as "abhorrent to the conscience of the American people," having then let the Army struggle through the painful business of court-martialing and convicting the lieutenant, and

---

* Really a concession to notions of identity, decency, etc., not quite dead—a holdover from the days when people didn't have to wonder who they were because they thought they knew.

having meanwhile auscultated the electorate to find out what it felt in its "heart," Mr. Nixon's own "heart" changed too. He now saw that young man in a truer, finer light—the light of mercy—ordering him to be moved from the stockade and announcing that he, the President, would "be personally the court of final decision in the case." One wonders what Lincoln, himself a most merciful man, would have thought of this proceeding—of the "heart" of all of us, in this strange era.

It remained only for some prophet to come along who would explain us entirely in terms of externals, of our environment—*things*. Huxley began the movement, satirically, with his *Brave New World*, but Alvin Toffler may have written its definitive work. *Future Shock* is a "now" book—in subject matter, in its underlying meanings, in its incessant use of words such as "thrust." For instance:

"The fact is that the entire thrust of the future carries away from standardization—away from uniform goods, away from homogenized art, mass produced education and 'mass' culture. We have reached a dialectical turning point in the technological development of society." In his view we have entered an age of superspecialism and superindustrialization which most of us are too "past-oriented" to understand. Not only is the pace of change frantically accelerating; the multiplication of "life-styles" and the riot-growth of what he calls "sub-cults" have reached a point at which our common culture is effectively in dissolution. (". . . The fragmentation of societies brings with it a diversification of values. We are witnessing the crack-up of the consensus."*)

On the technological side, the "personalizing" even of such mass-produced goods as the Ford Mustang has become possible thanks to the flexibility of computer-controlled manufacturing processes. And at a time when many of the older large-circulation magazines have been going under, improvements in printing have revived small-scale periodical publishing (particularly in the teen-age and special-interest fields), as well as permitting survivals such

* Actually, the consensus he speaks of is long gone. What we are witnessing is simply a crackup.

as *Time* to get out "demographic" editions slanted toward particular audiences.

Thanks to these new production techniques, the man nowadays who wants to do his "thing"—to express or categorize himself by the products he buys—has a good chance of finding what suits him. Indeed, he may suffer from what Toffler calls "overchoice." (The hippie rural commune, based upon handicrafts and organically grown vegetables, is presumably a reaction against this largess.) And of course, the color telephone and tailor-made Mustang are only a beginning. In fact, Toffler tells us, agriculture and the manufacture of tangible goods will soon be a "backwater." The same applies to service industries.

After "psychologization" of the product, our next step will be "psychologization" outright—the marketing of experiences. The "happenings" of the '60s were a forecast of this development, as were the "accent" flights offered by TWA. "The TWA passenger may now choose a jet on which the food, the music, the magazines, the movies and the stewardess's miniskirt are all French. He may choose a 'Roman' flight on which the girls wear togas . . . Or he may select the 'Olde English' flight on which the girls are called 'serving wenches' and the *décor* supposedly suggests that of an English pub." (BOAC went further, offering to provide "unmarried American male passengers with 'scientifically chosen' blind dates in London" along with prearranged parties, tours of discothèques, etc. This "Beautiful Singles" program was apparently killed when it came to the attention of certain stick-in-the-mud Members of Parliament.)

Toffler describes a sort of psychedelic geisha parlor in lower Manhattan, which offered the clientele "balloons, kaleidoscopes, tambourines, plastic pillows, mirrors, pieces of crystal, marshmallows . . . a lecture by or about Marshall McLuhan" and finally an interlude of dancing with "guides" or hostesses "nude under their veils." This enterprise called itself "Cerebrum, an electronic studio of participation," and Toffler classes it as a precursor of "experiential" industries of the future. "In effect they will say: 'Let us plan (part of) your life for you.' In the transient, change-filled world of tomorrow, that proposition will find many eager takers."

The proposition itself is not particularly new, as Toffler is quick to point out. "One very old experiential industry," he notes, "is prostitution." He admits, moreover, to certain doubts; the environments created by the "psych-corps" may prove too heady for some folks. He proposes, instead, a "fifty-year campaign to erase hunger from the world . . . Such a pause might give us time to contemplate the philosophical and psychological impact of experiential production."

Granted that no contemplative pause may be imminent, what are we to expect next? Toffler takes a cautionary line: "If consumers can no longer distinguish clearly between the real and the simulated, if whole stretches of one's life may be commercially programmed, we enter into a set of psycho-economic problems of breathtaking complexity. These problems challenge our most fundamental beliefs, not merely about democracy or economics, but about the very nature of rationality and sanity."

However, aside from the possibility that the Good Life of Tomorrow may drive us off our rockers, Toffler is optimistic. The family, he says, is falling to bits, but we may soon have substitutes which are as good or better—for instance, professional child raisers who would relieve us of parental duties during our youth. Or we may look forward to having children at the end of our careers, thanks to the new genetics which will give us children more beautiful, intelligent, and healthy than any we might have produced ourselves. "Why not wait and buy your embryos later, when your work is over? . . . The post-retirement family could become a recognized social institution."*

Another novelty which Toffler discusses at length is the man-machine combination, or Cyborg. He quotes the late J. B. S. Haldane as saying: "Clearly a gibbon is better preadapted than man

---

* I am "past-oriented" enough to believe that parents in their sixties would find didy changing and night feeding a bit much. Moreover, the embryos they had bought would be becoming teen-agers as they themselves reached seventy-five or eighty—a family situation some might consider terrifying. Possibly one could just rent children on a five-years-with-option-to-renew basis.

for life in a low gravitational field such as that of a spaceship. . . . A platyrrhine with a prehensile tail is even more so. Gene grafting may make it possible to incorporate such features into human stocks." (I doubt that I would wish a prehensile tail on a child of mine, particularly if he was the first kid on his block to have one; but as Toffler remarks, not all of us move easily with the times.) Joshua Lederberg, a colleague of Haldane's, is as intrepidly forward-looking: " 'We are going to modify man experimentally through physiological and embryological alterations and by the substitution of machines for his parts,' Lederberg declared. 'If we want a man without legs, we don't have to breed him, we can chop them off; if we want a man with a tail, we will find a way of grafting it on him.' "

A Cyborg that seems particularly to fascinate Toffler is one descended from the Curt Siodmak novel *Donovan's Brain*. As his precedent, he cites a gruesome experiment done a few years ago at the Metropolitan General Hospital in Cleveland. There, a macaque's brain was separated from its body and kept alive by means of a blood supply from another monkey. "Said one of the members of the team, Dr. Leo Massopust . . . 'The brain activity is largely better than when the brain had a body' "—though how he knew that is not clear. Another member of the team, Professor Robert White, was quoted as saying, " 'We could keep Einstein's brain alive and make it function normally' "—going on, rather oddly, to remark: " 'The Japanese will be the first to [keep an isolated human head alive]. I will not, because I haven't resolved as yet this dilemma: Is it right or not?' A devout Catholic, Dr. White is deeply troubled by the philosophical and moral implications of his work"—unlike the Japanese, apparently.*

By analogy with modular "plug-in" architecture or the "plug-in" family (half-seriously proposed for executives who are continually being transferred but don't want to drag their original families along with them), Toffler finds the "plug-in" brain a not-too-distant possibility. "This is the direct link-up of the human brain—

* And why did he omit the Russians? Perhaps this was a nod not to their superior morals but to their inferior technology.

stripped of its supporting physical structures—with the computer. Indeed, it may be that the biological component of the super-computers of the future may be massed human brains"—the question, as in the old joke, being whose. Will prisoners or terminal cancer patients be likely to volunteer their brains, once the nature of the project has been fully explained to them?

To test this idea, I tried imagining my own brain "stripped of its supporting physical structures" and plugged into a computer. Like any amputee, I would experience the "phantom limb" phenomenon—in this case a whole phantom body. There I would be, dreaming of the physical self and the life I had once had, trying to remember how the world had looked and sounded and smelled, while the only thing keeping me from the lunacy that follows total sensory isolation would be this machine, asking me questions. What questions? It wouldn't want to know the square root of pi; it could get that itself, much faster. Perhaps I might advise it on China policy or tell it the dates of famous battles, most of which it would have to look up to make sure they were right. Unless the machine took time out to chat with me and give me refresher courses, I would begin to forget the little I know. And in my dark, featureless, stationary inner world, I would soon be overcome with despair. My answers to the computer would grow more and more fragmentary and incoherent. Finally somebody reading my print-outs would say, "Brain Number So-and-So (Social Security number) has had it," and they would switch off my blood and glucose, unplug me, and throw me away.

Toffler proposes some other interesting Cyborgs. For instance: "It may . . . become possible to combine the human brain with a whole set of artificial sensors, receptors and effectors, and to call *that* tangle of wires and plastic a human being." He is equally enthusiastic about our recent progress in "robotology." "Technicians at Disneyland," he tells us, "have created extremely lifelike computer-controlled humanoids . . . The robots chase girls, play music, fire pistols, and so closely resemble human forms that visitors routinely shriek with fear. . . ." He is so impressed by this electronic breakthrough that he permits himself the following flight of fancy: ". . . We shall face the novel sensation of trying to determine whether the smiling assured humanoid behind the airline reservation counter is a pretty girl or a carefully wired robot. The likelihood, of course, is that she will be both." In a footnote he adds, "Professor Block of Cornell speculates that man-machine sexual relationships may not be too far distant." I had thought that thanks to Drs. Masters and Johnson, they were already here.*

Getting down to more serious business, Toffler tells us that the multiplicity of choices offered by our new "personalized" technics are putting us under immense stress. His chapter subheads alone give a sense of the urgency of the situation. For instance: "Chapter 17. COPING WITH TOMORROW. Direct Coping . . . Personal Stability Zones . . . Situational Grouping . . . Crisis Counseling . . ." The last item in this list (Global Space Pageants) reads like an odd afterthought—a carny touch intended to brighten up what are obviously pretty depressing prospects.

In the end it is the carny touch that stands out in Toffler's work. One is reminded of the rage of "modern" ideas that swept Paris before the Revolution—of Pinetti's "amusing physics" and the Abbé Mical's Talking Heads. Toffler tells us a good deal about the technical marvels lying ahead and about controlling our own evolution (if that's the word for it), but the whole thing reads like a combination of *Saga* and *Popular Mechanics*. For him it is as though the past had never existed. He writes from a perspective not of six thousand years but of two decades. For all one can tell, he is as indifferent to history as our mysteriously ineducable college students or our barely literate general public. He appears to share the peculiar parochialism which makes us imagine that because we have the telephone and a few other distracting conveniences, we are unlike any other civilization that ever was, that there is simply no continuity between what we once were and what we are now.

Toffler's prose is as up-to-the-minute as his ideas. He speaks of "fruitful roles" and "accelerative thrust" and "the strategy of futureness"—the essence of the last-named apparently being to cash

* See also the ads in publications such as *Screw*.

in on the suffering present. For the present is, of course, what we're talking about; it just sounds so much less dramatic to say so.* People don't know how to handle the lives they've got right now—and that despite more leisure than they've ever had to devote to the problem. But they don't devote it to that; they watch TV or play footsie with each other's wives or chase the big buck or go skin-diving. And when the sheer nothingness and anxiety of it all become too much for them, they take up alpha control or Sentics or Transactional Analysis, or become UFO nuts, or join a rural commune, or simply start drinking a lot. On the ground that it may get worse before it gets better, one could call that condition Future Shock, although the phrase strikes me as misleading and somewhat pretentious.

The various culture neuroses Toffler describes sound equally trumped-up. How serious a problem, really, is "overchoice"? No one *has* to listen to ads or allow himself to be psychologically swamped by the largess in his local supermarket. Big Brother does not force him to spend his income on junk he doesn't want. One would have to say he suffers not from overchoice but from underthink. The evidence, anyway, is that he *does* want it; a surfeit of mass-produced goodies is precisely what we set out to achieve in this country, from about 1870 on, and such was our success that the rest of the world envied us for it. But we, meanwhile, have grown too infantile to know what to do with it. Indeed, as Toffler himself says, we are going to pieces under it.

But as I'm sure he realizes, the overchoice problem is likely to solve itself. With populations and industrial wastes accumulating at the rates they now are, it seems probable that even without the help of nuclear war, our present affluence cannot last much longer. Already capital is moving out of this country into cheaper labor markets. The dollar has weakened abroad to such a degree that countries we once raided for commodities are now raiding us, raising our domestic prices and pushing our inflation toward the runaway stage. And although our birthrate is slowing down, the signs still are that the expansion of our economy may not be able

* *Present Shock* is not much of a title.

to keep up with it. This, rather than the one envisaged in his book, may be the "dialectical turning point" we are actually reaching. Far from having to cope with the synthetic excitements he describes, Toffler's mass audience may be lucky enough to continue in any assurance of steady employment and three meals a day. The so-called energy crisis of 1973 may be a sign that for us an era of plenty is coming to an end. *Future Shock* is consequently a glimpse of wonders for most of us never to come, and one feels that its author must see that, must see how the odds actually stand—which is what gives his book its essential cheapness.

Not that the Tomorrow he forecasts would be much more bearable than the one seemingly in prospect. There is a certain hollowness in his talk about a "fifty-year campaign to erase hunger" and his concern that life in the Skinnerian wilderness may cost us our sanity. If we are presently to be doing with human brains what Drs. White and Massopust did with a macaque's, the time for humane second thoughts is clearly past. *Future Shock* itself contains few enough of them. What one senses, in visionaries like Mr. Toffler, is a sort of crude sophistication, a delight in the devious and the mechanical for their own sakes, characteristics that are already quite visible in our world* and could well turn the future into the nightmare he describes. One thing is certain: whatever course things *do* take, there'll be a buck in it for somebody—as Toffler's book (available in several colors, like the telephone) has demonstrated.

* As the Watergate defendants have shown, with their wigs and walkie-talkies and pellet guns. From some of their testimony, one got the impression that they undertook their mission in the spirit of slightly cracked Boy Scouts.

xi

The Conservation of Nonsense

When motivational research first broke into the news, it seemed that a spooky new power had been unloosed upon us. Just by flashing the word FIRE! on a movie screen, for an interval too short to allow the audience to know they had seen it, you could throw them into a stew of anxiety. Flash POPCORN! and they would all rush out to buy some. Vance Packard's Hidden Persuaders were said to be using a form of MR—for instance, to sell laundry detergents on TV by showing the product, a white gooey liquid, spurting languidly from a container motivationally designed to resemble guess what?

We were equally appalled to learn, in the '50s, of the Communists' invention of brainwashing. Starting from Pavlovian fundamentals, they were said to have devised a method of counter-conditioning whereby anyone's convictions about anything could simply be erased and others substituted for them. It sounded almost too simple, and perhaps it was.

What has become of these sinister innovations? Is MR now in general use but just not talked about much? Has brainwashing as a method of making forced political converts worked? Probably not.* The fact is that nothing comes of most electrifying ideas or

---

* In the latter case, the number of man-hours of browbeating and psychological torture required per convert may have been prohibitive, and some, I have read, even required reprocessing.

As for MR in advertising, the number of products one can somehow make into sex objects or other items of special interest to the Id is doubtless limited. The use of lust or fear to draw attention to the product is an old technique in any case and need not work subliminally.

technical novelties. People just cease to be electrified. Sometimes they fail to be from the outset. Around 1912, a woman named Pearl Curran of St. Louis, Missouri, began writing whole novels and books of verse on a Ouija board—works she said were dictated by the spirit of a seventeenth-century English peasant girl who called herself Patience Worth. Mrs. Curran was astonishingly productive, and several of the Patience novels were published, receiving fairly good reviews. One would have expected them to cause great excitement—possibly to set off a boom in automatic writing—but nothing of the kind appears to have happened. Mrs. Curran may just have been ahead of her time.

To take another, apparently paradoxical, example: ideologies that may seem to have been dinned successfully into the heads of millions can change quite abruptly (as the Communist Party line has often done) or even disappear (as Nazism did) without causing the faithful any great perturbation. We tend to overlook this fact because it conflicts with our *idée fixe* about the remarkable powers of propaganda. One of the greatest triumphs of the Nazi propagandists was to convince us of the irresistibility of their methods—to such a point that long after they had failed we continued to believe in them. The miracles they worked with state-controlled radio, though dead in the minds of most Germans, are vivid still in ours. In 1950, the dawn of the TV age, Bertrand Russell suggested that there might be no limit on the extent to which populations could, as he put it, be "scientifically manipulated."

I doubt that that is actually the case. The very fact that propagandizing people demands such enormous unceasing efforts must mean that the process is rather inefficient. And of course, the basic premise of its enthusiasts cuts both ways: if we are as readily persuadable as they think, we are as readily dissuadable, which is why propagandists have to keep everlastingly at it. The truth is that apart from certain kinds of nonsense, mostly valetudinarian or religious, we have few strong preferences in ideas. Our convictions, like our behavior, are mostly a matter of protective coloration. It is therefore easy for those in power to be misled into thinking we are wildly enthusiastic about a particular credo, when in fact any official view that does not grossly infringe upon our self-interest is perfectly agreeable to us.* No one in either country seemed much taken aback when Russia and the United States, having been all but declared enemies from 1918 to 1940, suddenly became allies in 1941. For us ordinary citizens, capitalist or Communist, no really sacred article of faith was involved, although to have said so publicly might have been unwise.

Besides, it never troubles us that our leaders are illogical; we are so used to inconsistencies in our own thinking that we more or less expect them in theirs. It is this toleration of the contradictory which makes us liable to "scientific manipulation," our usual criterion being not the sense which the Party line seems to make but the vigor with which it is promulgated. Our ability to accommodate ourselves to irreconcilable notions is not, as snobs like Mencken supposed, a matter of simple stupidity, since in every era a great many intelligent men (Mencken included) have held quite peculiar opinions. The notion that only madmen are perfectly consistent is not a clinical truth but a way in which the sane save face.

Very early on in life, and almost without knowing it, we give up any attempt at making complete sense. We tell ourselves that that is because knowledge is too vast for us to know all of it, or too scanty to permit a real synthesis, but those are not the main reasons. We accept our inconsistency because we find ourselves so often obliged to come to terms not only with superior external forces but with superior internal ones, in the shape of our own fear, lust, avarice, etc. Being so often forced into rationalization, we give up and accept it as a way of life.

Moreover, the nervous system is so constructed that any radically new idea or event touches off a certain amount of fear—not because such ideas or events are threatening (often they are not), but because we don't know how to classify them at all. Instead of

---

* Who could have foreseen that Representative Nixon of Alger Hiss days would become President Nixon, traveling to Peking and Moscow in 1972? Who was really surprised when that happened?

fitting into some existing slot in our minds they simply float around, generating a diffuse agitation or "arousal." One way we try to calm ourselves in this situation is by forcing the comparison between an unclassifiable item and one already on file. A mysterious disk-shaped object in the sky is a "flying saucer." Identification by analogy is probably our earliest, most automatic, and most fallible method of thinking. It is also one of our more trustworthy defenses against seeing the new for what it is—a defense in the strict psychiatric sense, in that it sacrifices objective accuracy to restoration of the emotional peace. This initial fearlike response to strange or novel events, which the Russians somewhat misleadingly call the "orienting reflex," is an enormous hindrance to learning on our feet. On occasion (as the UFO literature seems to show) it can even make us hallucinate.

Given that newness is a problem in life and that we have these innate obstacles to dealing rationally with it, it follows that nature must have equipped us with some more reliable faculty or how would we have made such small progress as we have? That faculty is imitativeness, a disposition so strong one might include it with the rest of our instincts.

Our most basic characteristic is not, I suspect, love of mother, loyalty to the tribe, or even egoism; it is lack of originality. One can think of dozens of reasons why natural selection should have bred up that characteristic in us. Mimesis was perhaps the one sure way around our natural resistance to learning anything. As such, it is very efficient. Nobody catches on quicker than a good copycat. In addition, mimesis favored social cohesiveness from the outset, just as our inborn fear of the unfamiliar guaranteed that the members of one tribe would forever be prepared to hate and pounce upon those of another—or for that matter, upon eccentrics, foreigners, etc., in their own midst.

To those of us with the knack of rising in the tribe, imitativeness (in others) ranks among the highest of virtues, often being known as loyalty, devotion to duty, honor, obedience, etc. Kings, dictators, heads of corporations, teachers, priests, nannies, and of course generals all love a ready imitator, and are usually at some pains to ferret out and eliminate those who are not, thereby continuing the good work of natural selection on into civilized times.

Granted that this analysis is roughly correct, the wonder is not that nonsense has survived or lately begun a recrudescence, but that we have ever managed to escape from it, or from the trap of endless repetition we call custom. Among the things that have kept some civilizations from ossifying are disaster (invasion; conquest by others), practical innovations (which often insidiously modify everything), or plain ennui. One trouble with societies in which men are forever shouting, "Amen!" or "*Sieg Heil!*" is that they become terribly boring.

The problem is more acute in secular tyrannies, but even the ecclesiastical are not immune. In the same way that dictators are driven to conquest to hold their domestic audience, the clergy have frequently felt it necessary to promise miracles or catastrophes to come. Armageddon, the return of Christ, the end of the world by fire might be regarded as rather desperate measures designed essentially to maintain interest. It is a tribute to the powers of supernaturalist nonsense that faith, over the centuries, has withstood the nonoccurrence of predicted marvels* far better than Nazism or Bonapartism withstood the nonoccurrence of ultimate victory.

Having seen some of its psychological *raisons d'être*, we are now in a position to analyze and classify nonsense itself, one approach being to arrange it along a spectrum from most to least ephemeral. At the most ephemeral end lies what we call fashion. Most fashion has no very deep roots—no unique instinctive appeal or what Jung would call "archetypal content." What creates fashion is chiefly our mimetic tic, so that fashion itself can be, and often is, perfectly arbitrary. In her memoirs the Baroness Cécile de Courtot mentions that about 1801, the Parisian hatter Thierry made a bet that he could design a hat "in the very most absurd shape imaginable" and make it the rage. "These are tall cylinders of black felt, smooth as mirrors, and look exactly like chimney pots." As

---

* So far as I have heard, astrologers in India were not put out of business when the end of the world, which they had predicted for 1964, failed to take place. And it is *since* that time that astrology has become so big with Young America.

fashions go, this one has proved quite long-lived but may still pass, the high hat surviving today chiefly on the heads of diplomats, tropical potentates, and first-nighters at the opera.

At the opposite end of the scale lies religious nonsense—by which I mean not the word of saints and prophets but the official theology supposedly inspired by them: the claptrap of professional ecclesiastics. Between these two extremes of durability lie the systems of political belief known nowadays as ideologies.

One can immediately see that while ideologies have of necessity some "archetypal content" it is not as compelling as that of organized religion. For with few exceptions (Judaism being one), most churches promise a life after death, thus meeting *the* requirement for indefinite survival (i.e., of the doctrine as well as the believer). Most political ideologies cannot offer as much, except in the halfhearted *kitschy* way the Nazis did with their talk of Wotan. The appeal of statism in the German or Roman style is to men's more proximate needs—for instance, their need to torture, rob, and kill others.*

Therefore autocracies must produce results, and go on producing them, unless the populace can be as utterly crushed as it seems to be in present-day Spain or Portugal. The great vitality of movements such as Nazism is to some extent an illusion. They appear to have the authority of revealed truth, but in reality represent a form of the Social Contract. So long as a majority can be convinced that the revolutionary program is working, it is "true," and any number of fanatics are available to carry it out. When events act to tear apart that consensus—when, for instance, defeat on the battlefield shows the regime's doctrines to be "false"—a system of political beliefs that has commanded the evident loyalty of millions can crumble and disappear with extraordinary speed.

Cynics noted that after the fall of the Third Reich, hardly a single Nazi other than those in the dock at Nuremberg could be

---

* Fascism might be defined as a form of society in which crime has become a state monopoly. We tend to think of it as the work of hoodlums who have managed to take over the government, when in reality it may be the only alternative for societies such as ours, in which private crime has gone out of control.

found in all of Germany. But actually, of course, that was so. Circumstances had simply canceled the "set" or will to believe that had once caused Nazi ideas to be acceptable, even to highly educated Germans; while another instinctive reaction, fear for the self, made the cancellation retroactive: nobody had *ever* believed in them. That particular Social Contract had gone into the shredder and, like certain documents pertaining to the Watergate affair, exculpated all concerned by its disappearance. In the same way, after the defeat of the Axis powers in 1944–45, Italian Fascism evaporated and the emperor of Japan withdrew to his palace, living on as if in a museum whose chief exhibit he had suddenly become.

Up to the moment when sheer fact finally smashes down such ideological fortresses, the instincts that created them may be further inflamed, intensifying public devotion to the point of madness; i.e., the less our ideas work, the more failure and fear make us incapable of devising alternatives, the more we "fixate" our original mistakes—a principle to which American foreign policy during the past two decades* may have owed its remarkable consistency. The same mechanism accounts for the fact that regimes just about to be overwhelmed by foreign enemies seem never more secure in the loyalty and ardor of their rank-and-file, many of whom will soon be acting as their hangmen.†

If by nonsense one means arbitrary ideas—essentially mistakes— it is clear that nonsense has a feature our ordinary mistakes do not. The latter are apt, in the natural course of things, to correct themselves. Show a farmer it is in his interest to plow along the contour instead of straight up- and downhill, and sooner or later he will probably do so. In the meantime, he is not likely to become violently angry and denounce you as a Commie saboteur for suggesting such a thing. Contour plowing is simply not that kind of issue (though fluoridation of water, for some reason, is).

Nonsense, on the other hand, is not self-correcting. Quite the reverse; it is cemented in place by forces far more powerful than

* From the Truman through the Johnson Administrations.
† As happened in the case of the ever-popular Mussolini.

those of mere logic. Because they have arrived at a view of things that enables them to manage the Id, religious men often have a serenity of spirit which is highly deceptive. They appear to accept small reverses or even large ones equably, to move through life as though invisibly armored. But if one makes the mistake of questioning certain key notions on which that psychic stability rests, the man only a moment ago so calm and reasonable may turn into a most dangerous maniac.

The second feature of nonsense which distinguishes it from ordinary simple error is that it tends to become an edifice. A farmer who plows straight up- and downhill is not likely to have concocted elaborate arguments in support of that practice. It has merely proved, over the years, a convenient way of working. Unless he is an organic farmer, he is not apt to have a mystique about the perfect way of doing anything. Religious and political beliefs are unfortunately not like that. They do tend to grow into complicated structures and (in the case of religions) may then endure for centuries, in the face of the most threatening evidence or even of overt heresy and insurrection. The collapse of such structures, when it finally occurs, creates an impression that mankind has made a great leap forward in intelligence. Nothing of the kind, of course, has happened. It is just that citizens of an era which has managed, finally, to put certain of the delusions of the fathers behind it are apt to be so dazzled by that event that they fail to see what its authors have in mind as a sequel.

The principle of the conservation of nonsense applies in particular to religious ideas because of their unique power to placate the Id. To some degree, however, all nonsense has this feature; and once any idea has been around long enough, even reasonable men are apt to be impressed and to suppose it may be true. For centuries the Chinese have believed in acupuncture; therefore there must be something in it.* On the same principle, any number of

* And for the moment, by some reports, there is—which recalls Sir William Osler's suggestion that we should by all means use new drugs before they lose their efficacy. I am told, incidentally, that Osler himself once investigated acupuncture. (He recommended it for lumbago.)

ancient beliefs tend to persist into later times—sometimes disguised or overlaid with minor innovations; sometimes (like acupuncture) pretty much unchanged. It is as though *nothing* men had once taken seriously—witchcraft, *mana* ("vibes"; aura energy), transmigration, divine or malevolent Providence—was ever dropped from our repertoire. Religions in particular repeat one another, hiding old rituals in new. The gods never die; they are simply renamed.

Jung would attribute this phenomenon to what he called "archetypes."* I would attribute it to a poverty of ideas. There is only a certain range of messages acceptable to the Id, and we have been able to think of only a certain number of ways of phrasing them.

An important peculiarity of nonsense is that however passionately we appear to believe in it, we never do, quite. For in acceding to the demands of instinct, mind develops an uneasiness of its own. Our intelligence is, among other things, alert to its own mistakes. And since error, as such, can be a threat to our survival, it is logical that our psyches should be so organized that when we become even vaguely aware of our own mistakes, we react with anxiety. This circular arrangement, in which fear may generate systematically erroneous wishful notions, which in turn generate an awareness of error and so, by feedback, still more fear from another source, may explain why "conflict" or emotional unease is so inescapable a feature of our lives.

It also explains why the wildest, most arbitrary forms of nonsense are likely to inspire the most fanatical adherence. For in the nature of the case, the believer feels himself especially vulnerable; willy-nilly, his intelligence tells him he is—his response being to keep himself perpetually "dynamic" and worked up. His safety lies not in thinking, obviously, but in doing. He gets the sacred message down by rote, as Communist friends of mine got their Marx, and thereafter never examines it, never looks inward, but devotes himself to useful and reassuring tasks such as correcting wrong thoughts in those around him. It is not merely the spirit of dissent, but its content which threatens him. Hence intelligent dis-

---

* Roughly, inherited ideas or racial memories, comparable to instincts.

senters are much more to be feared than stupid ones, and intelligence alone may be grounds enough for preventive action.*

It follows that the inner conflicts bred by nonsense readily become outer and often on a colossal scale, resulting in those holocausts in the name of the True Faith of which history is so full. Nor is it surprising that religions in particular should inspire this sort of militancy, and that generations of clerics should busy themselves creating huge superstructures of dogma out of the (usually simple) utterances of the saints.

An evident source of these metaphysical exertions, if not the chief one, is our fear of death. Confronted by the knowledge that we must die, and by the mystery of what, if anything, lies beyond, we are put in a psychic predicament which other creatures are spared. It is perhaps untrue to say that animals do not "reflect" or that they have no awareness of themselves. The important point may be that they become reflective or self-aware only on occasion, when prompted by present circumstances. They do not seem to have the faculty of continuous, as it were self-propelled, thinking. Their thoughts accordingly do not have the generality of ours, and in particular take no account of the distant future. They may learn to dread certain signs as meaning "you may die,"† but the generality "all creatures must die" apparently never occurs to them.

Unfortunately for us, we have inherited the same basic psychic apparatus but have added to it the faculty known as mind, whose actions, though often wildly inaccurate, are also incessant. The result is that in us, thought alone—for instance, the thought of death —*can* chronically inflame the instincts and their corresponding emotions, thereby chronically dislocating mind's own workings as I have described. Moreover, the will to survive is possibly the most

---

* One can hardly think of a society, including our own, that has not regarded it with suspicion—so that when the earlier, more benign triumphs of science were followed by the Bomb, we greeted that event almost with relief. We were free to dislike and distrust intellect again.
† Really as touching off painfully violent fear and activation, a largely innate response which they fear as such. There is no evidence that the idea of death figures in their thoughts.

powerful of any, and the generality "we must die" the most un-challengeable, from which it follows that *the* great fount of non-sense—greater even than sexual love—is the uneasiness we feel in confronting the idea of death. Unless that is somehow brought un-der control, unless death can be made to seem a passage to other forms of existence, we can never be at peace; it becomes, so to speak, the background of everything we do, in relation to which all happiness, all our feelings of security or accomplishment, are mere episodes. We may with effort shut death out of our thoughts but it is always there, waiting to be brought back by a thousand reminders.

To settle this harrowing question of our own mortality, we *must* therefore devise a more satisfactory hypothesis than common sense in fact permits, and few religions of any scope have failed to pro-vide one. Indeed, it is doubtful if they could have established a hold on us or maintained it for long without doing so. One might suppose, then, that the only religious issue on which men would become fanatical is this one. But of course that is not so. It is not enough for seers such as Jesus Christ to hint at survival after death.

For one thing, mind, the error detector, may become suspicious of the news that all of us will live forever. So the idea of immor-tality must needs be elaborated into a doctrine which, just because it is one—widely known and argued and fought over—is felt by everyone to be the more believable. Medieval churchmen accord-ingly evolved a complete eschatology, including minutely detailed programs for salvation and two sorts of afterlife, one for the good and one for the evil.

But with this it would appear that Christ's injunction that we should love and forgive one another has become tainted with self-interest to the point of making our concept of virtue almost mean-ingless. For now human goodness is no longer an end in itself but a means to the most passionately desired of rewards, eternal exist-ence. (Note, too, that under this system, even the evil are given some sort of afterlife; which means that in this one you can err pretty badly and still not risk all.)

This elaboration has in fact been the principal business of ec-clesiastics, the more rational, compassionate side of Christianity having resulted chiefly in some centuries of perfunctory poor-relief. Since the main result of Church doctrine was to put goodness on the wrong basis and to judge it by the wrong standards—those of orthodoxy rather than those of evident virtue*—it is no paradox at all that Christians should repeatedly have exterminated their brethren in wars of faith or set up special institutions whose function was the torture and murder of deviant believers.

Because of the principle I have described—namely, that men can never feel secure enough in ideas which they know in their hearts to be ridiculous—enforcement of correct religious views necessarily became a major undertaking of the clergy. For not until no one is left to challenge them are the faithful absolutely safe from the assaults of reason. Better a converted sinner who persists in his sins than a virtuous heathen who may dispute you. The real slogan of proselytizers is not "Show them the Way!" but "Get them to agree!"†

In medieval Europe, agreement consisted in acknowledging, and acting as though one believed in, quite complex formulas for guaranteeing the soul's safety. Any other formula, since it implied doubt of the orthodox one, was not to be countenanced. Not only did those who strayed in this way risk their heavenly reward; their lives on earth might end quite suddenly too, and good riddance, in the opinion of the devout. For under this moral system, the greatest of undesirables is not the pagan but the heretic—the man in your midst who knows full well what he should believe but all the same goes around doing the Devil's work, questioning established ideas or, more subtly, by the unspoken comment of his actions, undermining the faith of others.‡

* Realists will maintain that the gentleness and forgiveness urged by Christ were not rational—meaning that these virtues are scarcely possible, and if possible would prove suicidal to those who practiced them. But the sort of competitive realism we do practice may work out no better—indeed, not as well. What true Christian would have hit upon the Bomb as a solution to the problem of survival?
† Almost the first thing the conquistadors did on this continent, after killing Indians, was to get the survivors to "take the Cross." The natives (as they still do in Guatemala) might go on with their older forms of worship, but the main point had been gained; they had agreed.
‡ This was the view we held of Communist "fellow travelers," especially during the late 1940s and early '50s.

The laity had reason to detest such people. As a good Christian, one feared for one's own soul as much as, or possibly a little more than, for the souls of others. A heretic could conceivably trick one into forfeiting it, which meant that many felt heresy to be a quite personal crime—an attack on everyone's eternal prospects including their own. Thus a crusading zeal for the faith was ultimately as selfish as the nationalistic zeal of later times, the arguments in defense of it being even more high-flown because of the more blatant moral contradictions they were required to cover.

Very few of the intricacies of medieval theology could have been logically derived from the things which Christ himself said— it being, of course, chiefly in the minds of his distracted vicars that these sprang up, along with much else not describable as Christian or even sane. However, Christianity, while still a living faith, had two things to recommend it: Almost in spite of itself, it taught certain moral principles of real value. And it acted, so to speak, to centralize nonsense, creating a state monopoly whose effect was to lift from men's minds an immense burden of uncertainty and dread.

Some will maintain that the Church did nothing of the sort— that it acted to create more fears than ever it set to rest. In fact it tried to do so, but not immediately. (Witches, for example, were treated rather leniently in the early Middle Ages.) And if one looks at the sequence of events, say, from the time of Gregory VII, in the eleventh century, to the Hussite wars in the early fifteenth, it appears that the doctrinaire ferocity of the clergy developed gradually, as if in reaction to the gathering exuberance of their parishioners.

This general rise in spirit, or spirits, which the Church had helped bring about manifested itself in the twelfth and thirteenth centuries not only in the new world of the chartered towns but in a thriving literature, vernacular as well as courtly—in romaunts and superb poetry and the work of men such as Roger Bacon or the remarkable Ramon Lull.* Impressive and promising though they

---

* Lull, himself a churchman, is said to have anticipated computers in his *Ars Magna*, which envisioned a universal logical symbolism into which all problems

were, these developments spelled trouble. For in proportion as men were relieved of ultimate doubt and thus freed from some of the constraints imposed upon their thinking by fear, they inevitably began to question that body of nonsense to which they owed their new *sang-froid*. For the Church, this turn of events prophesied disaster, since it meant that a faith too secure and untroubled today might well lead to agnosticism and collapse of the ecclesiastical power tomorrow.

It was perhaps for that reason that the "open" period of Christianity was short-lived, and that just when the Medieval Synthesis, as some call it, was reaching its apogee in the thirteenth century, the punishment of heresy began to be far more systematic and severe than it had been, say, in the days of Bernard of Clairvaux. Had St. Francis (who died in 1226) been born fifty years later, it is quite probable that he would not have died a natural death. As it was, his order was immediately corrupted,* while those few of his disciples who set out to follow his example were treated as public enemies and done away with by the usual methods.

The meaning of these developments seems to be clear enough. Having too thoroughly relieved its flock of certain ancestral fears, the Church was obliged to reinstate them in the form of an intensified fear of itself. Too many internal obstacles to thought having been removed, certain external obstacles now had to be devised, if only to keep those who did think for themselves from encouraging the same bad habit in others. With admirable realism, clerics such as Innocent III and Gregory IX (under whom the Inquisition was formally established, in 1233) may have reasoned that while faith

---

could be translated. His ideas influenced Giordano Bruno and Leibniz. His romance *Blanquerna* was still read in the eighteenth century. He is said to have been a great traveler and linguist, as well as a sincere and gentle Christian who believed that the way to make converts was through reason and good example. The reaction against him was surprisingly slow in coming. He lived until 1315, when (as one writer puts it) "at the age of eighty he achieved his longed-for goal of martyrdom."

* As Bertrand Russell says in his *History of Western Philosophy*, St. Francis' successor, Brother Elias, was a libertine. The Franciscans became "recruiting sergeants" in the Guelph-Ghibelline wars, and in several countries conducted the Inquisition.

robs the thought of death of its terrors for many, the immediate prospect of it, especially when coupled with torture, threats of eternal damnation, and the whole solemn ritual of expulsion from the ranks of the blessed may simply be too much for men—which on the whole proved to be quite true. For centuries afterward, a few in each generation—the German Mystics, Jan Hus, the Lollards—offered themselves up as sacrifices to the Better Way, but the majority never strayed. Nonsense was inviolate.

One result was that the education which the Church somewhat unwisely offered long remained, as it were, frozen in the minds of its recipients. Classical learning, roughly from the fourteenth until the eighteenth century, had the blessing of both First and Second Estates in part because, as practiced, it was entirely safe. To study and make marginal comments on the work of the ancients—to put great stress on mastery by rote and little on factual analysis or original ideas—guaranteed culture as an ornament of the state* while minimizing any embarrassments it might cause as a vehicle of present truth.

But of course a situation so delicately balanced could not last. Little by little the habit of thinking spread; the scope of thought increased and its accomplishments accumulated, but always under the cover of a most exquisite tact. Descartes, in the seventeenth century, is said to have felt considerable nervousness, the implications of his ideas being in fact far more serious than were those of Galileo's. Giordano Bruno, who came earlier, had been rash enough to criticize Aristotle and support Copernicus. (He was executed in 1600.) Malpighi, possibly the most gifted experimental physiologist of the time, managed to live an officially blameless life, becoming in his old age physician to the Pope. It was found at his death, however, that he had willed his papers to the Royal Society in London, as though from an awareness that his work might suffer a fate he himself had escaped.

---

* Buckle, in the second volume of his *History*, remarks that "there was another class of dictators . . . the old classical scholars and commentators who . . . were respected as being by far the most distinguished men Europe had ever produced. . . . It was generally believed that ancient history possessed some inherent superiority over modern . . ."—which in the sense meant here was definitely true.

The Reformation may be regarded as a consequence of several of the older Church's mistakes, the chief of which had been to teach the laity any of the real principles of Christianity. For not only did these provide men with certain tools and incentives for thinking; they also, inevitably, showed the Church itself in a bad light. Not that the Protestants, having made capital of Catholic excesses, failed to commit similar ones. The persecution of witches, which reached a peak in the sixteenth and seventeenth centuries, was as vigorous in Protestant lands as in Catholic. And in seventeenth-century Scotland, the Presbyterian common clergy, although brave and patriotic when it came to resisting the English, were also the most unsparing of tyrants, who spied upon and terrorized their parishioners, subjected them to five or six hours of fearsome sermonizing on Sundays, excommunicated many for trivial offenses, compiled endless lists of sins (swimming on the Sabbath was one), and through the medium of the elders and the Kirk-session (a kind of Inquisition), meddled in the affairs of the whole community. The Scots of that period probably knew the Devil better than did any other people in Europe.

Apropos of the longevity of religious, as compared with secular, systems of nonsense, it is interesting that Russian Communism, now a bare five decades old, is already finding itself in the same difficulties that began to trouble the Church of Rome after some eight centuries. The faithful are getting restive; the very airtightness of Communist doctrine guarantees it. Given that amount of absolute certainty from the cradle, rising young minds are going to be too free to think.

For the weakness of any ideology is precisely that it is too Skinnerian; it offers only earthly "reinforcements." The man who challenges it risks his life but not his eternal life. The man who breaks with his traditional religion risks both. Therefore ideologies are always more precarious and rightly rely on terror as a basic method of governing.*

In our civilization, it was not until the eighteenth century that

* Democracy, being an ideology but a permissive one, requires a true rational consensus or a people still subject to the restraints of religion. In democracies lacking either, the citizens are apt to begin terrorizing one another, forcing the state finally to terrorize them—i.e., to cease being a democracy.

the Old Nonsense finally began to weaken, and not until the twentieth that the whole Western world started drifting into agnosticism. To historiographers, this is a familiar sequence. All civilizations, they tell us, come finally to a Time of Troubles, when the faith of the fathers passes and a period of skepticism, materialism, and general turbulence sets in. Denied the consolations of the old religion, men seek them in new forms—in Mystery Cults and psi therapeutics. Old regimes are brought down, and the revolution, exported, results in successive wars of conquest, ending usually in the victory of one great power over the rest. This is the period of Contending States—in the modern world, of the emergence of ideologies. These last have no content,* representing reversions to a barbarous autocracy à la Hitler or Caesar, whose appeal is that they simplify the life of the average citizen. More correctly, they simplify his thinking; nor is that done against his will. He *demands* it. The *Simplificateur Terrible* is his own creation—the superbeing who will make existence "meaningful" for him, brighten his material prospects, relieve him of all responsibility except that of being a good follower.

An analyst of nonsense might at this point be inclined to say that if history is really cyclical, it is so because it represents a kind of inner battle—mind's successive, and as yet always unsuccessful, attempts to fight its way clear of the ancient rule of conditioning and the Id. For reasons I have described, this struggle begins with the great religions, which, nonsensified and perverted as they always are, nonetheless contain certain essential psychological truths. Of these, the most basic is that man, alone among creatures, is inwardly divided and can unify himself only at a cost of continual pain and effort. He alone is self-made; to aspire is not his option but his fate.

Because a few men in every civilization, including the saints or

---

* This being especially true of Fascism. The Marxism of Russia and China may be a different phenomenon—in Russia's case, a kind of Reformation in which the religious element is still present despite all efforts to kill it. In China a whole new culture may be struggling to be born, the function of Marxism there being to wipe out the old by massive brainwashing. What course either of these revolutions will finally take is impossible to guess, but they are not the same and not natural allies.

true founders of its faith, have recognized that fact, great religions, no matter how abused, have always brought great achievements and at least a few Universal Men in their train. They have also brought a hope of freedom, but not freedom in the sense in which Everyman understands it. It is not the freedom to *do* as he likes that is crucial, but the freedom to *be* what he feels he should —a human, no longer ruled by the Skinnerian beast inside him.

At bottom, this is what the notion of Free Will comes down to. We sense that the "I," the rational-imaginative self, has an autonomy proper to itself, which can and must be won if we are not to live perpetually in the "darkness of sin"—which is to say as animals driven by our own adaptiveness and haunted by the knowledge of our servitude, our *partiality*.

Stripped of its supernaturalist nonsense, what the idea of the soul and salvation—of grace—really stands for is this state of inner completeness. If so, it was Rousseau, not the Puritan fathers, who was deluded. It is not by surrendering the "I" but by achieving it that man arrives at the "oceanic sense," through a self-possession which opens both inner and outer worlds to the eye of the mind. Falling short of that state, as we find we are doing today, we console ourselves by repeating, endlessly, that really it was never in us to achieve it.* We despair of "intellectualizing" and seek the oceanic sense in the only other way available to us: through release and a passive experiencing of the unconscious—in drugs, in TM, in the "dark otherness" of sex.

But that is, in effect, to abandon the human in ourselves for the automatic and the animal, to become what Professor Skinner says we are. And in that we seem to be doing what other civilizations before us have done. At what should have been the height of our powers, we are opting for a half-deliberate barbarity. And like its predecessors, our culture shows signs of receding into Alexandrianism, becoming a temple object reserved to a special caste which understands it really no better than the rest of us. What the political results of these changes will be is easy to guess; indeed we

---

* Hence our innumerable theories proving the feebleness of Ego, the superiority of gut knowledge, etc. Hence Skinner.

THE NEW NONSENSE

have already seen some of them, in the revolutions of the Right of this century.

So reason appears to be losing once more, repeating a cycle one can trace as far back as the Hundred Schools of Philosophy in ancient China or the Hyksos in Egypt. Arising in clouds of non-sense, great civilizations seem condemned to ebb away in nonsense again, the saviors of the end—the god-emperors—echoing the saviors or betrayed God of the beginning.

Perhaps, after all, reason is not up to the victory—not because it is so weak but because, thanks to thousands of years of natural selection, the Id is so strong. Therefore plain intelligence may not be the problem. If it were possible to raise the I.Q. of whole pop-ulations overnight, the result might well not be a golden age of rationality but simply an intensification of our present struggle for personal or tribal advantage. Most of us today would say that that *is* the problem: no matter what its powers as a computer, the rational self is no match for Superego and Id. The fact remains, however, that only a small percentage of the men in any civiliza-tion have been given the chance to become human in the sense I have tried to define here—so until a majority have been given that chance and failed, it is too soon to say our prospects are hopeless.

In the meantime, there is no denying they are rather poor. Christianity never made Christians of more than a handful of us. And today the Renaissance ideal of universality, and the Vic-torian, of universal reason, are as good as dead. The specialist mentality cannot understand what these ideals meant, and the men of the New Nonsense don't want to. More and more, *à la* Toffler, we see our world only in the thin present—like primitive men, as Ortega y Gasset said, risen suddenly in the midst of a very old civilization. America, the country where it once seemed likely that a majority *would* be given the chance to become human, has fallen victim to a pragmatism whose consequences no one could have foreseen. The rational "I" became too pruned-down in us, developed on too narrow a base, making us the most childlike of modern nations, capable of amorphous inquisitiveness into almost everything but incapable of much genuine interest or depth of understanding.

Being childlike, we have hope and even a kind of innocence still, are clumsy sophisticates and uneasy in our libertinism. But it is among us that the new magicians are thriving and the next wave of the revolution has begun. The Second Religiousness stands on our street corners in Hare Krishna or the Jesus Freaks. Father Freud is dead, and the Terrible Simplifiers of our psychic problems now tell us we can solve them by fighting and screaming. In therapy, in our popular entertainments, in real life, the whole move is toward baldness, a most brutal simplicity. But childlike and residually idealistic as we are, we resist, not understanding what is upon us, not quite sure it is all as easy as the gurus and porn pushers and one-factor theorists make it seem. It is not too late for us, but very nearly.

The New Nonsense—really bits and pieces of the old, brought back and given a "now" look by entrepreneurs who know their market—arises when men, having abandoned faith for reason, find the task of living by reason too difficult for them. The rational consensus degenerates into enlightened selfishness, then into selfishness outright. Rousseau's solution to the human predicament was to let each be his God-given self; Skinner's was to set up scientific controls, guaranteeing "automatic goodness." We have tried a mixture of both, and neither has worked. At that point reason, defeated, retreats still further, from radical egoism into radical subjectivity.

A generation is rising now determined to see what it wants to see—believing in karma and "vibes" and the infinite healing powers of sex; thinking it can go back to nineteenth-century rural life if it chooses, that it can play at disaffectedness or revolution or mystical withdrawal indefinitely, that it is without obligations except to itself, that in a world of the savagely competent it can disdain competence, that it can let lapse a precision of thought and language and an accumulation of knowledge which men have labored centuries, and often at the cost of their lives, to amass— believing all of this, moreover, in perfect innocence, sure that only good will come of it. Whom the gods would destroy, they first make simple—simpler and simpler.

In Mind Control courses, the teacher reads to the congregation from a photocopied Good Book. As the faithful "go to their level" (the alpha state) he intones the lesson for the day, telling each that he is going "to a deeper healthier level of mind," that he has, thanks to Mind Control, such remarkable powers he can heal himself or others merely by willing it, can project his thoughts to other planets in the solar system or to other solar systems in the galaxy, etc. Many verses end with the statement "And this is so."

The same inflexible incantatory style developed years earlier in the psychoanalytic movement,* and in the case of such practitioners as Dr. Janov, may be the key to their therapeutic success. As another psychiatrist, Anthony Storr, remarked: "Janov has one card up his sleeve which few of us more skeptical theorists can match. He is absolutely sure he is right. Again and again he makes remarks of an unbelievably dogmatic kind. Primal therapy is not only the best cure for neurosis, it is the only cure." ("And this is so.")

The totalitarian tone of Janov and Schultz and Casriel and others like them is not incidental. They are to Freud roughly what Hitler was to Bismarck; simpler, more brutal-minded men. The intricate and subtle are no more their "bag" than their patients'. *All* original writing, according to Dr. Bergler, is based upon a suppressed desire to plagiarize from others. *All* adult neuroses are of early parental origin and can be cured by "recovery of the repressed" and screaming. Learn to control your alpha rhythm and all psychic powers will become yours—ESP, healing-at-a-distance, visits to previous incarnations, astral spaceflight. The trick is to take one key idea, as Reich did with orgone, and expand it into a universe. (Orgone *filled* the universe, which was just as good.) It must offer relief of anxiety in some form, preferably in the form of promises of a life to come;† glimpses of hidden spirit worlds interwoven with the everyday one; dimensions along which the trapped, tormented self can escape to find itself again—reborn, on

---

* Freud was, of course, continually excommunicating disciples who had developed unsound views. And anyone who has been in orthodox analysis, as it used to be called, knows at first hand the dogmatism I am talking about. Few supposedly scientific disciplines have set so quickly and so hard—in part no doubt because what the laity was paying for was not progress but certainty.
† Bergler and Regardie, and even Encounter, fell down badly here.

a higher plane. And it must be basically simple. Transcendence and simplicity are the thing. In Hitler's Germany whatever was wrong was due to the Jews and Versailles. But in the mystical union of National Socialism, Germany would transcend itself, would become invincible, wiping out all opposition everywhere, establishing a sort of Valhalla on earth. One heard it in the primal scream of the great rallies in Nuremberg.

It is not a coincidence that so many of the quacks of Mesmer's day were also revolutionaries; nor is it accidental that the New Nonsense and the so-called Young Revolution reached simultaneous peaks here in the 1960s. There was, as I pointed out, far less real cause for revolutionary discontent in America during the past decade than there had been in the Depression thirty years earlier. What distinguished the two eras was the degree of psychological erosion we had undergone in the meantime.

In those critical years, the last vestiges of our faith were perhaps passing; and even as that happened we were exposed (in the case of Belsen and Auschwitz and Dresden and Hiroshima) to the spectacle of what men could and would do as simply adaptive animals, trying to live under a system of "automatic goodness." In the same period we seemed to experience a sharp rise in anxiety* —which is to say an increase in the pressure of primitive emotion of all kinds. Some of that anxiety drained itself off by conversion into anger, producing a sudden rash of militancy (Women's Lib, SDS, etc.). No one would deny that many of the evils protested against were real, but the protest itself had an extra something behind it—such that if the militants were suddenly given all they demanded, one felt that they would be quite balked and let down and become even angrier.† Among Fem Lib people or in the

---

* It was then, roughly in the '50s, that we began speaking of it, after Auden, as an Age of Anxiety.
† In the financial section of *The New York Times* (Sunday, August 6, 1972) it was reported that the vice-president of an executive-placement agency had been canvassing various people including feminists, trying to find lady executives—the trend in business apparently being to hire more women for the sort of top-echelon work once reserved for men. Here is the comment reportedly made by Betty Harragan of the Association of Feminist Consultants: "Suddenly these male chauvinist pigs are picking our brains and then passing themselves off as experts on women's rights."

Weathermen and SDS, one found the same Terrible Simplifiers as were appearing in psychotherapy—dogmatic one-factor theorists who were prepared to *écraser l'infame* by their own special means and would stand for no back talk from the laity. A revolutionary era, in short, is one in which a huge surplus of emotional energy has piled up to the point at which it *must* find an object. The first result is an epidemic of the New Nonsense; the second, a series of splinter revolutions; and the third, perhaps, *the* revolution.

It is presumably when the more minor, trial solutions to the anxiety problem have failed—when the Weathermen have gone and the campuses lapsed into apathy, when Fem Lib gets more concessions than it really wants, when Mind Control and scientology have lost their magic and Scream is but an echo—that the time is ripe for *the* revolution, the Terrible Simplifier who, if we will only surrender all our freedom and responsibility to him, will bring about magical improvements in every department of our lives and give us, en bloc, a new sense of worth and purpose. His vocation is to do for us what the Church did long ago—to centralize nonsense in himself, enabling us once again to throw our troubles on the Lord.

It is hard to imagine a Napoleon or a Hitler arising in this country, but the psychological preconditions for such an event clearly seem to exist here, especially if we compare America in our day to France in Mesmer's.* The comparison suggests that what I have called the New Nonsense is essentially an interregnum occurring between the collapse of the Old Faith and the forcible establishment of the New—the "ideology."

Just before the French Revolution, changes were taking place in the social and intellectual lives of Frenchmen quite similar to those we see in the United States now. In the 1780s, seemingly at the apogee of the Age of Reason, Paris was swept by bizarre fads. Alongside the very considerable science of the day, there appeared that "astonishing rabble of quacks and angry cosmologists" I spoke of; and as their audience grew, the audience for genuine science noticeably diminished. In the same period, the salons rapidly be-

---

* Some will be quick to point out the differences. I am aware of them. Nor do they mean the similarities have no meaning.

came more "democratic," and the egalitarian tone of Mesmer's clinics was particularly remarked on.* Political ideas were strangely interwoven with mesmerist doctrine, and a number of theories, including Mesmer's, postulated universal fluids or orgonelike radiations which could bring health and virility to those who learned how to tap them. The boulevards fairly buzzed with nonsense, but of a kind very different from the pronouncements of men such as Bossuet, back in the days of *le Roi Soleil*. The productions of the 1780s were new to the French imagination, a riot-growth of odd ideas or theoretical devices—cosmologies, programs, "laws" of man and society, definitions of the Good—many of which had grown out of Voltaire and Rousseau the way that orgone and Scream and scientology have grown out of Freud. It is above all this multitudinousness which characterizes the New Nonsense. Compared with the Gothic creations of theology, it perhaps lacks grandeur, but more than makes up for that in vitality. Springing up as the old orthodoxies die but before those to come have yet taken shape, it is more various and ephemeral than either, flourishing for a brief brilliant season like a swarm of autumnal butterflies.†

It is a pity that in Rome there were few chroniclers of a mind to record the gaudy fancies which possessed men during the last decades of the Republic. We know that Egyptian and Oriental religions were spreading among the masses, just as Stoicism, long before, in the time of Scipio Aemilianus, had spread among the educated, both phenomena being an apparent response to the passing of the old faith. Some of the Mystery religions were evidently quite savage, involving flagellation and ritual bloodletting, and the era as a whole appears to have been most unsettled.

In his *History of the Roman Republic* Mommsen speaks of the "anxious suspense" and "gloomy perplexity" of the multitude, and concludes with this passage:

---

* See above, page 63.
† For of course, the *petits maîtres*, the Mesmers and Hörbigers and Janovs, have no place in the big event when it comes, and are lucky enough if they know that, taking their money, like Mesmer, and scurrying off into obscurity. Those who fail to understand their role as protofigures—symptoms—are apt to wind up as Danton did, with their heads in a basket.

Restlessly the wandering imagination climbed every height and fathomed every abyss where it fancied it might discover . . . new light among the fatalities impending. . . . A portentous mysticism found in the general distraction . . . the soil which was adapted for it and grew with alarming rapidity. It was as if gigantic trees had grown by night out of the earth, none knew whence or whither, and this very rapidity of growth worked new wonders . . . [seizing] like an epidemic on all minds not thoroughly fortified.

Not that all the nonsense of our own day is as grim (although the satanism now reportedly widespread in America, England, and Germany and the recent cults of human sacrifice on our West Coast have some resemblance to the savage faiths Mommsen describes). But the climate of distraction is definitely there. The gigantic trees are growing again.

In *Couples* John Updike describes his characters as "suspended in . . . one of those dark ages that visit mankind between millennia, between the death and rebirth of the gods, when there is nothing to steer by but sex and stoicism and the stars." He omitted to mention nonsense, for most of us a beacon as enduring as any. Like the instincts, it may change somewhat in its outward manifestations, but in principle and in basic content it never does. The instincts being conservative, it is conserved.

So long as intelligence and true imagining never decisively win —never persuade us of the powers they obviously have—the bulk of mankind will look to nonsense, living by its steady lunatic light and thinking themselves God's chosen for doing so. Professor Skinner could have saved himself a lifetime of theorizing had he bothered to read forty lines of the Grand Inquisitor.

Notes

1. T. C. Rennie *et al.*, *American Journal of Psychiatry*, Vol. 113, pp. 831–37 (1957). The study covered 1,660 New Yorkers of upper, middle, and lower income groups who lived in the same (one mile square) area of the city. Signs of neurosis and psychosis were most frequent in the lower and middle groups. Anxiety was considered prevalent at all levels, but especially so at the topmost.

2. "Man is not born wicked," according to Voltaire; "he becomes so [just] as he becomes sick."* In *Emile* Rousseau puts the case more strongly: "The fate [of men] of all ages is to suffer. Upon being born, the baby cries; his infancy is passed in weeping. At one moment we upset him, [at another] we caress him to calm him; at one moment we threaten him, [at the next] we whack him to make him keep still or arouse his [presumably fearful] imaginings or subject him to those of others; no sooner do we do something to please him than we make a thousand demands on him. We teach him early to wish, [only to] subject him to the wishes of another. Without any middle ground (*point de milieu*) he must either do the bidding of others or make them do his; his first notions are those of servitude or of dominance. Before knowing how to talk, he gives orders; before having the power to act, he obeys; and sometimes we punish him before he is in a condition to understand what he has done wrong (*en état de connoitre sa faute*). Thus early do we instill in his young heart the passions which we later attribute to his nature; and having been to some trouble to make him bad, complain at finding him so."†

Except that it involves no concealed racist bias, the foregoing perfectly states the ideas underlying our present environmentalism. The

---

* *The Portable Voltaire*, p. 228.
† Rousseau, J.-J., *Oeuvres complètes*, *Tome IV*, Editions Gallimard, Paris, 1969, p. 69 (Translation mine).

latter seems to assume that there are no innately unpleasant elements in human nature, only acquired ones. (The fact, if it is one, that Rousseau put his own children, by Thérèse Le Vasseur, into an orphanage may have enabled him to persist in this peculiar belief.)

3. In Chapter I, I mentioned the crime statistics released in 1973 by the Nixon Administration, showing that in the previous year crimes against property had declined, whereas murder and aggravated assault—senseless crime—had increased.

The trend of crime figures for the 1960s was generally upward. See for example, *The New York Times,* Tuesday, August 27, 1968, which carries on pp. 1 and 16 a story covering crime across the nation for 1967 and another covering crime in New York City for the same period.

The first story quotes two criminologists, L. E. Ohlin of Harvard and M. E. Wolfgang of the University of Pennsylvania, to the effect that the FBI's figures (of which both men in the past had been somewhat critical) were probably reliable. Ohlin said: "Although I'm pretty good at explaining crime increases, I simply do not have an explanation for this. Some part of it must reflect a change in the readiness of people to resort to armed attack against strangers."

Another *Times* story (Sunday, October 29, 1972, Sect. 1, p. 55) begins: "College students who are being mugged, raped and robbed with 'alarming frequency' are now demanding more protection from the campus security officers they once called 'pigs.' So said John W. Powell, executive secretary of the International Association of College and University Security Directors, at a conference that drew 85 campus security officials from leading Eastern campuses to Pace College here last week." (The story is datelined Pleasantville, N.Y.)

On August 11, 1967, *Science* (v. 157, p. 663) carried an article entitled "Riots: The More There Are, the Less We Understand" (by Robert J. Samuelson). In contrast to Professor Wolfgang, who (in *The New York Times,* Sunday, September 3, 1967, Sect. 1, p. 40) attributed the rise in violence in part to southern migrants to the cities who brought with them "violent traditions," the *Science* article says:

"The idea that recent migrants from the South, bitter and frustrated at their lack of success in Los Angeles, helped stimulate the [Watts] riot may be a myth. The authors found that 60 per cent of the sample (70 per cent of the men) had lived in Los Angeles at least 10 years when the riot occurred."

In Watts, "socio-economic level [of the rioters] showed little relationship with measures of discontent" but "life-style" and discontent were correlated (which sounds like a contradiction). Samuelson is reviewing a UCLA study made after the Watts riots of '65. He closes as follows: "The UCLA study, and a few others in existence, raise more questions than they resolve. Its conclusions, if correct for Watts, may not apply to other cities. And even its findings about Watts 1965 may no longer be true of Watts 1967. This summer's violence has been too widespread and yet too random to suit simple explanations. Each new disturbance amplifies uncertainty and leaves room for almost as many theories as there are disorders."

Boston's *Phoenix* for August 3, 1971, carried a lead story beginning: "It was Monday afternoon in North Woburn, seven fire bombs had already been thrown and J. was walking down toward the intersection of School and Main streets. He was smiling and carrying a six foot club. 'Look what I found in the woods,' he said, pointing to the club. 'When the pigs come after us tonight, I'll be ready.' "

The article goes on to describe a kind of revolutionary crisis in Woburn, between new affluent parents and their kids who "drank beer, committed petty crimes and balled in the woods." A running battle developed between young people and the police. "The kids were saying the final score was 17–10. . . . They were talking about 17 arrests to 10 fire bombs. The arrests cost a few thousand dollars in bail but the bombings cost $1 million in damages. The kids figured they'd won." One evidence of their victory was a picture, accompanying the article, which showed the smoking ruins of Brown's fertilizer warehouse, though in what way the destruction of that building furthered the cause of the Young Revolution is not immediately clear.

In *The New York Times* (Sunday, April 20, 1969, Sect. 1, p. 49) there is an article quoting Dr. Philip G. Zimbardo, professor of psychology at Stanford, as follows: "What we are observing all around us . . . is a sudden change in the restraints which normally control the expression of our drives, impulses and emotions. . . . Conditions which foster deindividuation . . . make each of us a potential assassin."

One of the more insane examples in my files was reported by a psychologist, George R. Bach (*The New York Times*, Sunday, September 3, 1967). According to Dr. Bach, "murders by 'super-coverts,' or persons who suppress aggressive instincts, outnumbered murders by persons who showed aggression by more than 3 to 1. 'The killers are very nice guys' he said, 'and they used the punishment of death to take out their frustrations in trying to love or be loved.'

"Secrecy and deception, he said, are other factors. He cited as an example a woman who killed her husband because she secretly objected to his social ineptness during their vacation. 'She was devoted to a love ideology which he wasn't aware of and it slowed the progress of their lives,' he said." Whatever that may mean.

No less idiotic was the outburst of mass violence that occurred in Pittsburgh on October 17, 1971. According to the next day's *Boston Evening Globe*: "Newsmen reported two apparent criminal assaults—in full view of hundreds who cheered the assailants—displays of public lovemaking, nudity and drinking. At the height of the melee, a police desk sergeant said he had calls reporting about a dozen rapes.

" 'This isn't a riot. It's a goddamn orgy,' a motorcycle policeman said during the disturbance which left the downtown area in a shambles. More than 100 persons were injured and 300 others were arrested. . . . There were scattered shootings but only one reported wounding. . . . At least 30 stores were looted and 30 or 40 more were burned. Newsmen counted another 20 autos with roofs that had been crushed by the destruction-bent crowds. . . . The wild celebration created the worst traffic jam in the city's history. At its height, cars were backed up for eight miles on one major freeway into the city and for six miles on another. . . . The melee ended 10 hours after it began when flying wedges of riot-equipped police, some with dogs, slammed head-on into the crowds and drove them from the downtown section." The occasion for all this uproar was the victory the Pittsburgh Pirates had just achieved in the World Series.

4. Rousseau: "If we consider the frightful disorders which printing has already caused in Europe, and judge of the future by the progress of its evils from day to day, it is easy to foresee that sovereigns will hereafter take as much pains to banish this dreadful art . . . as they ever took to encourage it." M. Rousseau goes on to quote the Caliph Omar who favored burning the library in Alexandria, since if its books were contrary to the Koran they should be burned, while if they seconded it they were superfluous. "This reasoning has been cited . . . as the height of absurdity, but if Gregory the Great had been in place of Omar, and the Gospel in place of the Alcoran, the library would still have been burnt, and it would have been perhaps the finest action of his life."

Also, on the same topic: "As the conveniences of life increase, as the arts are brought to perfection and luxury spreads, true courage flags, the virtues disappear; and all of this is the effect of the sciences and of those arts which are exercised in the privacy of men's dwellings."

(From "A Discourse on the Arts and Sciences," in *The Social Contract and Discourses*, pp. 151 and 145.)

5. The way rationalization works—the way partly or totally concealed desires or prohibitions, usually with the force of some instinct behind

them, decide what we shall think and what we shall see or fail to see —is marvelously shown by an experiment reported some years ago by a Dr. Lewis Wolberg (*Transactions, Second Conference on Problems of Consciousness,* Josiah Macy Jr. Foundation, 1951, p. 79).

Several people were hypnotized and given the following instructions: "When you awaken you will find next to you a bar of chocolate. You will have an insatiable desire to eat the chocolate . . . but at the same time you will feel it is wrong for you to have the chocolate, that it doesn't belong to you, that you must not eat it." The subject was then commanded not to recall that he had been given these suggestions; i.e., they were to operate on him in the posthypnotic state in the same way in which "repressed" memories or very old conditioning acts upon our everyday behavior. Here are some of the results:

". . . One man, as soon as he came out of the trance state, began to talk about the need to respond to the hospitality of those one visited, even to partaking of delicacies in the room without necessarily being invited to do so. He then reached over, picked up the bar of chocolate, slipped the paper off and began to eat it. As he did so, his face wrinkled up and he said, "This tastes bad; is it spoiled?" . . . When he had consumed a quantity, he excused himself . . . went to the bathroom and vomited up the chocolate." Wolberg noted that this man "had for some years suffered from a psychosomatic problem resembling gastric ulcer."

Another man, whom Wolberg called a "psychopathic personality," made what appeared to be an instant conversion of anxiety into anger (my assumption being that when he violated the command not to eat the chocolate, his first response was probably fearlike). "When he awoke, he grabbed the chocolate, violently tore off the wrapper, threw the wrapper against the wall, smacked his lips and ate the chocolate in an extremely defiant and . . . aggressive manner."

A third subject "seemed to have no emotional response at all, talking calmly and glibly. I asked him, 'Would you like a bar of chocolate?' He replied 'What chocolate?' I said, 'The chocolate right next to you.' He looked at it and retorted 'There is no chocolate there.' I insisted that this was not so. He exclaimed 'Are you kidding me?' I lifted the chocolate and held it up, and he said 'Why, all you are holding up is your bare hand.' When I dropped the chocolate, he shrieked 'My God, I heard something drop but I can't see anything.'"

6. See Frank Edwards, *Flying Saucers, Serious Business;* also Edward U. Condon *et al., Scientific Study of Unidentified Flying Objects,* p. 496.

7. *UFOs: A New Look,* A Special Report by the National Investiga-

tions Committee on Aerial Phenomena (NICAP), Washington, D.C., 1969, p. 3.

8. *The UFO Evidence*, Richard H. Hall, editor, National Investigations Committee on Aerial Phenomena, p. 129.

9. Edwards, *op. cit.*, p. 5.

10. *Ibid.*, pp. 75ff.

11. *UFOs: A New Look*, p. 4.

12. *Flying Saucers, Serious Business*, p. 87.

13. Philip Klass, "UFOs 'N-rays' and Pathological Science,' unpublished; personal communication.

14. *Ibid.*

15. Philip Klass, "On the Credibility of UFO Witnesses," unpublished; personal communication.

16. D. H. Menzel and Lyle G. Boyd, *The World of Flying Saucers, passim*.

17. Philip Klass, *UFOs Identified, passim*.

18. *The UFO Evidence*, pp. 32 and 162.

19. *Scientific Study of Unidentified Flying Objects*, p. 248.

20. *The UFO Evidence*, pp. 39–40.

21. "UFOs, 'N-rays' and Pathological Science"; Martin Gardner, *Fads and Fallacies in the Name of Science*.

22. Klass, *ibid.*, p. 12.

23. *Flying Saucers Here and Now*, Bantam Books, 1968, p. 55.

24. *Flying Saucers, Serious Business*, p. 44.

25. Personal communication, Raymond E. Fowler (Chairman of the Massachusetts Subcommittee for NICAP).

26. D. R. Saunders and R. R. Harkins, *UFOs? Yes!*, p. 172.

27. *The World of Flying Saucers*, pp. 232–33.

28. Reported in the *APRO Bulletin* for January, 1964.

29. *NICAP Investigator*, March, 1971, p. 3.

30. *UFOs? Yes!*, Appendix A, p. 242.

31. *UFOs: A New Look*, p. 18.

32. Pages 68ff *et passim*.

33. *The Strange Death of Liberal England*, 1910–1914, p. 120.

34. Life in the communes is probably the best working model we have of the sort of world the New Left would set up if it could dispose of the present one. And the evidence from the communes is that talkiness, aginnerism, and a general refusal to do the dishes are the same problem as elsewhere. David French and his wife ("After the Fall," *The New York Times Magazine*, Sunday, October 3, 1971) joined one on the West Coast, finding it to be full of argumentative Fem Lib types and people determined, in their togetherness, to minimize in-

timacy or cooperation. Not to be a chauvinist, not to be involved at all, seemed to be everyone's objective. "It was a shock," French writes; "where Elena and I had come to The Community to deepen our own relationship and extend it to others, we found the entire idea of serious relationships under fire." Later he notes: "With relationships not an objective, the idea of relationship around work became irrelevant. Instead, people sought activities that expressed their own special apartness. Crafts were in favor, since they were personal things, done alone. . . . As for the work that paid the bills, the same centrifugal forces applied. . . . Most people didn't work at all, preferring to live off the foundation money or checks from home." (The Community had in the beginning gotten a substantial grant.)

The emotional tone of The Community was if anything colder than that of the "straight" world. "Compassion was held to be condescending. Favored instead as a basis for interpersonal style was a sort of brutal honesty that forced distances between people. . . . We came to realize that everyone was in flight, that The Community was bound together largely by its negativism." One day the Frenches went to a nearby prison to visit with the prisoners. "The people we saw were open and eager to communicate . . ." On their return to The Community they found "people were lying around on the floor as if paralyzed, talking with their customary detachment about Women's Liberation. It was shattering. *Here* were the imprisoned . . . 'There's too damned much verbiage around this place' someone once said to [one of the members]. 'You and I had better have a long talk about this' he replied."

French described The Community's pets as "freaked-out creatures howling and whining and snapping for attention" and its children as "brittle, supercharged, alienated." It was forbidden for any member to enjoy special respect because of his knowledge or greater age and experience. For such members "it seemed an unwritten law that they were never *never* to appear to know more about anything than the rawest escapee from some middle-class suburban home. On the other hand they *were* allowed to do the tedious administrative work . . ."

A young friend of mine who in 1970 visited six communes gave substantially the same report.

Bibliography

Abetti, Giorgio, *The History of Astronomy*, Henry Schuman, 1952.

Adams, Henry, *Mont-Saint-Michel and Chartres*, Houghton Mifflin, 1933.

Anand, B. K., *et al.*, in *EEG & Clinical Neurophysiology*, 3: 452–56 (1961).

Baker, Robert H., *Astronomy*, D. Van Nostrand, 1930.

Bergler, Dr. Edmund, *The Writer and Psychoanalysis*, Brunner, 1954.

Buckle, Henry T., *History of Civilization in England*, 3 vols., Longmans Green, 1885.

Chesler, Phyllis, "The Sensuous Psychiatrists," *The New York Times Magazine*, Sunday, June 19, 1972.

Cohen, Daniel, *Myths of the Space Age*, Dodd Mead, 1967.

Condon, Edward U., *et al.*, *Scientific Study of Unidentified Flying Objects*, D. S. Gillmor, editor, Dutton, 1969.

Courtot, Baroness Cécile de, *Memoirs*, Henry Holt, 1900.

Dangerfield, George, *The Strange Death of Liberal England, 1910–1914*, Capricorn Books, 1961.

Darnton, Robert, *Mesmerism*, Schocken Books, 1970.

Edwards, Frank, *Flying Saucers, Serious Business*.

Encyclopaedia Britannica, 11th Edition, "Homeopathy."

Frazer, Sir James G., *The Golden Bough*, 1 vol. abridged, Macmillan, 1931.

Fromm, Erich, *The Crisis of Psychoanalysis*, Holt, Rinehart and Winston, 1970.

Gardner, Martin, *Fads and Fallacies in the Name of Science*, Dover, 1967.

Hartmann, Heinz, *Psychoanalysis and Moral Values*, International Universities Press, 1959.

Huxley, Aldous, *Collected Essays*, Harper and Brothers, 1958.

Janov, Arthur, *The Primal Scream*, Simon and Schuster.

Jones, Ernest, *The Life and Works of Sigmund Freud*, edited and abridged by Lionel Trilling and Steven Marcus, Basic Books, 1961.

King, Francis, *Rites of Modern Occult Magic*, Macmillan, 1970.

Klass, Philip, *UFOs Identified*, Random House, 1968.

Koestler, Arthur, *The Roots of Coincidence*, Hutchinson & Co., 1972.

Kulik, L. A., "The Tunguska Meteorite," from *Source Book on Astronomy 1900–1950*, Harvard University Press, 1960, pp. 75–76.

Larousse, *Encyclopedia of the Earth*, Prometheus Press, 1961.

Lawrence, D. H., *Phoenix*, E. D. McDonald, editor, Viking, 1936.

Lawrence, D. H., *Studies of Classic American Literature*, Doubleday Anchor Books, 1953.

Lefebvre, Georges, *The Coming of the French Revolution*, Princeton, 1947.

Ley, Willy, *Watchers of the Skies*, Viking, 1963.

Lifton, Robert Jay, article in *Yale Alumni Magazine*, January, 1969.

Lockyer, J. Norman, *The Dawn of Astronomy*, M.I.T. Press, 1964.

Loeper, Dr. John J., *Understanding Your Child Through Astrology*, Paperback Library, 1971.

Lyttleton, Raymond A., *The Modern Universe*, Harper, 1956.

Maliver, Bruce, "Encounter Groupers Up Against the Wall," *The New York Times Magazine*, Sunday, January 3, 1971, pp. 2ff.

Marcuse, Herbert, *One Dimensional Man*, Beacon, 1964.

Menzel, D. H., and Boyd, L. G., *The World of Flying Saucers*, Doubleday, 1963.

Menzel, D. H.; Whipple, Fred L.; Gerard de Vaucouleurs, *Survey of the Universe*, Prentice-Hall, 1970.

Mommsen, Theodor, *The History of the Roman Republic*, 4 vols., Everyman's Library, New York, 1930.

Mumford, Lewis, "The Megamachine," *The New Yorker*, October 17, 1970.

Needham, Joseph, *Science and Civilisation in China*, vol. iii, Cambridge, 1970.

Norbeck, Edward, *Religion in Primitive Society*, Harper & Row, 1961.

Ortega y Gasset, José, *The Revolt of the Masses*, Norton, 1932.

Revel, Jean-François, *Without Marx or Jesus*, Doubleday, 1971.

Riesman, David, *The Lonely Crowd*, Yale University Press, 1950.

Rousseau, Jean-Jacques, *The Social Contract and Discourses*, Everyman's Library (J. M. Dent and Dutton), 1923.

Rubin, Jerry, *Do It!*, Simon and Schuster, 1970.

Russell, Bertrand, *History of Western Philosophy*, Simon and Schuster, 1945.

Russell, Bertrand, *Unpopular Essays*, Simon and Schuster, 1950.
Sargant, Dr. William, *Battle for the Mind*, Doubleday, 1958, p. 195.
Saunders, D. R., and Harkins, R. R., *UFOs? Yes!*, Signet, 1968.
Skinner, B. F., *Beyond Freedom and Dignity*, Knopf, 1971.
Steiner, George, *Language and Silence*, Atheneum, 1967.
Stendhal (Henri Beyle), *The Life of Henri Brulard*, Vintage, 1955.
Sullivan, Walter, *We Are Not Alone*, Signet, 1966.
Toffler, Alvin, *Future Shock*, Bantam Books, 1971.
Trevelyan, G. M., *English Social History*, Longmans Green, 1944.
Trollope, Frances, *Domestic Manners of the Americans*, Vintage, 1949.
Velikovsky, Immanuel, *Ages in Chaos*, Doubleday, 1952.
Velikovsky, Immanuel, *Worlds in Collision*, Dell, 1967.
Voltaire, *The Portable Voltaire*, Ben Ray Redman, editor, Viking, 1949.
Wilson, Edmund, *To the Finland Station*, Farrar, Straus & Giroux, 1972.

Index

French revolutionary, 74, 82
Livermore, Calif., 145
Lloyd, Emily, 147*n*
Lockyer, Sir Joseph N., 163, 171, 183
Lollards, 254
London, 204
Lorenzen, Coral, 140
Los Angeles, 114, 266–67
Louis XIV, King, 19
Louis XVI, King, 67–68, 70–72, 83
love, 194, 197
Love Generation, 202*n*
Low, Dr. Robert, 153–54
Lowry, Malcolm, 205*n*
Lysenko, Trofim D., 32
Lyttleton, Raymond A., 172
Lull, Ramon, 252–53

MacDonald, Dr. James F., 148
machismo, 196
Macmillan Company, 185*n*
magic, 212, 213
magnetism, 61, 180
Maharaj Ji, 103*n*
Maharishi, 218
Mailer, Norman, 205, 209
Maliver, Bruce, 48–51
Malpighi, Marcello, 254
mammoths, 168, 180, 181
Manhattan Project, 212
manna, 176, 180
Manson, Charles, 17, 202*n*
Marat, Jean Paul, 69, 82
Marcuse, Herbert, 75, 81, 82, 109, 111, 207, 223
Marie Antoinette, 63, 64
Mars, 37–40, 138, 139, 153, 170, 220
Marx, Karl, 24, 28, 248
Massopust, Dr. Leo, 235, 239
Masters, William, 55
Masters and Johnson, 18, 204*n*, 237
mathematics, 183, 210
Maxwell, Clerk, 107*n*, 109, 207*n*

McCarthy, Joseph R., 201
McCarthyism, 112, 185*n*, 215
McLuhan, Marshall, 82*n*, 102, 233
McMinnville, Ore., 141, 148
medicine, 65, 76, 77, 113, 134, 147*n*
Medum, Egypt, 171*n*
melancholia, 16*n*
Mencken, Henry L., 78, 81, 242
Menzel, Donald, 140, 142, 155, 175*n*
Mesmer, Franz Anton, 60, 61–64, 74, 75, 133, 135, 218, 262
  clinic, 62–63, 263
  and French Revolution, 185, 261
Mesmerism, 21, 61–65, 73, 81, 113
  membership, 185
  mesmeric tubs, 62, 63
  and spiritualists, 64–65
meteorites, 142, 150, 173–75
Mexico, 138, 170
Mical, Abbé, 65, 237
Mill, John Stuart, 23, 24, 27
mimesis, 243
mind, 25, 100, 206, 208–10, 248–250, 257
  and conscience, 93, 190
  and Id, 79*n*, 197, 204, 248, 256
Mind Control, 26, 34–43, 52*n*, 88, 209*n*, 259–60, 262
  brain waves, 35, 59
  organization, 64, 218–19
minorities, 104
Mirabeau, Comte de, 67, 68, 75
Mommsen, Theodor, 51, 78, 263–264
moon, 178–80
morality, 27, 57, 98
moral revolution, 30, 78, 98
Morgan, Helen, 29–30
mortality, 15. *See also* fear of death
Moss, Dr. Thelma S., 130
Mossberg, Walter, 85
motivational research, 240

philosophy, 51, 210, 224
Pinetti, Joseph, 65, 237
plagiarism, 221, 222, 260
plane crashes, 125–27, 129
planets, life-supporting, 156
Plath, Sylvia, 210*n*
Pleasonton, Augustus, 113
Poe, Edgar Allan, 28, 192, 193, 205
Poland, German occupation, 80
Powell, John W., 266
precognition, 128
Presbyterian Church, 255
Prismatic Ray (Lloyd), 147*n*
prostitution, 234
Protean Man, 102
Protestants, 44, 66, 78, 229, 255
Provence, 197
psi-energy, 131–33
psihypnosis, 131
psi phenomena, 9, 40, 77, 135
psitrons, 33, 128, 129, 131, 135, 226*n*
psi-war, 131, 132, 135, 136
psi weapons, 9, 131–32
psychiatrists, 46, 224
psychiatry, 55–56
Psychic Discoveries Behind the Iron Curtain (Schroeder and Ostrander), 129
psychic energy, 9, 135*n*
psychoanalysis, 14, 51, 52, 54, 55, 58, 100
    and dianetics (Scientology), 21, 53
    literature of, 222, 260
    and self-knowledge, 89
    in U.S., 44, 113
    Velikovsky's adaptation, 161, 193
psychoanalysts, 58, 226
    use of horoscopes, 64, 213
    and Velikovsky, 159, 161, 183
psychodrama, 44
psychohistory, 46*n*
psychokinesis, 33, 129–31
psychologists, 55, 134
psychosis, 265

psychotherapy, 55–56, 58, 159, 262
psychotron, 132, 133, 135
pyramids, 168, 171

quacks and quackery, 53, 58, 64, 69, 76, 87, 113, 147*n*, 184, 185, 220, 221, 224, 262
quantum physics, 133

racial memories, 181, 248*n*
radical egoism, 59, 99, 259
radical subjectivism, 57, 59, 86, 88, 90, 99, 203, 259
rational consensus, 22, 23, 29
rationalization, 89, 90, 96, 100, 224, 242, 268–69
reading skills, 76, 104
reason, 29, 32, 46, 59, 87, 96, 107–8, 132–33, 210, 215–16, 259
    and astrology, 213
    vs. fantasy, 86, 90
    and free will, 25
    and Id, 258
    and instinct, 24
    intellectual attacks on, 81, 82, 86, 107–8
    and Machiavellianism, 94
Regardie, Dr. Francis I., 221, 226, 260*n*
Reich, Charles, 59, 81, 82
Reich, Wilhelm, 58, 135, 159, 215, 216
    character armor, 47, 48, 52, 59
    etheric force, 133
    orgasm key to well-being, 47, 56
    orgone box, therapy, 47, 52, 59, 62, 77, 220
    orgone energy, 21, 61, 260, 263
Reichenbach, Baron Karl von, 133, 135
reincarnation, 34–35
religion, 51, 80, 113, 224, 247–251, 255–57
    decline of, 15, 22, 66, 74, 78, 99*n*
    in France, 66, 74, 80

scientology, 14, 21, 34, 35, 52–54, 64, 77, 214, 263
Scream, 44, 47, 48, 114, 209n, 212, 262, 263
Scream Therapy, 219, 224
SDS, 261, 262
seismographs, 174
Selby, England, 157
Senmut, 162, 163, 165, 179
Sentics, 114, 238
sex, 34, 55–56, 189, 195–96, 198, 199
  compulsive sexuality, 100
  sexual revolution, 17–18, 106
Shakespeare, William, 189n
Shoo-king (Shu Ching), 161
Siberia, 168, 173–74
Silva, José, 37–40, 42, 218
simplification, 44, 181, 182, 184, 256
Siodmak, Curt, 235
skepticism, 21, 22, 86, 98, 115, 256
Skinner, Burrhus, F., 24, 223, 239, 255, 264
  conditioning vs. free will, 25, 45, 257
  and the Ego, 92, 95, 100, 101, 229
  man's "automatic goodness," 56, 57, 259
Smith, Adam, 218
Snow, C. P., 106
Social Contract, 57, 73, 245, 246
Society of Universal Harmony, 64
Socorro, N. M., 141, 145
Sontag, Susan, 210n
space, 137, 156
space station, 139
space travel, 36–37, 152–53, 157
Spain, 31, 32, 245
Spectro-chrome Institute, 113
spiritualism, 113
Spitzbergen island, 148
Stalin, Josef, 31–32, 76, 125
Steig, William, 215
Stein Gertrude, 208, 209n
Steiner, George, 79n

Stevenson, Robert Louis, 205n
stoicism, 95, 263
Stonehenge, 163, 178, 179
Storr, Anthony, 224, 260
Student Academic Freedom Forum, 217
Students for a Democratic Society: see SDS
Sullivan, Walter, 156
Sumeria, 164, 171, 181
Superego, 25, 52, 92–96, 98, 99, 190, 258
supernaturalism, 33
superstition, 14, 28
Surrealism, 199n
Su-shu Huang, 156
Symmes, John, 113

tarot cards, 58
Tau Ceti, 138, 156
teen-agers, 17, 104–5. See also hippies
telepathy, 119, 126–29, 131–33. See also ESP
teleportation, 33
television: see TV
Tesla, Nikola, 138
Thomas, Dylan, 205n
Thoreau, Henry David, 114
Thorp, Willard, 104
thought projection: see ESP
tidal waves (tsunamis), 167, 168
Time magazine, 206n, 217, 233
Tocqueville, Alexis de, 112n
Todd, Dr., 138, 139
Toffler, Alvin, 59, 88, 232–39, 258
Totem and Taboo (Freud), 159
Toynbee, Arnold, 226
Transactional Analysis, 114, 238
Transcendental Meditation, 26, 35, 52n, 219, 257
Treash, Robert, 179, 180
Trent, Paul, 141, 148
Trollope, Mrs. Frances, 112
Trotsky, Leon, 92
Truman, Harry S., 112
Turner, Glenn, 219–20
TV, 206, 238, 240